Climbing Trees
Beverley Campbell

To My Beloved Grandpa.
You've walked beside me all my life. Thank you.

Climbing Trees
Print ISBN: 9781761097034
Ebook ISBN: 9781761097041
Copyright © Bev Campbell 2025
Cover design by Graham Davidson

First published 2025 by
Ginninderra Press
PO Box 2 Bentleigh 3204
ginninderrapress.com.au

Chapter 1
Barefoot white child.
Southern Rhodesia. 1962

The corrugated iron roof is warm, and its undulations curve beneath my bare feet. The trees above are scattering their crisp end-of-summer leaves, some of which have been raked and piled near the compost heap.

Grandpa's voice, gravelly from too much smoking, calls out to me, 'Bread's out of the oven—come down from there, Child.' I'm somewhere I shouldn't be. The roof's resident cats have had kittens; some are snuggling greedily as they feed. I can't stay away.

I scamper over the roof, drop onto the water tank, and slide down the side pipe into his arms. 'You really shouldn't be up there, you know?'

Grandpa's not angry like the others would be. I laugh, wriggle free and dash around the corner towards the aroma of fresh bread filtering out the kitchen door, along with the voices of Mummy, Nanna, and Great Gran. I stop and watch them chatting together in the warmth of the wood stove. Freshly turned butter sits on the worn table, and loaves are tipped from tins and shrouded beneath tea towels—crispy brown tops with fluffy white insides.

Nanna's pouring tea, with milk first, followed by the rich brown brew, leaves trapped in a polished silver strainer. A saucer of weak tea is on the ground for our fluffy ginger cat, Bluey, who's parading between legs, his purr revving. Nanna sees me.

'You were up on the roof again, weren't you?' She straightens up, her voice firm as her corset, and turns to my mother. 'Norma, you should give that child a hiding! How many times has she been told to stay off the roof?'

Great Gran stamps her walking stick on the lino in agreement and Mummy's bottom lip vanishes between her teeth. The three of them are ganging up on me, a common occurrence, and I know that soon a wooden spoon will connect with my bottom.

'That bread smells good,' Grandpa says. His long shadow falls as a protective cloak around me. 'Is the small loaf ready for us to have?' His weathered forearm rests over my shoulder. I examine his bad tattoo from WWII in Burma, his arm hair embedded in ink, sunburnt skin, and the nicotine stains on his fingers. Nanna forgets about me as her hands deftly place starched serviettes. We are 'proper' despite our pole and daga house built of tree trunks and mud. Her brown eyes rest on Grandpa and me, and then on Mummy, who's slicing the bread. 'Come on, let's sit so we can all enjoy afternoon tea,' she says. 'Hurry up before the bread goes cold!' Grandpa takes my hand, and we move into the room to sit side by side. I look up at him; he's smiling past me, with soft eyes at Nanna. He's saved me from a hiding, *this* time.

Nanna always says, 'Sit up straight, stand up straight,' and I do. I try to listen and do as I'm told, but it's hard. The outside is calling me.

Mummy says, 'You may leave the table, Beverley. Don't go to the compound!'

How did she know *that*? I slide off the wooden chair, the lino's cool beneath my bare feet, and walk through the kitchen with a straight back. Now I run, barefoot across the yard, past the dairy buildings where Nanna churns the butter, down the path between the turkey pens and veggie garden, through the tall grass over my head and I'm here, at the compound.

Little children like me are playing. I join in, pushing wire-crafted cars with bottle-top wheels along roads smoothed in the mud. I've got a collection of little metal cars, but I keep them in a box in the wardrobe. These wire ones are better. Women stand over fires, their strong arms stirring sadza in huge black pots. I know Mummy will smell the smoke on me later, and I'll be in trouble. But, Grandpa's home, *he* will save me.

And we start to eat. I reach into the pot with my right hand, as the mafazi's have told me to, and scoop a chunk of sadza. *See I listen sometimes.* It's so hot. Quickly I roll it between my fingers and then dip the ball into the pot of beans, steaming beside the fire, and giggle with my friends. It tastes so *good.*

I'm tired, it's hot. Grandpa tells me the rains will come soon—and I am too full for lunch now. Mummy's going to be cross with me.

Girty finds me. She's not happy.

'Picanin missis, I look all over for you!' She grabs my hand, her dark fingers wrap around mine, all dirty and white, and our palms squish together as she leads us along the narrow path, her skinny black legs moving fast, flashing coffee souls at me. She's angry. I forgot to tell her where I was going.

'Sorry, Girty,' I say.

She glances over her shoulder. There's a wide smile of brilliant white teeth on her black round face. I'm forgiven. She pulls me towards her. 'I'm your nanny; you must be with me.' I nod my head. Nanny? What's that? Girty's my friend!

Girty scrubs my filthy hands under the outside tap near the water tank. 'Eish, dirty,' she mutters and leads me to the kitchen door. I run into the dining room. Lunch is finished. I've missed it. Mummy gets up fast and walks towards me, she's got her cross face on! I look around for Grandpa, but he's not here. Panic grips me, and Nanna says, 'Give that child a hiding!'

Great Gran stomps her walking stick, and Mummy snatches a coat hanger from on top of the ironing basket and grabs hold of me.

'No, no!' I shriek and *whack,* she hits me. My skinny body writhes under her grip. The wooden coat hanger strikes my legs, my bum, and I scream, 'Grandpa!'

'You can yell all you like! He's up the yard fixing the borehole pump!' Mummy says and whacks me even more.

I break free, flee out the back door and run over the red dirt, past the fruit trees... and there he is.

'Grandpa!' I cry and his arms are around me, his hands on my hair and a clean hankie swishes over my face. I hiccup.

'Let's go and see how the turkeys are doing,' he says and leads me towards the pen where the vain creatures are gobble gobbling and strutting.

***

The next morning, I make sure to wait on the verandah for Girty as I'm told to. I *don't* want another hiding.

It's nice out here, in the shade, sitting on the wood floor with Nanna's maidenhair ferns behind me, their elegant leaves cascading over the sides of the rusty half drums they're planted in. Bluey's coiled asleep, a ginger heap, in the last one. I hear Nanna's steps coming along the partially enclosed verandah and *bang*, the screen door slams behind her. I knew it! She's seen Bluey.

'Get off!' She says lifting the huge long-haired cat and dropping it on the ground. 'Just look at my beautiful ferns, you've flattened them, again!' Her fingers run through the fronds, lifting the delicate leaves as she tut-tuts under her breath.

Silly Bluey, you should have slept in the golden shower fence along the driveway, perfectly hidden among the hanging orange bell-shaped flowers and leaves. I suppose the early morning sun on the ferns was too good to miss.

Nanna's at the end of the verandah now. I watch her unlock the door to the Post Office. 'The only brick place here,' says Grandpa, and she goes inside.

The first Post Office customer pulls up. As he leaves, red dust puffs match the red bricks of the Post Office, and he calls out, 'Tot siens!'

I giggle to myself. Nanna can't speak a word of Afrikaans! She adamantly claims that she's not bothered with learning *that* language, but we all know it's not that she doesn't *want* to. It's because she *can't* pronounce the distinctive guttural words.

And I'm still waiting for Girty. But I'm not bored. My eyes wander over the large open area beyond our front yard, to the left where the abattoir is. I like going there, but the workers chase me away because they are killing cattle. Sometimes they let me watch the dead ones being hung by their hind legs and cut up. It's fascinating to see all the layers peel away. And after a while they say, 'humba picanin'.

That's when I visit the old man sitting in a shed next door and perch on a chunk of wood opposite him, watching him work. He grins at me, bends his head and continues carving. My fingers itch to touch his grey, woolly hair, which is longer than most. He squints in sunlight streaming through the door and pays close attention to the sharp metal tool that he's using to carve detailed animals and trees onto the dead cattle horns. These he makes into vases, using chicken wire scrunched up to hold flowers, and ornaments, all mounted on wooden stands. He polishes the horns until the varied browns, creams, and blacks gleam. I like the black parts best, they look like Girty's skin when it's wet; it's beautiful. I gaze at my nut-brown arms and think about my white tummy. Would I get sunburnt if I was black? Better not ask Mummy.

Next door is another house. I don't know who lives there. On the far side, opposite me, is a long low-slung abandoned building that used to be a shop of sorts a while ago. Its verandah is decorated with cobwebs, dust, and bird droppings. Swift swallows flit in and out, feeding their begging chicks in mud-built nests.

We live in a mud house too and we also have an outside 'P.K.'—that's what Nanna says is the polite word to use instead of 'toilet'. I don't like using it, no matter what word I use, way down there behind the trees and near the compost heap. It smells.

Behind the abandoned store a bush path winds through the long grass to the Gadzema Railway siding. Goods trains mostly stop there and every evening a worker brings us the siding keys for safekeeping.

Another car is leaving the Post Office. I watch as it drives away towards the train tracks. That's the way off the farm. Over those tracks, sometimes we turn right and travel a few miles along a strip road, over a narrow one-way bridge, to the gold settlement, The Giant Mine. There's nothing giant about it now as the gold is almost depleted. A mound of 'fool's gold' rubble lies near one of the buildings, through whose murky windows I've watched liquid gold being poured into small crucibles. There are a few houses, and a Clubhouse, surrounded by low scrub where a swimming pool, plonked in the ground, frequented by frogs, water scorpions, and us kids, and we all enjoy it.

Turn left after the train track and we drive through Gadzema. Not much here either except tired buildings, a store, a garage, and a few houses sitting beside the strip road. Grandpa tells me stories about gold being discovered in 1867 and that Gadzema means 'Shining Place'. *I guess that's because gold is shiny.*

'Beverley,' he says, 'You should have seen this place during the 1930s and 1950s, it was a great village full of miners, politicians, poker players, and daredevil pilots who landed their planes near here. Imagine that, all those people?' This is where he usually sighs, 'Those were the days, your great-grandparents were here back then!'

I don't understand all the things he tells me, but I hear about the two hardware stores, the fabric shop, the Club, and the Hotel. 'We had everything we needed.'

Now, it's a quiet place we pass on our way to the town of Hartley, named, Grandpa says, after a hunter called Henry Hartley who shot an elephant. 'When that huge animal's tusks gouged the ground, gold was found there,' he tells me. I guess that's why there's a Giant Mine!

See Grandpa, I do listen to lots you tell me, even though I climb onto the roof.

***

Whenever we drive through Gadzema, Grandpa is alert. I know he's on the lookout for Mr Passaportis's Pekingese dog pack which ambushes cars, and today they chase us, running out from the long grass, again.

'Here they come!' Grandpa says, 'One of them is going to get knocked one day!' He mutters a few extra low words.

Thump! 'Yip'. Grandpa pulls off into the dirt beside the strip road and opens the car door. As he gets out, the pack rushes at him with proud tails curling over long coats, snub faces and teeth snapping at his ankles.

'Is it dead?' I call out of the window.

'Yes, Beverley, stay there,' he replies above the barking.

I slump in the seat and finish the ice cream he bought me in town; dead animals are just a fact of life to me. Grandpa shoots duiker (native antelope) regularly out in the lands when they come to eat the young maize shoots. We are not supposed to shoot them, so when he does the Africans are quick to help butcher them. Some meat is hidden under frozen turkeys in our deep freeze, and the rest goes into the cooking pots in the compound.

I hear yelling and lean out the window. Grandpa's standing near an open screen door; Mr Passaportis is standing on the top step shouting, arms gyrating like he's doing a Greek dance. Grandpa shakes his head, turns, and walks slowly back towards the car. The Pekingese pack has subsided and Mr Passaportis slams his door.

Grandpa sighs, lowers himself into the driver's seat and mutters, 'I always said one of them was going to get hit someday.'

He tips my chin, 'Let's see your face,' and wipes away any trace of ice cream around my lips. Then he winks at me. Ice cream is our secret! He starts the engine and pulls onto the strip road. I hang my head out the window and look back at the lumpy bundle of fur beside the front door where Grandpa gently laid it. He said one of them would get clobbered one day, and that day is today.

After dinner, we gather in the sitting room. Table lamps are lit and the TV is boring. The warmth of the day is still with us. Grandpa's in his favourite chair. He taps his pipe bowl scattering the stale contents into the ashtray, repacks it methodically, strikes a match, and draws, encouraging the flame downwards.

'Dad, you're quiet tonight. Everything alright?' Mummy says and looks up from her knitting pattern. Great Gran, Nanna, and Mummy are all knitting, each set of needles clicking an original tune.

Grandpa draws on his pipe, exhales, and smiles at her. 'Yes, Norma, everything is just fine. I'm enjoying watching you all.' Mummy nods her head and continues knitting. 'These socks are for you, Dad,' she says quietly.

'That's a lovely thought to end the day with,' he replies.

Chapter 2
Grandpa, Girty and me.
I'm five soon.

Girty's waiting for me in the kitchen, her hands wrapped around a tin holding sweet milky tea that she's slurping with delight. Nanna would say, 'Don't slurp your tea,' but we both do if she's not around. Girty grins at me over the rim as she finishes. Fingers intertwined, we run out the backdoor into the end of winter sunshine to play away the day.

'Lunchtime... Beverley, Girty,' Nanna calls from the kitchen door, her voice reaching us where we are sitting on the hard ground in the shadows of a water tank that towers over 20 feet on wooden supports.

'Come, we wash hands now,' says Girty putting down a lump of wet clay. Red remnants stick to her ebony fingers and stain her cream palms. My little white fingers are red too. Scattered around us are small moulded misshaped clay animals; long dry thorns create cow and rhino horns or tusks for elephants. It's the only way to identify what we've made.

'Don't want to, we're making animals!' I protest.

Girty makes an *eish* sound between her teeth. I know that I'm being difficult. 'Mine's better than yours!' I say to annoy her more.

'We go, now,' she announces with some authority.

'Dirty Girty, Dirty Girty,' I shout running between the water tank's stilts. This will make her angry for sure. If I want to get her mad, this is what I call her.

She grabs my hand and pulls hard. This is not my Girty. I look up. Wide eyes stare at me from her ebony face that's alive with fright. Then

I hear loud snapping sounds. 'Balekka, Balekka!' (run!) Girty screams, dragging my unresisting body as around us, wood snaps and cracks. Scary shadows distort and chase after us.

With our skinny knob-kerri knees pumping, bare feet slapping the hard dirt, we balekka towards the pathway between the house and a detached two-room building. The sounds of termite-eaten wooden supports splintering echo behind us, and the ground shakes beneath our feet like thunder rolling. The tank crashes to the ground. It splits in half and water explodes up and outwards—a roaring river swirls after us between the two buildings.

Girty yanks me sideways up onto the verandah.

Torrents of water rush past, muddy, frothing, and lapping at the verandah edge and on towards the tree where my tyre swing hangs. It's like when the rains come and the dry vlei (river bed) floods in seconds.

Girty pulls me close to her skinny body. Her chest is shuddering against my face as she smooths my hair. I look up at her. She's crying. Huge tears snake through the dust on her face making shiny train tracks on her cheeks.

'Eeeeh, picanin missus,' she keens, rocking back and forth.

'I'm sorry I called you names, Girty,' I say and hug her back.

Later, the water tank halves are dragged beyond the outside toilet and now lie under a large thorn tree, where yellow weaver birds dart back and forth, gathering grass and weaving their snake-proof nests on the outer skinny limbs of branches. Their entrance tunnels face the ground and the nests hang from a woven cord, little grass baskets that come alive with chicks that eventually launch themselves, and just know how to fly.

This is now one of my favourite spots to play and I can also protect the weaver birds. The picanin boys, with their mean catapults, sneak up from the compound. Their aim is deadly. They grip their wooden slings, pull back the old tyre rubber and release stones that kill the birds.

'Ikona!' ('No!') I shriek and run at them. The boy's skinny arms wave their catapults high above their woolly heads, as I jump to snatch them. They're faster and bigger than me. This futile chasing lasts a few minutes and then I shout, 'I'll tell the boss!' This gets their attention, they're not worried about me, but telling the boss is another matter. They bound away jeering towards the compound. It's a battle between us. Sometimes I manage to snatch a catapult which I gleefully throw into the fire that heats our hot water. Then I do a little victory dance that they can see!

Two weaver chicks launch into flight too soon. I scoop them up before the picanins do and retreat to the kitchen and insist that the boys make me a cage to keep them safe. Grandpa assures me they are easy to feed and will soon fly properly. He shows me that the inner edges of their beaks are almost hard, so they are nearly fully grown.

A few days pass and Grandpa says, 'They can fly now. Later this afternoon, when we get back from town, we will let them go near the thorn tree.'

This is exciting, they will fly free. We return from town and I race into the kitchen. The birds are gone.

'Where are they?' I ask the boys, but they don't answer or look at me. I stand by the empty cage and pick up remnants of fluffy feathers.

Grandpa turns me away and says, 'Go and find Nanna.' As I leave I hear him talking, in a low voice, to the kitchen boys. He's angry. I know the birds are dead.

***

Grandpa's gone to town, Mummy's at work and Nanna's in the Post Office. I'm supposed to be in my room resting after lunch, which is so boring. Instead, I sneak out and climb onto the roof, being very careful to walk slowly so Great Gran doesn't hear me. If she does and tells Nanna and Mummy they will probably 'give me a hiding' with the wooden coat hanger or the back of a hairbrush. They say, why hurt our hands when it's my bottom that needs to hurt? This is a risk because Grandpa's out and can't save me. So if they chase me and I run shouting, 'Grandpa, Grandpa,' at the top of my lungs, he won't appear, as if from nowhere, saying, 'Now leave the child alone!' This makes Nanna and Mummy mad.

It's the kittens on the roof that are the attraction I can't resist. There are three litters, and about 10 kittens have their eyes open and are stumbling around on wonky legs getting too close to the roof edge. I dash around snatching them up and returning them to their mothers. My anxiety is growing. The dogs are lurking below, with eyes bright and tongues lolling, drooling, just waiting for kittens to fall. It's a never-ending cycle. Kittens are born, they explore, fall off the roof and the dogs rip them to shreds. Suddenly, the dogs are in a frenzy. I've missed one and now it's too late.

Later, I gather up the kitten's remains and carefully wrap them in a scrap of material. There's a spot near the compost heap where the earth is soft. It's my private kitten cemetery. Little graves, little glass jars of flowers and little wooden crosses. I keep it looking pretty. Mummy ignores me, she's got no patience with my graves. Grandpa finds me now kneeling, crying and he wipes my eyes with his hankie. 'Come on Beverley,' he says, 'let's go inside.' He takes my hand and we walk towards the house. Grandpa stops for a few moments and gazes thoughtfully at the roof. 'They keep falling off, Grandpa,' I say, sniffing. He nods and we stroll on, side by side. Grandpa always makes me feel better, and I do now.

Several days later I see Madala, the garden boy, sitting on the ground by the tap with a small drum he's filling. I wander over and I peer in. Newborn kittens are swimming in a circle round and round in the current of the gushing water. I'm mesmerised. Madala tries to shoo me away, but I don't listen. I know what's happening.

'Ena fele?' (They die?) I ask.

'Ja, ena fele,' Madala replies, 'humba picanin.' (go away little one)

I shake my head and sit beside him in the shade of the fruit trees and wait, having decided this fate is kinder for kittens than being torn apart by dogs. I'll dig more graves.

***

We only have little dogs on our farm. Most of our friends have very big dogs and I'm scared of them. My favourite is Noddy, a corgi with a short tail, he's mine. There are two others, a black dachshund called Whooo, and Pansy, a long-legged tan and white bitsa (mixed breed). Each has a designated sleeping spot on the enclosed, partially walled, and screened verandah.

'Have you locked Whooo up, Dad?' says Mummy one evening as she arrives home from work.

Grandpa's sitting in his favourite armchair, pipe in hand, which he abandons and hurries from the sitting room, calling back over his shoulder, 'Quick, Norma, come and help find him!' The screen door at the end of the verandah bangs shut behind them.

Mummy and Grandpa are looking under the trees, bushes and any hiding spot that Whooo might have chosen.

Nanna appears and calls out, 'It's too late, he knows it's a full moon. You're not going to catch him now!'

Grandpa returns to the house in disgrace, with Mummy behind him complaining about not getting any sleep tonight.

'Eric, that dog should have been locked up after lunch,' is all Nanna grimly says.

As the house lights go out and everyone settles in bed, we hear, 'Whooooooo, Whooooo, Whooooo.' That little black dog will howl all night at the full moon. There's no point going out to try and find him. As soon as someone opens the door, he falls silent and blends with the night! That's how he got his name.

***

Every few months the dogs get angry with each other. I don't understand why but they start circling each other with low rumbling growls. This is the preliminary round that lasts a few days and progresses to teeth-baring and much snapping. Then raised hackles and stiff-legged strutting in aggressive circles. Now we all know it's getting serious. Grandpa twists some newspaper into tight lengths, and we wait.

Suddenly they're at it!

'Eric, Eric, the dogs are fighting. Quick stop them!' shouts Nanna.

Madala has turned the hose on them; to no effect. The dogs are in a frenzy ripping at each other in the dust. Grandpa grabs the newspaper twists, flicks his lighter and ignites them. He tosses several burning twists into the melee. The dogs are soaking wet and the fire drives them apart. The burning wads splutter, and extinguish in the puddles and the bloodied combatants retreat, with drooping heads, to their beds amidst the odour of singed hair and smouldering smoke.

Nanna emerges from the house carrying the pepper shaker and advances on the wounded trio. They cower in the knowledge of what is about to happen.

'Serves you right. Look at the mess you're in!' She admonishes them and proceeds to douse the many oozing wounds with pepper. Now the dogs are all sneezing and whining. 'Silly lot!' are her final words as she and the pepper shaker go inside. This is Nanna's favourite remedy for bleeding wounds. 'Clots the blood,' she informs her human patients too, and they also sneeze.

***

Noddy is vicious, but I adore him. We have to watch him when strangers come to the Post Office because he's quick to bite. He knows all the regulars. The Africans have a healthy respect for this little dog too.

One morning I'm up in the mango trees inside the turkey run, sitting on my leafy perch, chewing ripe mangos, with an elevated view of my surroundings and the narrow dirt path running past me to the compound. It's interesting watching the Africans coming and going, whilst I hide here flicking mango skins and seeds at the turkeys.

A group of mafazis (ladies) with picanins are at the tap filling assorted containers with water, laughing and chatting their voices rising and falling on the breeze. Lembu (material) is twisted into a coil that they put on their heads as a cushion to balance their water containers.

Small containers for picanins, very large ones for mafazis. It's a noisy collaboration that ensures each picanin's container is well balanced. Then they get to the mafazis.

Huge water-filled drums create a balancing act as they collectively lift each one onto a head. Now, there are three mafazis left, who crouch close; two lift a drum and place it on the third's head and she remains crouching to help lift the second drum. These two mafazis, balancing their drums, then lift the third drum. Much shouting, instructing, and grunting ensues from those watching and waiting until the drum settles on the final head and their strong legs strain to stand.

It's done. Barely a spill.

They form an orderly, raucous line walking past me in the Mango trees, along the pathway to the compound; the oldest first, hips swaying, some with babies tied on their backs, down to the youngest, at the rear balancing little tins and jugs on little heads.

Noddy is hiding in the long grass at the edge of the path, camouflaged by his cream and tan coat. I've only just spotted him, he raises himself. It's too late to stop him. If I shout it won't make any difference. As the last balanced teapot head passes him, Noddy launches barking and dashing between their legs.

Shrieking, screams and cries mingle with rapid barking. Water containers crash to the ground and the dignified column disintegrates into a mass of bodies fleeing down the narrow pathway. Noddy stands proudly in the puddles panting, his stubby tail wagging. The hullabaloo diminishes as the group reaches the far end of the path. They shout angrily at Noddy. Much later the picanins scurry back, wide-eyed, their heads swivelling as they look out for the dog and gather the small tins and roll the larger drums down the path. They will return later and I'll lock Noddy up!

I must remember to wash my face later too. If I don't, mango juice around my lips will tell tales of where I've been.

Chapter 3
Cranky Great Gran, Tickies and Bad Words

(Lydia Elizabeth Walker née Clarke 1876–1964)

'Bitch.' *That's a naughty word!* Now, I'm paying attention.

Great Gran mutters, 'Bitch' again, almost as if she's alone. But she is not. Nanna's crouching at her feet, head down, and not saying a word. My elephant ears are working overtime. Nanna would usually say, 'I can feel a breeze, Beverley, go and play!' But she doesn't know I'm here, hidden behind Grandpa's favourite chair. I've been watching Nanna going back and forth carrying assorted items and placing them near Great Gran's chair: a bowl of steaming water, clean towels, soap, and finally a small box. It's comfortable here, the textured material against my cheek, the polished wooden armrests curving gently from view, with hints of Grandpa's pipe wrapping around me. It's cosy and safe and I can almost feel his arms holding me.

I should not be here.

From her favourite chair, Great Gran is also watching Nanna. 'Thank goodness she can't get around,' Mummy frequently says. Nanna kneels on the floor, carefully removes Great Gran's stocking and places her feet in the bowl of water; beside which lie nail clippers and other implements. I know Nanna is fixing 'bunions', whatever they are. I only know that they're on her feet.

Great Gran's saying that bad word over and over. Nanna is not looking up. If I can hear her, Nanna can too. I wish I wasn't here. *Grandpa, come back. I know you're fixing the borehole pump. I can't call you. Come back, please.*

'Mum, what are you doing that for!' exclaims Mummy from the doorway. 'I said I'd do the bunions. Mum, get up. Please.' Mummy's angry and upset. Her voice and face tell me that. *Thank goodness you're home, Mummy. I dare not tell you the naughty word. You will be even more cross if I do.*

'Norma, I don't want you doing my bunions! Iris can do them,' says Great Gran. Her voice is strong, and she's alert. Did she know she was saying rude words? Maybe.

'Well, Gran, that might be the case, but Mum's not well. I don't give a damn what you want! When your bunions need doing, I'll do them!'

'Norma, it's fine, I've finished,' says Nanna drying Great Gran's feet. 'Please put her stocking on for me.' Nanna's tired, I can hear it in her voice. Great Gran shouts, 'You do it, Iris! Don't you touch me Norma, you disrespectful girl! Get away from me.'

'No, I won't!' says Mummy. 'You're going to let me or go without your stocking!'

Mummy takes Nanna's arm and helps her up all the while glaring at Great Gran, whose lips are clamped shut as she glares back. It's a battle of wills and Mummy wins. She pulls the stocking over those bunion-free feet, very firmly.

They leave the room, carrying the bowl and towels. Great Gran's eyes follow them. She stamps her walking stick hard on the lino floor. 'Two bitches!' I hear her say and hug closer to my hiding spot.

Then, a whisper reaches me, 'You can come out now, Beverley.'

***

Great Gran spends most of her day in the sitting room. It takes two people to get her out of bed, dressed, and seated, and she has a crocheted blanket over her knees on cooler days. From there, her cantankerous old lady's eyes follow us about our daily business, her sharp ears listen to distant conversations, and her stamping walking stick asserts authority along with her strident voice calling for attention. She can be difficult.

Everyone knows she's in 'considerable pain'; an excuse Grandpa uses for her bad behaviour. Nanna and Mummy do not tell tales about her to Grandpa. She is his mother, and they show him that respect.

'Iris. Get me my chlorodyne. Iris, where are you?' shouts Great Gran, each word punctuated by thumps on the lino with her walking stick. Nanna appears from the kitchen with a glass of water in hand, picks up a small brown bottle from the dresser and adds drops to the water that disperse in a muddy trail.

'More, put more in! I'm in terrible pain. Hurry up!' Great Gran snaps and glares at Nanna. 'You never put enough in.' Nanna adds a few extra drops, only her pursed lips betray her thoughts.

Great Gran's hand trembles as she drinks the murky water, sighs, closes her eyes and says, 'Thank you, Iris.' Nanna touches her shoulder, adjusts the crochet blanket and then walks away. Quietly, I make myself scarce.

These conflicting gestures and expressions confuse me. Nanna's angry when Great Gran shouts, but is kind to her. Is it because of 'the pain' that all the adults discuss? Is that why she can't walk or get out of bed unaided—the one Mum says Great Gran slept in with Great Grandpa next to her, dead—and needs help to use her commode in the bedroom that smells bad sometimes? It's confusing, but I know what she thinks of me because she tells me. Sometimes, I'm a 'naughty girl' who 'needs a hiding' and sometimes, I'm a 'good child, here's a tickie (threepence) for sweeties' but generally I 'should be seen and not heard.' That's the one I like. It allows me to stay and 'flap my ears'!

Today, maybe I'm a 'good child'. Great Gran is half smiling at me. An earlier dose of chlorodyne has put her in a good mood.

'Come here Beverley,' she says, her voice soft. I'm suspicious and hover a few feet from her, recognising the overture of a game she likes to play. Sometimes I win, sometimes she wins.

I observe her trying to gauge her mood: one hand grips her walking stick; not by the handle but part way down the shaft, the other is extended towards me, fist closed. Does it conceal a tickie? I consider my options and examine her grip and fist. When was the last time I was rude? Great Gran remembers things like that! If she has a tickie hidden in her fist, can I snatch it and jump back before her stick hits me? Or, will her palm uncurl, empty? Then, I'll lose focus, be slow to jump and she will whack me!

'Here Beverley, a tickie for a good girl!' She says, interrupting my thoughts. Her head tips towards her fist, her arthritic fingers uncurl and it's there: a shiny small tickie, beckoning me.

I leap forward and snatch the warm coin. *Whack!* Her stick connects with my leg! I shriek, stumble out of her reach and retreat, limping. Great Gran's stout frame is wobbling with silent laughter. From the doorway, the tickie on show between two fingers, I stick my tongue out and do a little dance. She shouts, 'Iris! The child needs a hiding!' I'm not worried, Nanna will ignore her! This time it's a draw. Tickie to me, successful *whack* to Great Gran.

We always eat at the table, set with polished silver, polished serviette rings, and steaming tureens with lids. Standards are maintained, despite our house, where tree roots occasionally bulge under the lino. Meals appear from the wood-fired stove, also used to heat a variety of irons for pressing clothes, and which warms the kitchen in winter and is too hot in summer. Great Gran insists on sitting at the table for dinner. Moving her there takes two people exerting considerable effort; she sits at the head, next to a small window that affords her a perfect view of the sitting room TV, which she watches while eating, very slowly. No one leaves the table until we are all finished, and no one will say *anything* to Great Gran, that's called being rude!

So, we all sit in restrained silence.

Chapter 4
Daddy Comes To See Me.

Soon, Daddy will be here, again. Everyone will be happy to see him. Except for Mummy. His last visit taught me to hide my happy voice from her, and that I love the swing he put up for me. I can't *wait* for him to get here. Excitement bounces around inside me and I forget that Mummy isn't going to be pleased.

'Daddy's coming to see me, Mummy, did you hear?' I chortle while dancing around. 'Grandpa's just told me!' He's trying to tickle me and Mummy's staring into the distance, ignoring my antics. She's not hearing me. I gently tug her full skirt.

'When's he coming?' I gaze up at her. She's beautiful.

'I've forgotten,' she says drawing on her cigarette and pushing my hand away. 'Ask Grandpa, he knows.'

'Norma!' says Grandpa. He ruffles my hair, 'Tomorrow, he'll be here tomorrow. Off you go and play.' I linger long enough for my 'elephant ears' to hear him say, 'No need to be like that Norma, she's just a child. You might not like Denny's visits, but *we* do. Be polite too!'

'Gran won't, don't see why I need be!'

'For the child, *that's* why!' Grandpa replies, 'Denny excuses your Gran.'

Grandpa sounds stern. This is not how he usually speaks to us. But, he and Nanna like Daddy, so it's alright.

I run across the yard to my swing—an old car tyre cut up and fashioned into a seat with sides. Daddy made it the last time he came to visit. He'd climbed the tree, stretched out across a branch, high up, and secured long chains that dangled to hold the seat. I'd stood below shouting for him to be careful and he'd teased: 'I'll squash you if I fall and that will save me!' Later, he pushed me on that swing and my feet yearned to be tickled by the green leaves. 'Higher, higher!' I'd shouted and Daddy had called back, 'Touch the leaves with your toes.'

Now he's coming and will push me again, even though there are no leaves on the tree.

***

Tomorrow arrives and the garden boy alerts me. 'The boss's train is here.' I race down the path, through the long grass, to the railway siding. The train has pulled up. There he is. 'Daddy Daddy!' I shriek, hopping from one bare foot to the other in the red dirt. He scoops me up and hugs me hard, I hang back in his arms and touch his face. He is real and *here*. I'm so happy and his long-lashed brown eyes love me.

The siding boys unload a white bath, a washbasin, and a toilet. There's much pointing and joking over these items as Daddy negotiates with them to carry them to the farmhouse.

Down the narrow bush path, in a chongolola line, we go. The boys follow Daddy and me, singing as they go, and carrying the enamel bath, basin, and toilet above their heads. The long grass is swishing as we make a grand entrance to the farm. Daddy pays them. Their cream-coloured palms accept coins amidst belly-rolling laughter and hand-slapping. Tonight, at the shabeen (beer hall), they will laugh, even more, recounting the story of the crazy Mukiwa (white boy) and his bathroom goods!

Only one person is not happy about the arrival of Daddy with his enamel goods, and that's Great Gran, whose lack of amusement and opinion is heard by all.

'What was good enough for me is good enough for you lot!' She shouts. 'Get him out of my house. Is he sleeping next to the sewing room? Norma, you tell him!' No one agrees with her so she continues, 'Eric, I told you, he's not putting those things in the bathroom!'

The tirade fills our ears. The household ignores her. Grandpa talks to her calmly, 'Mum, we need a proper bath and toilet *inside*. Denny's been good enough to bring them from Bulawayo, and do the work!'

Grandpa's words are ineffective and Daddy just keeps on installing the bathroom luxuries. Out goes the old narrow metal bath, loved by me for the long sloping back that is great soaped up and used as a slide. I'd swish down that slide and water would fly over the edges onto the floor. Mummy loved that bath too, she'd lie there, book in hand, stretched out with her toes just touching the end – soaking, smoking, and reading.

Now there will be no more holding our noses while we use the hole-in-the-ground wooden seat P.K. way up the back near the compost heap. The night potty is gone from under our beds, replaced by a flushing toilet with a wall water tank and a long pull-chain. We are in awe of the bathroom. Fire-heated hot water is now flowing into the new bath and hand basin.

Great Gran runs out of voice and sulks in her permanent chair in the sitting room. But if anyone stops to listen, she starts to shout again. Anyway, she has a commode in her bedroom and is bathed by Nanna in her bed. So why does she care?

***

Daddy decides it is easier to eat his meals outside under the trees, that way he can keep away from Great Gran. This evening he's sitting on the verandah with Nanna and Grandpa, who is enjoying his pipe, and I'm sitting on the floor at his feet. The screen door bangs and Mummy comes out carrying two poured beers. She hands Grandpa one and holds the other out to Daddy. The fluffy white foam rises above the pewter tankard rim, condensation beading on its outside.

Daddy looks up at her, 'No thank you, Norma, I've got my coffee,' he says.

Her laughter fills the air and in a funny voice, she says, 'Oh, that's right Denny, you don't drink. How silly of me to forget! Suppose I'll just have to enjoy it, won't I?' She sits on the edge of the verandah, puts the tankard down and pulls cigarettes and a lighter from her skirt pocket. 'Might as well enjoy a cigarette too,' she adds and flicks the lighter. 'I'll make sure the smoke doesn't drift your way,' she says and exhales.

Nanna gets up, 'Norma, perhaps we should go inside, the mosquitoes are going to come out soon.'

'Not just yet Mum, I'm enjoying sitting here,' says Mummy.

Nanna goes inside and Grandpa says, 'Denny, what's your opinion of this move by Britain regarding independence for Northern Rhodesia?'

'Eric, it's a disaster if you ask me, I…'

'Oh for God's sake, who wants to talk bloody politics on a lovely evening like this!' Mummy interrupts. She gets to her feet and leaves with her beer and cigarette.

Grandpa sips his cold beer. 'Denny, I want to say how much we appreciate the new bathroom, very good of you.'

Daddy's smiling. 'My pleasure,' he says, and sips his coffee.

And then Daddy is gone again. I cry.

Mummy says, 'Don't carry on like that! You'll make your face look ugly!' Grandpa's warm beside me; he's looking at Mummy who suddenly keeps quiet. He coughs. Mummy frowns. 'That's a "smoker's cough,"' the adults say.

***

Months later, Mummy and I are in the sewing room. It's one of the two-room buildings detached from the main house. It's where Daddy has to sleep when he comes to visit. Sunlight slants in from the open verandah. Outside, a stiff late-winter breeze kicks up small puffs of red dust. The sewing machine hums along, eating up yards of fabric under Mummy's nimble fingers. It's Saturday, so she isn't at work, but her hands are not idle for long. In her spare time, she sews and knits. She makes all our clothes.

'I've lost my thread,' I murmur in disgrace.

Mummy reaches down, rethreads my needle, and passes it back with the scrap of material my nearly five-year-old fingers are trying to stitch.

The machine hums. 'I've lost it again.'

Mummy stops, squints at the eye of the needle, re-threads and knots the cotton ends together. 'There,' she says, 'Now you won't lose it.' I smile up at her, this is nice. Mummy is beautiful with soft brown eyes that change with her mood. They sparkle when a jest reaches her perfect lips. When she laughs, it's a tinkling sound that makes everyone smile.

'Finished!' She flicks the dress over her bent knees and plucks the garment into place with her long-painted fingernails. It's lovely: fitted bodice, puff sleeves, a full gathered skirt of soft pink fabric over fluffy petticoats. It's a fairytale dress. For good. Not a 'play outside' one. My little fingers stray over the fabric and her thoughtful eyes meet mine.

'Your father's coming to see you,' she says, her lips compressing, like when she's pricked her finger with a pin.

'When?' I ask in a careful voice, the one I use for *may I leave the table?* Rather than the one that wells in my throat, wanting to shout, *yippee!* I've learned to keep that happy voice to myself when Mummy mentions Daddy, which is hardly ever.

Concentrating on the dress, she continues, 'In a few days. He's taking you to Ladysmith and Durban to see your Granny and cousins. He's coming on the train.' She pauses, looks out the door, and then quickly adds, 'You'll drive to South Africa from Bulawayo.' I've no idea where Bulawayo is, but I do know where the train arrives and that's an easy place to be.

Nanna knits me a bolero of pale pink angora wool to match the dress. Soft wool sprouts like candy floss over the soft garment. She explains, 'This is your dinner dress and bolero for when you stay at the Palmerston Hotel in Durban. Remember your manners, and put your serviette in your lap.'

***

Grandpa shakes Daddy's hand as he gets off the train. We walk to the farmhouse, I'm running along the path ahead calling to Nanna, who comes out of the Post Office. She hugs Daddy and they are all chatting away. Daddy's hand finds mine and I try to pull him away towards the swing. 'Let him have a coffee first, Beverley,' says Nanna. The tea tray is ready and I see Bluey the cat lounging on the counter just waiting for his saucer of weak tea. It's adult time, I'll just have to wait! This is extremely exciting because we are going on holiday and I'm going with Daddy on the train!

Everything is great until the next day. Daddy is holding my hand, saying goodbye to Nanna and Grandpa. My suitcase is upright on the ground beside him.

Mummy? I can't see her. Where is she? Mummy! I pull away and run fast through the house, silently searching; she's not inside. Maybe she's outside in the sewing room.

There she is! Tears dripping off my chin I fling myself into her unsuspecting lap and push my face into her bust. She's here.

Firm hands move me away. She stands up, looks down, and fluffs out her crumpled skirt. It's yellow, and I launch into its gathered folds where laundry soap lingers. It's where I want to be.

She grasps my hands, untangles my fingers, and steps back. Gone is the fabric and scent, the memory of them hangs in the space around me. Her extended hand protects her skirt and she says, 'Stop it! Just stop it right now!'

'I don't want to go,' I sob. My chest is hiccupping.

'Oh, for goodness sake! You've been going on and on about your father coming. I've made you nice holiday clothes. Now go on, he's waiting!'

Oh, Mummy, I loved sitting by your side while you sewed those clothes, loved the feel of your brisk hands pulling them over my body, making them fit and you saying, 'Walk over there so I can see. Keep your back straight!' I walked back and forth, doing as you said, warm in your gaze and praise;

feeling fingers at my knees, measuring the hem. But now the clothes are packed into my suitcase.

I don't want to leave you. It all sounded exciting until now. Why are you angry with me? Is it because I'm crying? I know you don't like that, but I can't stop. Maybe if I do, you'll hug me.

She stands very still. Tears continue to leak down my face. She smoothes her water-spotted skirt, sighs, and turns away lifting a lit cigarette towards her lips. Smoke trails around us. Her rigid profile is all I see. Grandpa's shadow darkens the room. He's in the doorway.

Without a word, he takes my hand and leads me away into the sunshine towards the old water tank, where Daddy is standing. His long shadow leans towards me, beckoning. 'How about we walk to the train together?' Grandpa says. He squats, his folded hankie flicks and blots my tears.

Hand in hand we walk silently, past Bluey in the hedge, past the Post Office, over the road, and down the narrow path to the siding. The train is waiting. Daddy lifts me into the carriage and a large door bangs behind us. He opens a noisy sliding door, and we go into a room with green leather seats. 'This is our compartment, where we will sleep,' Daddy says. I kneel on the seat and hang out the open window, Grandpa's looking up at me. He seems sad. Maybe I should stay with him? I try to smile, but my bottom lip quivers. He winks at me. I giggle. Grandpa looks better now, so I know it's OK to go.

The train jerks. The massive black wheels churn and we gather speed. Ragged picanins race alongside, leaping and laughing until they can't keep up anymore, and Grandpa becomes a dot, far away. The bundu hurries past our window. I hang my head out and start to sing. That makes it feel like home.

***

Durban is so busy! Cars and people are everywhere; we book into the Palmerston Hotel.

Daddy's unpacking and says to me, 'Now, Beverley, when we are in the room you call me Daddy. OK'

I nod my head

'But when we go out, you're to call me Denny. Got it?'

'Yes, Denny.'

'No, Daddy here and Denny outside!'

'Yes, Denny.'

After several more tries, he gives up.

I never get it right! Or maybe I just don't want to, so Daddy can't chat with the ladies who might like him better without me!

***

We go for a walk along the beachfront, I long to run along the sand, but then Daddy points and says, 'Look rickshaws, come on Beverley, let's go for a ride!'

I try to pull him away but Daddy keeps walking towards them. I'm scared. The rickshaw man's so tall wearing a headdress of multi-coloured beads, shaped like a fan, and it towers above his head, and on top of that ostrich feathers reach even higher. Two curved cow horns, decorated with blue, red and white beads, curve upwards and two curve downwards over his chest, covered with a beaded cloth that falls past his waist. Around his shins cow tails hang and as he walks towards us, bells jingle with every step. He leaps into the air, shrieking and waving his cowhide shield and a spear. I almost scream!

Daddy pulls me towards a brightly coloured cart, with two huge, decorated wheels, seats, and a canopy that covers our heads.

'This will be fun,' he says and hoists me into a seat covered with cushions, and climbs in next to me. The rickshaw driver grabs two long poles attached to the cart and begins to jog along the street. His bells jingle and people are pointing and staring. This is OK. Suddenly, the driver shrieks loudly and tips the rickshaw back. His cart's now rolling down the street with us almost on our backs, he's high in the air, feet dancing and jingling and still shrieking. Daddy's laughing. I'm screaming. But it is *fun!*

For dinner, I wear the special dress Mummy made, with the Angora wool bolero Nanna knitted. Daddy manages to tie a large white bow in my hair and I feel special and grown up when we sit at the dining table, set with silver and serviettes in rings.

Daddy orders curry and tells me, 'Curry to make me cry, the hotter the better.'

'I'll have curry, please.'

'No, you won't eat it.'

I get difficult, and Daddy, with a cross face, orders me curry.

I don't eat it.

***

We've already visited family in Ladysmith and I played with my cousin, Cindy. Now, here in Durban, we go to see Granny who lives at North Beach on Marine Parade. It's wonderful to be with Daddy. She doesn't say anything about my visit with Mummy and I just know to keep quiet too.

I remember that visit, Mummy and I were on holiday in Durban. She made me special clothes to wear and we played at the beach with the coarse white and fine pepper-black sand beneath our feet. The sand stuck to our skin refusing steadfastly to rinse away even under the gushing taps. It didn't matter. We walked happily along the Corso, splotched with patchwork black sand, past shops overflowing with buckets and spades in brilliant colours, calling me in to touch them and gaze.

A beach photographer, who displayed his photos in a kiosk for people to buy, followed us every day. He clicked and snapped until Mummy agreed to pose on top of a wall. She looked beautiful standing there, in her structured bathers, her shapely long legs crossed at the ankles, flaunting frills over her hourglass hips. Another time we posed with our faces framed through life-size cardboard caricature boards with scenes from Hawaii and a Jailhouse. And then one day she snatched his camera and took his photograph and we all laughed. We bought that photo too, with a lot of others, on the last day. Now those photos live in our home, and in my mind.

One afternoon while walking along Marine Parade, Mummy suddenly stopped, her attention focused on an old lady turning into a doorway. There was something vaguely familiar about her to Mummy and then she said, 'That's your Granny, your father's mother.' Her face was thoughtful and I knew to be quiet. She grabbed my hand and we walked quickly into the same building. We went up several floors in a rickety close-the-grill-door lift and paused in the hallway before Mummy hurried forward and knocked on a door.

It opened. Granny was standing staring at us. Mummy was very still.

'Oh my goodness!' Granny said, her hands trembling and reaching towards us. 'It's you, Norma, and Beverley! Oh my!' She took Mummy's hand and pulled her closer. 'Norma, this is such a wonderful surprise, come in! Beverley, let's look at you child!'

Tears wobbled in her eyes and they embraced.

It was 1962, and I was almost five years old.

Chapter 5
There Are Three Men In My Life.

There are three men in my life. Grandpa, my protector from 'a hiding', who loves me and buys me secret ice cream treats. Daddy, who comes to visit with hugs, pushes my swing high and sends presents. And there is Carl, who also visits and always buys me *Noddy* books, and reads to me.

***

Carl comes to visit when it's dry or not raining too much and the roads are passable. His farm is further out than ours, over a lumpy crater-filled road that makes our teeth chatter, or so wet and slushy that we can't get there. Grandpa enjoys Carl's company, and this evening, they're outside drinking Castle Lager beer and smoking, their deep voices filter to me where I'm lying on the ground stroking Carl's dog, a tan and white collie who rubs her narrow nose into my face. Her name is Annatoria! What a funny name for a farm dog, but she is beautiful.

The sun sinks as a searing ball towards the horizon, its dying blaze skulks behind the darkening trees and bushes that merge into a flat sepia mass. Then, in a final explosion of orange across the sky, it sizzles and rests; gone. Chirping birds jockey for space in the trees and settle. The first nightlife emerges as bats weave their silent flight like fast shadows in the moonlight, frogs and crickets begin to tune their instruments and small creatures sneak out to eat.

Two cigarette tips glow behind me and their voices rumble. It's comforting. Mummy and Nanna come onto the verandah banging the screen door, disrupting our harmony. There's the soft scuffling of Africans from the compound gathering, some squatting, others keeping the children close. Their outlines, like cut-out shapes, are distinguishable in the seeping sitting room light. But I can see their lovely white teeth when they laugh. It feels comfortable with us all together.

The dogs are locked inside. Great Gran is helped outside, with two walking sticks, and sits quietly in the shadows.

Nanna pulls me onto her lap and wraps her arms around me. I relax into her ample bosom, enjoying the warmth and her heartbeat near my ear. She doesn't often hold me.

Carl walks into the velvet dark, strikes a match, and an orange-yellow flame stands tall, illuminating his face. A fuse is lit. The Catherine Wheel fizzes, spinning rapidly, tossing ever-changing brilliant sparks, flames and brightness, a hissing show chorused by the wide-eyed, faces. Then it's done. Momentary quiet. Then suddenly there's cheering and clapping, amidst the floating smoke and sulphur smell of rotten eggs.

Now he lights a rocket which soars upwards, exploding to our mingled cries of awe. The show continues and finally, Grandpa and Carl bring out the sparklers. One is placed in each of my hands, little black hands reach for theirs. They are lit and we run together, waving spiky spitting sticks, swirling patterns shine on our innocent faces and like conductors, we wave our arms around and orchestrate our shrieks in the night. And as the sparklers fizz to an end, I look at all the African faces around me and feel like I belong. Belong right here. It's Guy Fawkes 1962, and I'll be five years old next week.

***

Not long after that, we go to Salisbury for a day trip. It is exciting because we don't go to the city often. Nanna and Mummy walk from shop to shop. We have tea and milkshakes in a café, and I use my best manners. We return home with parcels, including a new doll and a pair of black shoes for me.

'I'm glad to see you got Clarkes,' says Grandpa looking at my new shoes, safe in their box. 'Norma, I still think she's too young for school!'

'Dad, when I got home the other day, Beverley and Girty greeted me from their hiding place under the table. I couldn't tell who was speaking.

She sounded like a picanin!' Mummy seems cross. 'She needs to go to school, I know it's a year earlier than most, but she'll manage.'

How am I supposed to sound? Picanin? Aren't I one anyway?

My 'elephant ears' have let me down until now. Normally I'm good at lurking and gathering information. School. This is news to me. The confining sensation of the new shoes being pushed onto my feet returns and I recall the shoe lady saying, 'Put some newspaper in the toes and they will last all year.' It makes me anxious. I retreat to my bedroom, hold my new doll—now named Elizabeth—and leaf through my favourite *Noddy* books from Carl. These are safe things to do. Later, I'll go and climb the mango trees and think about why I'm like a picanin and not supposed to be. Anyway, who cares if I am?

During mango season, I climb these trees and taunt the turkeys by throwing mango skins amongst them. *Gobble Gobble Gobble,* they go, and with wings flapping, they scurry after the treats. I toss the mango seeds I've chewed on into the squabbling bunch, usually managing to hit the most aggressive birds. Grandpa doesn't like me to do this, so most of the time I don't throw the seed hard.

Along with chickens, turkeys are an important source of income for us. Grandpa says, 'People prefer the turkeys with white feathers!'

How do they know if they had white feathers, once they're frozen? It's a bit like the picanin thing, isn't it?

Today the boys start preparing the turkeys and chickens for sale. They've long given up chasing me away saying, 'humba, humba,' accompanied by flapping hands that make me laugh because they look like turkeys flapping their wings. Sitting in the shade of Grandpa's fruit trees, I watch them chop off the bird's heads. Decapitated, round and round they run spurting blood until they collapse in red feathered heaps. The boys think it's funny. Within hours, the birds are plucked, packed, and frozen.

***

The rains will arrive soon. October is hot. The earth bakes day after day, its red cracked skin gasping for moisture. We call this suicide month!

The wind kicks up dust and heat lingers into the night. Everything is waiting for the November rains, when huge cumulonimbus clouds will march over the horizon, their flat-bottomed bases angry, black-grey, rising in towers to off-white. The sun pierces through and streaks across the sky. They rumble, like Matabele warriors preparing for battle, beating spears on animal hide shields, echoing, on and on. Then the warriors engage. Lightning spears fly, slicing jagged holes through the darkening sky. The feet of a thousand men pound the earth; it vibrates. Shields crash together roaring in our ears.

Suddenly the rain falls. Huge plops smack into the dust so hard that miniature explosions of red rise. Then the deluge begins and the roaring fills our ears and pounds on the corrugated iron roof, demanding that we listen. I run outside and dash around wildly, my arms flung wide and face upturned. It's *wonderful* to be wet. I love the mud squelching between my toes and puddle-jumping in the rain!

Now the earth heaves with nature. The air fills with small white-winged ants that are suddenly everywhere. Their lacy wings detach, and scatter in the breeze and the ants scurry searching for new nesting grounds. The birds peck and feast on them. Under trees, the Chongololos (African millipedes) appear and their hard shiny bodies slink along on hundreds of small feet. If you touch them they coil up tight. I collect them in a paper bag, and chase after Mummy, 'I've got a present for you!' Her face lights up until she opens the bag and sees the Chongololo's twisting and writhing inside! She shrieks and tosses them away exclaiming, 'Siss!' I do agree with her. They are quite smelly since they've pooed in the bag!

In a low tree grove, huge snails emerge from the wet earth. So large, that their creamy white shells overfill my palm, and their slimy, shiny trails squiggle over the leaves and twigs. I touch their albino heads and waving antennae and watch them shrink into the safety of their mobile homes.

Within days, green shoots erupt over the barren veld creating a grass vista and the narrow winding footpaths are sharply defined. The naked, hard-thorned acacia trees sprout leaves and milky soft thorns, their brittle limbs with grey thorns no longer rattle in the wind. The vlei (shallow, intermittent lake) beds flood and torrents of water gush over the eroded ground and rocks, and between the gnarled exposed tree roots. The landscape is soft now, with flowing water and lush greens. It's as if the earth beneath our feet sighs, saying…. thank you.

***

It's Sunday, Mummy and Nanna want to go for a picnic, on the banks of the nearby Umfuli River, and I'm about to learn a valuable adult lesson. They know Grandpa isn't interested and will refuse to take them. Nanna says to Mummy, 'Let's see if it works, you start.'

Start what? I follow them into the sitting room.

'I think the Umfuli must be flooding,' says Mummy as if Grandpa's not there. 'We've had so much rain!'

'It's not,' says Grandpa; he's listening to the radio.

'Well, Dad let's hope you're right, otherwise I won't be off to work tomorrow.'

'Sorry, Norma you will be going. It's not going to flood yet.'

'Your father's right,' says Nanna. 'Although, when Mrs Jones stopped in for eggs she said it's going flood for sure. But then who knows with her!' My sharp ears didn't hear that! Is Nanna fibbing, surely not.

A few minutes later, 'Ladies, how about we go and have a picnic by the river.'

The ladies grab the prepared basket—the hot water flask—and are out the door before Grandpa leaves his favourite chair.

'Come on Beverley,' he says, 'I've let them win again. They think I don't know what they're up to! I was going to take them anyway.'

Win *what?* I've missed something here! I guess it's some strange adult game they're playing.

It's lovely down on the banks of the river and we lie on blankets after eating. Weaver birds' nests hang over the water, and the local hippo yawns so wide I think he could swallow me! What huge, curved teeth.

I must remember to clean mine tonight.

***

Christmas season arrives and Nanna bakes the Christmas fruit cake in the wood stove oven, and makes a calico-clad pudding, with hidden silver charms and coins wrapped in greaseproof paper. It hangs, fragrant with brandy and spices that waft a promise of what is yet to come. In December, she will roll out pastry with Mummy and make soft-topped mince pies. I can't wait for Grandpa to untangle the Christmas tree lights so we can hang them up.

On Christmas Day we feast on a white feathered turkey and pull crackers. The best part is the pudding, when we seek out the coins and charms. Grandpa watches closely. They are hard to find under the cream and fruit. 'Beverley, look over there he says,' and points at the tree, and when I look back, wrapped coins and charms have miraculously appeared on my pudding plate.

Carl comes to visit at Christmas and brings me another *Noddy* book and reads it to me. Daddy sends a large box with wrapped presents that Mummy pokes holes in so she can peek and see. I forget about school until a few weeks later.

'Girty is leaving us now,' says Mummy one day. Girty is standing beside me, her fingers are clenching mine. They're hot and sticky.

'Why?'

'She's getting married and you're off to school next week. Grandpa is going to take you and pick you up every day.'

Girty hugs me and leaves. My best friend is gone. I cry a lot, but not where Mummy can see me making an ugly face.

Mummy takes me to school on the first day. She's made my uniform and I'm wearing the horrid new Clarkes shoes with newspaper-stuffed toes. Her hand is gone. I'm in a line with other children. I glance around, they are all so noisy, like the birds nesting at sunset, chattering in my head and it feels *strange*; and it's not just the place. Then it comes to me. We are all white. I've never seen so many white children before.

Tears gather and I search for Mummy's face, she's not with the others clustered together talking.

Inside, we have to sit at desks and look at the teacher. Through the windows, the trees in the playground beckon. I don't want to be here. This is school. I'm not impressed. I want to go home, run barefoot to the compound and play with my friends. Grandpa's waiting at lunchtime, by the gate, and we stop for an ice cream treat!

Some things are fun at school, we draw and play outside for part of the day. We listen to stories, and I like that. There's a 'Wendy House' and only clever girls are given a reward by the teacher to play there. I try hard, but some things confuse me. We are given coloured, different-length blocks (Cuisenaire rods) and are supposed to do something with them. I stare at mine with no idea of what to do. So I line them up around my desk and build a multi-coloured road. 'What are you doing?' The teacher says frowning. 'I'm building a strip road home. If I had a toy car it would be better.' It was months before I got to play in the 'Wendy House'.

We stand in a group and sing, 'Kookaburra sits in the old gum tree,' and make funny laughing sounds. No one knows what a kookaburra looks like. We must stand up straight to sing, 'God Save our Gracious Queen,' whoever that is! She must be important because we don't fidget or talk when we sing to her.

Small bottles of milk arrive in crates and wait for us under the tree in the playground. We all line up, take one and under the watchful eyes of teachers, peel back the foil top and drink warm *yucky* milk. It dribbles down the boy's shirts and we have little white moustaches to prove we've finished. Then we can play. Milk days are *awful*.

***

With Girty gone, I'm left to my own devices after lunch. This is a new experience, and I enjoy the freedom to explore. The best times to escape are when the adults are all busy. Times like when Grandpa is fixing the borehole down by the chicken runs, or Nanna, Great Gran, and

Mummy are sitting in a circle perming each other's hair. They smell like rotten eggs and that makes Grandpa glad to leave the house. They will be occupied for hours, so it's time to go.

The vastness of the bundu attracts me. As I get older, I begin to wander further from the main house. The maize fields swallow me, their green stems tower tall and I dart in and out playing hide and seek with imaginary friends. Dry vlei beds offer hours of scratching around for small bones, shed snake skins left in the tangle of exposed roots, interesting stones, broken bird's eggs, and feathers—all of which come home with me. I visit stagnant pools of water festooned with strings of frogs eggs and watch for tadpoles to hatch that will morph into small frogs that hop away. It's annoying to miss them doing that.

Today, I have an idea. Tin can in hand, I head for the pools of water and catch tadpoles. In a few days, they will be frogs because they've already got legs and stumpy tails. Back home, I hide them in the dairy in a large tray with sand, a few rocks, and water, and promptly forget them.

Several days later Nanna's shouting, 'Where did all these frogs come from!' I can hear her from the kitchen. This will earn me a hiding for sure. Quickly I run towards the safety of the mango trees.

***

Grandpa does the daily school run. He picks me up at lunchtime and we travel home on the strip road, bumping along, past the Passaportis's yapping Pekingese pack. After finishing my ice cream, I hang my head out the window and sing at the top of my voice. The wind whips the words from my mouth and scatters them over the trees. I'm *free!*

One morning Mummy says that Mr Sparkes is giving me a lift to and from school. Nanna's in hospital, something's wrong with her heart, my big ears hear, and they are going to visit her. It's far away. I don't know who Mr Sparkes is and I'm not going to ask. Mummy's already impatient with me. He arrives in a small red car. I climb in and he nods at me, then 'puts foot' (drives fast) towards town. My hands clench the seat. I'm terrified. Grandpa drives slowly; this strange man is driving too fast. The car jerks to a stop at the school gate and I stumble out. He's gone, wheels spinning and flinging clouds of dust. My legs are shaking, my heart thumping. Mr Sparkes picks me up. He doesn't speak and just 'puts foot' back to the farm. I stare at his profile, it's stern, and I'm scared of the speed, and him too. This man doesn't like me. What have I done to make him so angry?

That night, Grandpa's reading to me and I start crying. He holds me close and the day's events gush out. 'Who is Mr Sparkes?' I ask, 'Why doesn't he like me?'

'I'll make sure you never go anywhere with him again,' says Grandpa, his voice is calm, but I can feel his anger. Not with me, but with this strange man. I don't understand, and I don't care, because Grandpa's here.

Later, I hear Grandpa talking to Mummy. His voice is low and muffled, and Mummy's arguing loudly with him.

'I'm sure Beverley is just making it sound bad!'

Grandpa raises his voice and says, 'He scared her. That man is not to come here again! That's it, Norma.' I fold myself into the eiderdown and eventually go to sleep. Adults are so complicated.

Chapter 6
Two Daddys, A Wedding, A Baby, and Loompi

A potato flies past us, just missing Nanna, Grandpa, and me.

'Oh for goodness sake!' says Nanna, 'Someone pushed a potato up the car exhaust pipe, how foolish!'

The cheering crowd beneath the spotted shade of flamboyant trees, festooned with red blooms and feather-like leaves, begins to move away. We are all dressed up in our 'Sunday best' with shiny shoes, women wearing hats, men in suits, and everyone's talking loudly. Mummy looks beautiful in a pale green and cream full-skirted dress, its soft folds graceful around her knees. A white hat circled with flowers sits on her hair which is set around her ears. People cluster around her, and she climbs into a blue and white car—the one that shot the potato at us. It drives away, tin cans on strings clatter behind it. Nanna's fingers rest on my shoulder, and Grandpa is talking to grown-ups who are shaking his hand. I don't understand. Mummy's gone. What's happening?

Great Gran's happy to see us when we get home. Nanna's chatting away to her about how wonderful the day was, and then I ask, 'Where's Mummy?'

'She will be back in a few days,' says Nanna, 'Off you go and change your good clothes and put your shoes away.' I do as she says, I'll see Mummy in a few days. Grandpa still reads me a story every night, so everything is alright.

Later in the week, Grandpa buys me two ice creams after school and while I'm eating them, too busy to hang my head out the window and sing, he says, 'Mummy's come home.' Just as well my mouth is full of ice cream, I can't shout *yah!* Then he adds, 'There's someone with her, his name is Bill.' He tosses his cigarette butt out the window. 'Your Mummy married Bill, he's your stepfather,' he says. But I already have a father! I kind of understand, but Grandpa's busy driving so I don't ask, and besides the ice cream is melting.

The 'stepfather' is there next to Mummy when I careen into the sitting room and launch myself at her. Briefly, she embraces me and then she steps back.

'Beverley, this is Bill. Grandpa's explained that we are married?' She says holding Bill's hand, looking happy. I suppose I should look happy too.

I nod and shyly look at Bill. He's smiling at me. He's not like Daddy. Bill is shorter with Brylcreem in his hair. It's slightly wavy and has grey bits that sweep about his ears.

Nanna calls, 'Lunch is on the table.'

In the dining room, Bill sits in my chair next to Mummy. I hover in the doorway and Nanna points to Grandpa's chair next to her. Slowly, I walk around and sit beside her, with Grandpa on the other side of me. Mummy doesn't see, she's busy chatting with Bill, whose voice sounds strange.

After lunch Grandpa and I retreat to the sheds and the water pump—it's not working again, and he must fix it—beyond the fruit trees. Here I'm free to ask all the questions I want. Yes, he agrees, Bill does sound funny when he speaks—that's because he's from England—and has only recently arrived in Rhodesia. And yes, he does look older than Daddy, but I shouldn't mention that and better not talk about Daddy to him either. OK? Yes, if you say so Grandpa. So, the same as I don't mention Daddy to Mummy too? Now it's all sorted out in my mind. Mummy's married to Bill. Don't say he's older, keep quiet about Daddy! Is the pump fixed yet?

***

It's bedtime and I'm rummaging through comics on my bed, searching for a story that Grandpa will read to me. The door opens and I don't look up, 'Haven't found one yet!' I exclaim.

'Well, how about you show me some of the ones you have there?' says Bill.

I scoot back on the bed and stare at him standing beside me. This is unexpected. Grandpa reads to me. What do I say? Bill leans down, picks up a few comics and flips through the pages. 'I know these! They're from England. Here, what about this one?' he asks pointing to *The Beano*.

'Ok,' I say.

He reads to me in his funny voice. There's a whiff of pipe around him and it's strange because that belongs to Grandpa. Daddy doesn't smoke at all. Eventually, he says, 'Think that will do, shall I turn the lamp off as I leave?'

In the shadows, I examine him closely. A kind face, moustache, swept-back fringe, and blue eyes staring at me. He's doing the same to me. Staring is rude! Doesn't matter, I'm doing it though. We are sizing each other up. His moustache spreads into a smile, 'Want to see a trick?'

'Yes.'

'Watch my ears.' I wait, watch and then start to giggle. His ears are wiggling up and down all on their own! The giggles turn to laughter from both of us. I snuggle down and say, 'You can turn the lamp out now.'

***

Bill creates change for us all. The first thing is that the three of us move into Hartley. Leaving Grandpa is sad, I miss our drives home, ice creams and talking to him. He listens hard to me.

What's not too good is that there's a church in our street. Mummy now drags me out of bed on Sunday mornings and escorts me out the front door with instructions to, 'Go to Church, just down the road.' And with a puff of cigarette smoke, like Samantha in 'Bewitched', she retreats into the house while I consider the options of either hiding in the hedge or walking to church. If my friend, Sharon, is around we hide in the hedge. It's more fun with someone than alone.

The house enthrals me. It's modern. There are large bedrooms, a tiled bathroom, parquetry flooring – no tree roots poking through lino here – an electric stove, hot running water any time of the day, and a sitting room with an interior curved wall and another wall of full-length glass with doors opening onto a red concrete polished verandah. This is where we sit in the evenings. Mummy smokes, Bill has a cold beer, and we watch the world pass us by.

I miss Grandpa. It's not long before I notice that Mummy's getting fat and is wearing 'tent' dresses and I hear something about 'she's having a baby.' Baby talk is for when children are 'not around', but when I do manage to flap my ears, I hear frightening, mysterious things about having babies. 'She had a dreadful time, I doubt she'll ever have another' and 'That's the fourth one, she says her husband better stay away from her from now on!' Don't think I want to have a baby.

Mummy is happy. She plays her favourite records, and often when I walk in from school, Petula Clark is singing 'Downtown' in our sitting room, and Mummy's humming away wearing her red tent dress. One evening we all are sitting outside, and she suddenly says, 'Beverley, Bill and I are talking about baby names. Is there one you like?'

This is a surprise, I'm a 'seen and not heard child', only Grandpa and sometimes Nanna ask me what I like!

'Yes,' I say. 'Suzanna.' Where that name came from I have no idea. It just popped into my head and I blurt it out.

Bill draws on his pipe and Mummy frowns a bit, then says, 'Bit long I think, how about Susan, much nicer' And we don't even discuss a boy's name!

***

After a few months, we move back to the farm. It's great to be with Grandpa again, but Nanna is not well. She closes up the Post Office forever and needs to 'rest' a lot. Nanna isn't happy about having to rest and often refuses to do so, so Mummy asks her to knit for the baby, which she does, sitting on the verandah in the shade, well away from Great Gran, whose bunions Mummy says, can wait until she's able to fix them.

One afternoon Nanna calls out to me. I find her on the verandah. She pats the chair next to her where I sit and she says, 'You know Mummy went away yesterday?' I nod and wait, it's best to do that with adults. 'Well, she's had the baby. It's a little girl, Susan.'

Mummy and Bill soon come home and leave a blue pram, with a green netting cover, in the corner of the verandah, near the screen door that bangs. All the adults are happy and chatting. I follow them into the dining room where lunch is on the table. We finish the meal and Mummy says to me, 'Beverley, go and see if the baby is awake.'

Grandpa pats my hand, he's telling me to go. 'How will I know if she's awake?' Mummy laughs, that wonderful sound that makes everyone smile. I'm ashamed to be asking such a silly question. 'She will be moving… that's how you'll know, off you go, quietly.' I tiptoe towards the pram, peer inside and *there she is*, all wrapped up like a parcel in pink, wriggling! She starts to cry.

Mummy hurries along the verandah, pulls back the net and picks her up. I catch a glimpse of her small face. This is Susan. I'm six and a half years old and a big sister.

***

Susan is very sick. The house is gloomy, everyone's talking in hushed tones. I'm invisible with big flapping ears that catch as much as they can.

A minister's coming to christen Susan, it's important because she's going to die. The minister arrives. The adult rumbling voices get louder. Suddenly I hear Grandpa say very loudly, 'Get out! Get out now!'

Shoes squeak down the red, polished verandah floor and the screen door bangs. The minister's gone. Mummy and Nanna are upset, Great Gran has plenty to say too. And Grandpa's very angry. 'What a load of rubbish, just because her Godparents are of a different…' I can't hear and don't understand. But, what I *do* hear is that Susan is going to die, and now won't go to heaven. My world shrinks to be all about this. She's my sister, even if she cries a lot, I *don't* want her to die.

Susan does not die. Mummy joked for a long time that she lived because she wasn't christened and couldn't go to heaven! I'm glad she didn't go anywhere.

Everyone knows Susan is alive. Her shrill crying chases all the previous gloom out of the house. Mummy is either rocking her pram or holding her. When she's asleep, she's in the pram outside, under the trees, shrouded by a green net to keep the insects away. Bill hurries home every day and hugs her to his chest talking softly. I'm not allowed to hold her, she's too small everyone says, and nearly died. Now she has lots of medicine. Grandpa is worried about Nanna too, but he still listens and reads to me at night. I try not to bother him too much.

***

It's around this time that Grandpa says Daddy is coming to fetch me. He explains that Daddy enjoyed our trip to Durban so much that we are going again. There's no big fuss about holiday clothes.

I start to cry, and Mummy's angry. 'Stop making such a fuss and following me around with that face!' As much as I *want* to go, I *don't* want to go either. It's a tug of war I can't understand. I try to cling to her skirt but that makes her mad. It's her I can't bear to leave, even though she's busy with Susan and Bill. Daddy arrives, he's quiet and we leave, by train, the next day.

In Bulawayo, he's back to being the Daddy I know. We go to his house in Woodville and he has a surprise for me. On his last visit, he asked to borrow two of my 18-inch dolls. I'd agreed and here they are, in brand new dresses. Daddy says his friend made the dresses. One's a bride with a veil, the other is dressed in a Spanish red-frilled dress with a black mantilla. He says that they won awards at the Bulawayo Trade Fair. Whatever that is I don't know, but my dolls are beautiful and I say that I won't play with them now; they're for display.

That's not the only surprise. Daddy's asked Lenid, a house boy at the farm, to work in Bulawayo for him. Lenid has arrived with his wife and little girl, Beauty, and they move into the house at the far end of the two-and-a-quarter-acre property.

We know each other and I remember his wife bringing their baby to the house to show Nanna who said, 'Goodness, isn't she a beautiful girl!' So they called her Beauty. Dad explains to me that Lenid's family are from Malawi and they didn't fit in with the Africans living in the compound. This employment fixes that problem, and Daddy has a boy he trusts.

In the kitchen is a puppy in a wooden crate! Daddy has also brought one of Noddy's puppies, it looks just like my cheeky corgi but has a long tail. Nanna was too ill to chop them off and Mummy flatly refused to do so. Daddy calls her Lady. I love being here, it's as if part of the farm has come to Bulawayo with us.

Daddy makes a bed for me in the car and we drive all night to South Africa. When I wake up we are in Ladysmith, and I'm so excited to see my cousin Cindy again. From there, we go to Durban and visit the beach every day, and the area is familiar. Mummy brought me before she married Bill, but I don't mention that. This is the beach where the photographer followed us day after day snapping pictures and she held my hand as we walked. It feels very strange. And there's the building where Granny lives. Daddy and I go inside and visit Granny.

Then we are back on the train to Gadzema. My dolls are standing on the table in the compartment and Daddy's quiet, almost sad. In Gadzema, we walk through the bundu to the farmhouse, Grandpa's waiting outside. The next day, Daddy picks me up and hugs me extra hard and hurries away, back down the bush path. I won't see him again for almost six years.

***

Great Gran's been difficult all day, shouting for people and I run away with my hands over my ears and climb the mango trees. Tonight, sleep eludes her, ergo sleep will elude us all, and as the lights go out and slumber settles, she starts calling for help.

'Iris, Iris come here.'

Nanna dons her dressing gown—it's not proper to walk around in your nightie—and goes to see what's wanted. A drink of water. Done.

A short time later. 'Eric, Eric, I need you.'

Grandpa's as proper as Nanna, dressing gown on he responds. Toilet needed. Two people are required, Nanna and Grandpa.

A little later, 'Norma, come here, Norma turn me over.' Two people are required. Mummy and Grandpa.

Then it's water again, toilet again, turn over again, again, and again, until they all decide to ignore her at around 2am.

Great Gran is not giving up. She continues to call and shout. No one responds. Suddenly she's screaming. All the lights go on, and everyone's up. Great Gran's lying on her bedroom floor writhing with pain. In a rage, trying to turn over, she's fallen out of bed.

An ambulance takes her away. The hospital tells us she's broken her hip. She dies a few days later. No one cries. If Nanna and Mummy could have lit cake candles and shouted *hoorah* they would have. But they restrain themselves, for Grandpa's sake. But I do hear Mummy say, 'Gran died from a temper tantrum because the nurses wouldn't put up with her demanding ways!'

But, surely we need to be sad, like when the kittens fall off the roof and the dogs kill them? So I decide that I will cry, which is exactly what I do—loudly—with a photo of Great Gran on display in my room, to the amusement of Mummy and Nanna. I tell them, 'It's the proper thing to do! Aren't we supposed to be proper?' But, secretly the only thing I'm really sad about is the end of the tickie game.

Grandpa and I drive to a small cemetery, hemmed in by trees and a sagging strand wire fence that guards crooked metal crosses beside earth mounds. Some of these are decorated with plastic flowers under plastic domes, opaque with age. Someone did care, once. Dry winter trees stand tall and bare, brown leaves crunch under the 'boys' feet as they move quietly, with spades through the scant shade. Cape doves coo, 'Work harder, work harder' and from the car, I watch the boys begin digging, carving into the cold red earth, dry and hard beneath their scraping spades. Even though it's cool, their naked bent backs glisten black. Their voices are hushed, melodious murmurs. Normally, they would be laughing, joking or singing, their tones blending in harmony, and all would know they are here. They're quiet today. This is where we are going to bury Great Gran, near her son, 'Uncle Sonny, who drank himself to death,' as Mummy says.

***

And then there's a big shock. We are moving again, to a small town called Raffingora, something to do with Bill's work.

Mummy jokes and says the town's name is bigger than it is! She's right. A few houses, a general store and a butcher that also sells ice cream. There's a one-room school for KG1 and KG2 (kindergarten and first class). There's only one teacher and she walks up the street each morning collecting us kids, and we trail after her to the school building in the middle of a barren plot of land.

School is fun. We don't do much writing or reading, and lunch is a long playtime, and we learn to knit. I decide to knit a Golly for Susan. We go on nature walks and pick grass seeds for the teacher's budgies. It's like being on the farm.

There is one worry, though, about school next year. That's when all KG2 kids, including me, will go to boarding school. This thought makes my heart pound and I want to cry. I can't go away from Mummy.

I try not to think about it and concentrate on the Golly I'm knitting instead. Hopefully, Susan will like it!

The best thing is that Mummy isn't working. She's home all the time. This is a new experience for me. It's wonderful to run in the door at lunchtime and find her there.

Bill comes home for lunch too and the only problem is I won't eat my cabbage. It's disgusting, bright green—added bicarb makes it fluoro green—and it tastes awful. So I'm sent to my bedroom and told that I'm an 'ungrateful child, don't you know there are starving children in Africa!' Yes, I know that, and I still don't want cold cabbage.

'Stay in your room until your plate is clean!' Mummy shouts as I retreat down the hallway, carrying my plate.

After contemplating the starving children, I offer them my cabbage. They don't want it either. So, I open the window, carefully scoop up the soggy leaves, thrust my hand through the burglar bars and drop the cold green mass into the flower bed below. The gardener buries it for me. Then, plate in hand, I return to the sitting room and Mummy says, 'Honestly, I don't know what all the fuss is about, see your plate's clean, now.'

And I just say, 'Yes, Mummy.' That's how I eat cold cabbage in my bedroom, several times a week!

Susan is now a happy baby. She's pulling herself along, rolling over and laughing when we tickle her tummy. When Bill comes home he scoops her up, 'How's my little girl this afternoon?' He asks and then looks at Mummy, one eyebrow raised.

I hear her say, 'She's a clever girl, up on her knees this afternoon again. Not long until you'll be crawling, is it now,' Susan reaches for her. 'Come on, Mummy's going to let you have a splash in the bath, you'll love that! Look at your blonde curls, they're getting long and tickle my face.' Her fingers tussle those soft curls and she kisses Susan's nose. She squeals, her blue eyes alive with mirth, as she grabs at Mummy's neck.

Did Mummy ever say that to me? I think I had some curls too, but they were brown. No one helps me to bathe now. Grandpa used to watch me in the bath, slide up and down swishing water, wash my back and lift me out in a big towel. Now I have a bath on my own. When was the last time Mummy pulled me into her arms, hugged me and Bill read to me? I don't know. A long time.

Dinner is always a light meal, following our main one at lunchtime. Susan's in her highchair banging her spoon and flicking bits of mashed apples all over the place. 'Beverley, go and get a facecloth,' says Mummy.

'OK, Mum,' I say.

I'll be seven years old. Next week.

***

There's a small sausage dog in the front yard and when we open the door, it bounds inside, panting and tail wagging. He's soft and brown with large eyes and so friendly. We look up and down the street, but no one's in sight. Susan laughs and shrieks as the dog cavorts around her. Bill suggests we keep him if we can't find the owners. Over the next few days, I hurry home from school and there he is waiting, jumping around and licking my legs. Then he's gone.

Mum says, 'The strangest thing happened. A car pulled up and the dog jumped in. They were off before I got outside!' The house feels empty without him running around. I'm sad. He was a cute dog and Bill had said he could be mine.

The following day I walk home and the dog is back, barking and leaping at me. He's in my arms and Mum appears in the doorway. 'You'll never guess what happened,' she exclaims. 'A couple called by earlier and apologised for taking him yesterday. They'd lost him a few days ago in town and were so surprised to see him in our front yard.'

They told Mum that they were leaving the country and were taking Loompi (his Italian name) to the vet to be put down. They decided to first ask if we wanted him! Mum said, 'Yes!' So Loompi is now my Italian sausage dog!

***

We move back to the Farm before Christmas of 1964. The looming prospect of boarding school has vanished. In the New Year, I'll return to Hartley school and my friends.

The Christmas tree goes up in the dining room decorated with special ornaments and gifts that appear from overseas in boxes slathered with stamps we hardly ever see. Mum picks at the wrapping and peeps, then denies it, but everyone can see the Sellotape has been disturbed!

It's been a busy year. Susan was born and nearly died; Great Gran had a tantrum and did die, and we've been to Raffingora and back! And I've got a dog called Loompi, a silly name, but he's loveable, mine, and not vicious like Noddy.

Chapter 7
Bicycles, Owls, and Nanna Dies.

I know bicycles are important. Without one, most people walk, so no one cares if it's hard work pedalling uphill. You can carry lots too; chickens crammed into woven baskets, firewood and passengers seated on the handlebars or clinging to the rear—even a baby tied to its mother's back. They are valuable and expensive.

I don't have one.

Most Saturdays, around midday, we pick up Bill from the garage, where he's working in Gadzema. Often, he throws a pile of greasy spanners into a metal tray and pours Coca-Cola over them. It's amazing how shiny they are on a Monday morning. And to think we *drink* that stuff!

One Saturday he calls me to the rear of the garage and says, 'Have a look at what I've made you out of used spare parts.'

I can't believe my eyes. A bicycle!

It's scruffy with peeling red and yellow paint and rust poking through the once-white wheel guards. But it's a bicycle with tyres and a seat! To me it's beautiful! I want to run and hug him, but I don't. Bill doesn't hug me, ever. My hands cover my mouth, and I stare at him.

'It's the best present!' I exclaim and he's grinning.

He reaches into his overall pocket and stretches his closed fist towards me. 'Found this too, soaked it on Coke last week.'

His fingers open. In his palm lies a shiny bell. I lean forward, my fingers trail over the cold, age-pitted metal, and Bill coughs, his feet shift, and I take the bell from his hand. He gestures to the bicycle leaning against the rear wall, 'It will look good once I paint it,' he says almost gruffly. 'The only spare paint is pale blue, might put some stripes on it as well, like a racing car. Then attach the bell.'

I run my hands over the peeling old frame, 'It's great as it is,' I say.

But a few days later that second-hand, brand-new to me, bicycle's now pale blue with black stripes and a shiny bell, is mine. Bill rides it around our front yard before passing it to me. The only spare parts he didn't have were for brakes! But who cares!

I think I like Bill, quite a lot now.

***

This bicycle gives me even more freedom. Now I ride to the Giant Mine, a few miles away, to play and swim in the Club pool.

No longer do I wait for the mine kids to come to visit. Now I leave the farmhouse, pedal hard on flat ground over the railway lines—check for trains like Grandpa reminds me to—turn right, pedal downhill, a considerable gradient on one tar strip, and then gathering speed, I can freewheel over the single lane bridge with my hair flying away from my face, and get halfway up the steeper slope on the other side. From there I must pedal hard to reach the top, and then I'm at the mine.

The return trip is the same. Downhill momentum takes me over the bridge and sometimes as far as the railway line! Great. At least, most of the time. But there's a road rule. Bicycles must give way to vehicles, which means getting off the smooth strip onto the uneven rocky dirt verge.

The trick, before careening down over the bridge, is to make sure the road is clear for at least a minute or so. But on this particular day, I get caught flying towards the bridge by a bus coming from the opposite direction. I have no alternative but to swerve off the tar strip, bounce over the dirt verge, and crash into the embankment. I fly off the bicycle and land hard in long dry grass.

The bus, laden with passengers hanging out of the windows and chickens in cages tied on top, hurtles past me and I hear their laughter above the engine roar. The bicycle's wheels turn slowly as it lies on its side, almost mocking me.

The bike needs brakes. I might ask Bill about that, again. Maybe not. If I tell them what happened they will stop me from riding to the mine. Best to just have a quick clean up and hide the dirty clothes in the washing pile. No one ever asks about a few scratches on my face and arms!

***

As I said, bicycles are very important to most of the population. I learnt this only too well one night. Grandpa was driving us home from a wedding in Hartley before Bill arrived in our lives.

A small round light was coming towards us. 'Bicycle ahead!' Grandpa said.

From the back seat, next to Mummy, I watched the light through the dark; it veered off the strip road. As we drew closer, it suddenly remounted the strip. *Smack!* We hit it. Nanna shrieked, Grandpa said a bad word, and Mummy put her hand over my face. I could see through her spread fingers though. The rider slid over the car bonnet, his head smashed through the windscreen and his chin came to rest on the steering wheel.

'Eric! Oh, goodness have we killed him?'

'Wait here,' Grandpa said and he slowly opened the car door.

The African's wide eyes stared at us for a few moments, he jerked backwards through the smashed window, shook his head, slid down the bonnet, and stood swaying in the car's headlights. Small trickles of red glowed on his face and peppered his woolly head and his bloodshot eyes—from too much shabeen drinking. He stumbled towards his bicycle at the periphery of the light, mumbling, 'Blue light, Ipi lo (where is) blue light?' We didn't understand what he was searching for. Neither did Mr Markee—our African cook who had come with us into town—who had clambered out of the very back of the station wagon and was now beside Grandpa, trembling.

Our victim wasn't responding to any of their questions. We were all standing on the lumpy roadside dirt, our shadows distorted in the headlights, and Grandpa was trying to stop Mr Markee from shouting. Mr Markee was not only angry, but also mortified about the large wet mark down the front of his smart go-to-town pants, that we all ignore because that's called being polite!

Mummy had no shoes on. She gave them away to a lady who admired them at the wedding. Nanna was not amused about that, and Grandpa was trying to keep everyone calm.

The police arrived. They bundled the African into their wagon, tied his crumpled bicycle to the roof racks and told Grandpa not to worry about anything. It was an accident. As they shut the rear door, we heard the man say, 'Blue light, ipi lo blue light?' No one knew what he was talking about.

Grandpa said, 'Suppose we can go home now, hey Mr Markee?' And from the rear, we heard him say, 'Yehbo! Ena penga!' (Yes, he's mad!)

'We needed a new windscreen,' Grandpa said the next day.

That made me think about a few months ago, when what had been several small stone-caused stars on the windscreen were joined together by large cracks, like a road map, on another nighttime drive home.

The car was bouncing along, its headlights swaying over the strip road and nudging at the edges of the unseen bush. The breeze through the window and the sound of the engine were almost lulling me to sleep. *Bang!* Grandpa suddenly braked hard and pulled off the road. Something had been flung across the windscreen, blocking our view, and allowing only small fragments of light through. Grandpa opened his door slowly.

'Stay here,' he said quietly. I watched him lift something. 'It's an owl,' he said, 'neck's broken, poor thing.'

With care, Grandpa folded the bird's wings and laid it in the boot. He sighed as he got back in and I knew to be quiet because he was sad. If we'd hit a guinea fowl it would have been fine. We would have had a nice bird for dinner.

The following day, I asked the boys to cut the owl's wings off. They made a super display at the next Show and Tell at school. The teacher wasn't impressed, and the girls screamed and ran off, but the boys agreed it was great and examined the wings with me.

***

The house is quiet. You see, yesterday Nanna died, the 12th of February 1965. I trace my finger over that date on the calendar on the wall, a silly one with an English countryside scene. Maybe Nanna liked England because she went there when she was young, pity I didn't ask her about that. Grandpa says, 'We are British.' Aren't we Rhodesians?

One day she was here and the next she was gone. It was something to do with her heart. She will be buried somewhere far away in Salisbury, cremated, I'm hear—whatever that is. There will be a plaque in the garden that we will visit soon. Maybe she didn't want to be near Great Gran with her bunions. 'Who died exactly to the day, nine months ago,' says Mum.

I'm seven and a half years old, and so glad I'm big enough to remember Nanna.

I cry on my own. Grandpa's sad enough without seeing my wet face. Mum's sad too, with red eyes. Susan and Bill aren't upset, one's too young and the other too new to love Nanna.

Grandpa's lost the light in his life, he smiles but it's not the same, his voice is softer and he coughs even more now in the mornings. Mum's coughing too. Are they sick? Or is it from the cigarettes?

Grandpa's slipping away from us, from me. I don't understand his grief. But farm life goes on and keeps him busy. Between the borehole pump that breaks down regularly, the chickens, turkeys, and now rabbits to be checked on and secured at night, the veggie garden, the crops, and fruit trees, there is a lot to do.

'The Africans are stealing the fruit again,' says Grandpa. 'Come on, Beverley I'll show you my trick to stop them!'

Hand in hand we walk to the shed near the borehole. There he fills two metal hand-held sprayers with water and says, 'Now we add a few bits of soap.' He hands one sprayer to me and says, 'Let's go,' and chuckles to himself. I'm baffled. 'This is how we stop them stealing fruit!'

We reach the fruit trees and he says loudly, 'Now, Beverley, you can help me spray every tree. OK?'

We start pumping and spraying, fine misty water flies over the fruit and leaves. 'Remember, do not eat the fruit.' Pump... hiss... pump, bubbles floating... and even louder, 'It will make you very sick! You have to wash it in my special muti first, the one I keep in the house.'

'Yes, Grandpa,' I say, loudly too, and he winks at me. I know there's no muti, and it's soap from the kitchen we are spraying all over the place! But the Africans don't know that!

No more stolen fruit.

Chapter 8
There Are Terrs Out There, 1966.

They are dead. The Viljoens, farmers who live near us. 'Machine gunned down... Murdered.' These are fragments I hear and my evening greeting dies on my lips. I remain, unseen, in the doorway.

Bill's home early from work. Mum's home early from work. They're sitting at the dining table with Grandpa, their voices gusting like the winds before a storm, blowing with agitation, grief and disbelief.

Grandpa's voice shakes, 'Terr's got them. At their house, not like Piet Oberholzer on the road home.' He lights a cigarette. (Terrs: terrorists)

Mum's crying, 'No, all of them, surely not! The children?'

'Not the baby,' says Grandpa and adds, 'Or little Tommy, Nikky's at boarding school, thank goodness.'

Nikky! I know her. We've played together. Her Mum and Dad are dead? Their farm is somewhere around here.

They sit with their thoughts, in the cool air, cigarette tips glow intermittently red and smoke hangs listlessly, occasionally shifted by warm drafts from the wood stove, through the open door to the kitchen.

Mum is crying even more now, 'Oh Dad, it could have been us!'

Us! Tears gather in my eyes. Engrossed in their conversation, I'm out of sight. If I say anything, they will shoo me away. Mum's crying increases, 'Such a lovely family. How frightened they must have been!'

'I know,' he softly says, shakes his head and takes Mum's hand. 'The police are coming around just now to see us, it will be alright.'

Mum's voice rises. 'What can they do, Dad? That poor family just answered a knock at the door!' Her hands cover her face and she whispers, 'They shot them... shot them...' Disbelief hangs on each word.

Bill touches her shoulder and quietly says, 'Norma, Susan's awake. How about you go and get her?'

Mum swipes her fingers over her cheeks. Grandpa hands her his hankie and she shakes her head, 'I can't' she sobs, 'Nanny will get her. I need to just sit here.'

Mr Markee appears carrying a large tray set with traditional Sunday afternoon tea even though it's the middle of the week. China rattles as he places it carefully down, leaves and returns with a large sponge cake, his speciality, farm-made lemon curd oozing between layers and dusted with icing sugar. His usually grinning face, displaying his fake front gold tooth, is solemn.

He looks directly at Grandpa and says, 'Baas, tea, cake,' and leaves, shaking his head

Grandpa says, 'Thank you, Mr Markee.'

Even the Africans know already. 'Bush telegraph' is what we call it. Fast, efficient and exclusive to them.

I slide onto my chair. Sunday afternoon tea on a weekday, in mid-May. This is very scary. There's a gun propped against the table, Grandpa reaches for it.

'Suppose we had better clean this too,' he says.

Mum pulls the tray towards her. Milk splashes into the teacups and rich steaming tea flows, without the strainer, some into the saucers too, and a few tea leaves float. Mum would normally say strain them through your teeth. Nanna wouldn't forget the strainer, she'd not like this at all. No serviettes!

There's an uncomfortable hush. No bustling and banging in the kitchen, only a smell of bean soup; no voices outside calling knock-offs for the day, even the nesting birds in the mid-winter trees are subdued. The world is on mute, and as the sun sets, we become grey outlines at the table with our dark thoughts, sipping tea and picking at the cake.

A jeep pulls up outside. Doors slam. In the background, Susan's laughing in the bath, splashing. Grandpa turns the lights on, and we blink, like animals caught in a car's headlights, nearly always hit, they die. The fast ones flash away into the night, lucky. Are we fast?

Men in uniforms carrying guns, with serious faces and stiff bodies, walk on the property. Looking. The Africans are all in the compound. Fruit bats with miniature fox faces spread their wings, shadows flitting over trees where green mambas slither between now-dark leaves, and small duiker fold their spindle legs to settle and wait for dawn. We will all wait for dawn.

'Bring the dogs into the house. Haven't you got any big ones?' They ask.

'No, no big dogs here, they scare Beverley,' Grandpa says. I'm more scared of the terrs now than big dogs!

'Patrols will pass by a few times during the night to check up on you.' To see if we are dead is what they mean.

Grandpa calls Loompi into my bedroom and lifts him onto my bed. His soft brown coat is smooth under my fingers. 'Isn't this a treat? Loompi can keep you company tonight!' He's trying to smile, but I can see the frown between his eyes. Loompi curls up on my bed. He smells faintly of dip from yesterday when Grandpa had thrown all the dogs into the concrete dip run before the bellowing cattle were chased through. The dogs hated it! I smile visualising them swimming out and dashing up the concrete ramp, flicking water from their coats and rolling frantically in the dirt, rubbing their noses hard. Grandpa reads to me. The dog, faint dip smell and story all feel safe, for now. Maybe, we will be safe in our beds.

I watch Grandpa leave, through my bedroom door that's way down at the end of the verandah, and listen to his footsteps recede, slowly. I feel alone around the corner by the bathroom. Maybe the terrs won't use the P.K. and won't see me.

The patrols come at night. The dogs bark. Footsteps on the verandah pass my room. Grandpa and Bill are up, only Susan sleeps all night. I hear voices outside my room. 'They've slipped away, probably to Salisbury, into the outlying areas there.' They say.

And then Grandpa says the patrols need not come anymore. He's grateful, and says, 'You men come in the front and leave through the back door; the terrs come in behind you. Then we are dead in our beds, anyway. We do have a gun.'

So now the terrs will get us in our beds! Now at nighttime the adults are on edge. I hear Grandpa and Bill's footsteps and their murmuring voices on the verandah, where the lights stay on all night and insects batter themselves to death and are swept up in the morning.

We must lock the back door, which we never do. The men carry the gun everywhere. Sometimes my elephant ears are a curse. At eight years old there are still monsters *under* the bed, but now they are outside too.

***

After a few months, Loompi is evicted and joins the other dogs to sleep on the verandah. Laughter returns and Mr Markee flashes his gold tooth.

Grandpa says at lunch he's going out later into the lands to shoot a duiker. He hasn't done this for a while. 'All because of the terrs!' Mum says. She's upset and angry with the terrs, just like she is with the Germans who, 'Took your Grandpa away for years!' I don't understand that. And, Mum's also furious with Ian Douglas Smith, 'It's all his fault this is happening,' she almost spits his name. Bill and Grandpa disagree with her.

'Off now,' Grandpa says, as he picks up the gun and walks out the backdoor into the gathering shadows.

The Africans know to listen for the shots. It's their call to hurry and help. We are not supposed to shoot game (wild animals). The kill will be skinned, sliced and distributed fast. Our portions are always hidden under frozen turkeys in the deep freeze, and then it's roast venison for Sunday lunch!

Grandpa returns in the dark, his shadow spills into the kitchen under the bulb bright beneath a metal shade.

'What, nothing Dad? You were gone for ages!' exclaims Mum.

Grandpa unloads the gun and puts it on the kitchen table. If Nanna were here and saw that she'd say, 'Eric!'

'There were a few, took good aim…' He pulls his hand over his hair and looks at Mum. 'Bloody things not firing!' *A swear word!*

'What!' says Mum her eyes wide. They stare at each other. Mum's hand rushes to her perfect lip. After a few moments, she starts to giggle, her fingers fluttering now, perfect red nail polish. 'So much for shooting the duikers and terrs,' she finally splutters, 'Lucky duikers!'

'Sure, lucky duikers tonight!' They're both now laughing loudly, tears running down their cheeks. 'Think we should drink to that,' Grandpa finally says.

Bill walks in and asks in his very English accent, 'What's so funny?'

The two of them collapse into chairs, breathless. 'Sorry Bill, you had to be here!' Mum says. 'I've got a stitch in my side. Oh, let's all have a beer.' Adults are so confusing.

***

With the terrs no longer lurking in the adults' minds, Mum decides we should visit Aunty Ivy, Nanna's sister, who lives on a property called Forest Hill Farm, outside Rusape. Susan and I haven't met Aunty Ivy, but Mum tells us that she stayed there a few times during her school holidays. Auntie Ivy picks us up from the train station. She's so like Nanna. Mum's in her embrace, both have tears in their eyes and I sort of understand why Mum's come here.

The farmhouse is brick, not pole and daga like ours! And it's plastered too. A sweeping stairway with curving concrete sides, wide enough to sit on, leads to a large, covered verandah, and the front yard. The garden is dry and waiting for the November rains. Large stones edge the garden beds, which curve away under jacaranda trees with their purple blooms, soon to be overshadowed by the leaves. Assorted succulents survive in the heat, their winter flowers faded now, leaving stark dry stems stiff in the hot wind, and a few linger on in the shade—proud red hot pokers and golden shower orange flowers, which are prolific in the cooler months.

Behind the house, a kopje (small hill) slopes towards the cloudless sky. It's hard and rocky, with trees wedged between boulders and dry grass anchored in shallow soil. There's so much to explore when the adults are 'resting' after lunch.

That night we sit in the gathering evening grey. Crickets start to sing and the screaming cicadas go to sleep. I don't understand why the lights aren't turned on.

Aunty Ivy finally says, 'Robbie shouldn't be much longer, now.' And as if he heard her, a young man saunters into the room, his lean frame and angular face softened in the gloom.

'Hi, Norma. Super, you're here again. Be with you all in a bit, got to light the lamps, good train trip?' Mum waves her hand indicating just so-so; what would you expect with two kids?

Robbie lifts the glass globe of a paraffin lamp, rolls the wick up, strikes a match and lights the wick. A small yellow flame wavers as he replaces the glass, the flame leaps high and smokes, deftly he turns the wick down and a soft yellow glow filters over Mum and Auntie Ivy, their features partially hidden until more lamps are lit.

So this is Robbie, Auntie Ivy's son, Mum's cousin, and he has a sister called, Anne. She's married to an 'Air Force man' Mum says. Amazing what I learn by listening!

'I'll be back, going to fire up the generator,' he says.

Auntie Ivy guesses the question I'm not asking.

'We have a battery-run electric fence around the fruit trees and grape vines, keeps the pesty baboons away. Robbie turns it on once all the boys have left for the day. Norma, would you like to bath Susan?'

I'm wide awake. It's dark and late. There's horrible screaming, outside, it's going on and on. It sounds like people, more than one, are being ripped apart. Everyone is asleep. The dogs are quiet. The screaming stops. I come out from under the sheets. Am I the only one awake? I stare into the darkness. No lights to turn on. No one has gotten up. They would have if they thought there were terrs about as Grandpa and Bill did on the farm. Wouldn't they?

At breakfast, Auntie Ivy says, 'Norma, did that din wake you up last night?'

'Yes and goodness what a racket those baboons were making, the leopards were sure after them!' *Baboons! Leopards!*

'Baboons for dinner!' Auntie Ivy chuckles, 'You know the leopards used to come down from kopje and try to take the dogs off the back verandah. Those little fox terriers would start yapping their heads off and Henry, shooting light on his forehead, would rush out there and fire off a few shots.' She scoops bottled guavas into a bowl. 'We had a bountiful fruit season, bottled these and peaches.'

Mum reaches for the marmalade. Her elegant fingers swivel the jar around, she sighs and says, 'I remember your wonderful homemade jams and Forest Hill Peanut Butter. That was the best!'

Auntie Ivy smiles, it's one of those sorts of sad ones that adults do. 'Oh, Norma those were wonderful days. We grew peanuts and bought them from other growers. The women roasted them in a 44-gallon drum. Goodness, they knew how to get that just right, I can almost smell it.' Mum stays quiet, she's enjoying Auntie Ivy's reminiscing. I see her face soften, and I know she's thinking of Nanna. I miss her, even though she used to whack me with the hairbrush sometimes.

'You know those women were so quick at shelling and grinding nuts. I used an old coffee machine to fill jars, clever how things can be repurposed. Lids on, jars wiped, and Forest Hill labelled, all done here on the front verandah! And their singing! What melodious voices and they'd dance with such joy at the end of the day.' I love listening to the Africans singing, I don't hang out the car window and sing anymore when Grandpa's driving.

'Why did you stop?'

'It all got too much. Henry was busy with fruit, grapes vines, and vegetables. I was worn out packing, delivering or arranging that all over Southern Rhodesia. I gave it all up over 10 years ago now. You know South African Black Cat Peanut Butter was never sold here while we produced our Forest Hill Brand. We had a 'gentleman's agreement, Henry used to say. Ours was 100% pure peanut butter. We were proud of that!'

I watch them, quiet with their thoughts, and I know to be silent. 'And then Henry died a few years later,' Auntie Ivy says quietly. I guess that would be my Uncle Henry. Was I even alive then? Better not ask.

Suddenly, Mum snatches up a slice of cold toast, just how she likes it, and slathers it with butter and jam. I do the same.

'Robbie's walking with us up the kopje today. There are wonderful bushman paintings and it's years since you've been there, isn't it Norma?'

'Sure is. Susan will be fine here with the nanny.'

Aunty Ivy looks at me, tips her head sideways and says, 'Beverley, don't worry about the leopards. Robbie has a gun.'

I almost choke on my cold toast.

Chapter 9
Wedding, White Ants and The Dogs Are Gone (1965-1967)

Mum makes a Merry-Go-Round cake for my eighth birthday. It's in the centre of a table under large, shady Cedrela toona trees—where snakes like to slither—which stand in a line behind the house. Soon my friends will be here. It was all very exciting until a few days ago when my birthday gift, boxed up in brown paper with lots of stamps, arrived from Dad. Mum's got the box open and is reading my birthday card from him. She doesn't usually do that now I can read for myself.

She looks up and says, 'Your father's re-married. Her name is Frances,' she points to the writing. 'Look, here in your card, it says *love from Dad and Frances.*' Her finger jabs at the words and I take the card and envelope. The writing is small and cramped, not at all like Dad's large bold words. So that's why Mum opened it. Is that why Dad hasn't been to see me?

'And there's not much in this box either, he usually sends a lot more!' Mum's painted nails piano play over the cardboard edge tapping out an unsaid message. It doesn't matter how much is in the box. They've sent a pretty card with candles on the front, and Frances has written it too. Frances is his wife. I roll her name around in my mind and wonder what she looks like. Maybe he will visit me with her, maybe not, because Mum wouldn't like that.

'At least your father could have written the card himself! Or called to let me know about *her* before this!' And her hand flicks over the open box.

Why? You don't even *like* my father. It's all very confusing. I wonder what is wrapped up, it's a shame I'll have to wait three days to find out. Mum will cheat and unpick the sticky tape and know before me. It spoils the surprise if you do that. She abruptly shuts the box and briskly walks away muttering, 'So now you've got a stepmother.'

Like Bill is my stepfather? Do I call her Frances? Better not ask right now.

But it's a lovely birthday. Mum iced the cake, set my hair in rollers and teased it up like a grown-up lady. I don't like it—too late now—and she made me a new dress, and I've got a stepmother too. I hope Dad's happy; Mum isn't. That's too difficult to think about. My friends are here, so let's light the candles and sing 'Happy Birthday To You'. Life's a bit like my merry-go-round cake, up and down we go. This cake tastes good.

***

I remember another special cake, from about six weeks ago. Carl had invited us all out to his farm. Luckily it was before the November rains arrived and turned the dirt road to a lumpy, slippery sludge, so with October's suicide heat taunting us, and our windows down, hot winds messing up Mum's hair, we navigated the track to his house. I was excited to see Carl. He hasn't visited us much lately, so there were no more *Noddy* books, but I suppose he had already bought me the entire set and I'm getting older too. Or was it because of Bill? But he's Grandpa's friend too. We arrived and hurried into the thatched cool of his house. In the middle of the dining table, there was a white decorated cake. Carl had his arm around a slim, beautifully dressed lady with short dark hair who visited us at Christmas with him. Carl then said, 'Betty and I got married yesterday.'

Grandpa hurried forward with a smile reaching right up to his eyes and grasped Carl's hand. 'Wonderful news, Carl, just wonderful. Betty, he's a good man!' Betty smiled and hugged Grandpa. Mum was standing very still. Bill put Susan on the floor and hugged Betty too. His English voice filled the room, 'Well, I say, grand surprise Carl.

Congratulations.'

Mum moved past Bill, pulled Carl into her arms and kissed his cheek. 'Aren't you the dark horse then!' When she released him she turned to Betty and said, 'Never expected this after you vanished up to Zambia!' Her long arm, wearing the wide silver cuff Carl gave her, swept towards the wedding cake with a plastic bride and groom on top. 'You finally caught him!'

'No, actually *he* caught *me*,' Betty said with a smile. 'We hoped this would be a happy surprise, didn't we Carlos!'

'Oh, it sure is!' Mum said, smoothing her fitted skirt from her small waist down over her ample hips. 'I hope you'll be very happy. A bit isolated out here though?'

'Suits me just fine,' Betty replied in her clipped British accent, 'Shall we cut the cake, Carlos?'

'Yes Betty, lets.'

As she moved past Carl towards the table his smile froze and he stared at Mum for a moment, turned and wrapped his arms around his wife's waist, and together they cut their wedding cake. We all clapped. Carl was Betty's Carlos now.

On the way home, Mum said, 'Suppose there hadn't been any other offers until now! She must be over 30.'

'So are you, Norma,' Grandpa said quietly, to which Mum huffed, 'Really, Dad!'

Later on, Carl and Betty had a daughter, Louise. We visited the farm and I peered at her sleeping in her crib. *Her Daddy will read her* Noddy *books, tuck her into bed and hug her lots*, I thought. A small worm I can't name wiggled deep inside me.

'So now I have another daughter,' Carl said as he came up behind me. No one but me heard him, saw his hand on my shoulder or felt his warmth near me. It made the wiggle thing go away because I know that he loves me, even though he's not my Dad, and now never will be.

***

A few months later Bill is standing on a ladder in the sitting room. All we can see are his pull-up socks-clad legs. Most of him has been swallowed up by the manhole, and the moving torchlight and his mutterings tell us nothing until he clambers down the ladder. Dust and cobwebs grace his wavy hair, and he sneezes loudly.

'White ants! Eaten every bit of timber up there, nothing's holding up the bloody roof!' His fingers rake through his hair and he wipes the cobwebs on his shorts. 'Between the terrs and the white ants, Eric, we're done!' His matter-of-fact English accent is out of place in the African heat.

Done! What does that mean?

'Time to sell, Dad,' Mum says as she rubs Grandpa's shoulder, but he doesn't acknowledge her. Instead, he's looking around the sitting room, at Nanna's chair—now empty with her knitting basket still beside it—to his wide-armed chair below the window, through to the dining room where Nanna sat beside him. Where she laughed with mock horror when he asked guests to, 'Eat up everyone, otherwise we have leftovers for lunch!' And she replied, 'Eric!' I wonder if he's remembering the Christmas tree beside that table with its lights blinking, and the smell of roast turkey from the wood stove, white feathered are the best, and rich pudding with the hidden silver charms.

It's there, the meaning of 'done and sell' on Grandpa's face but I don't quite understand it, even though it's my reality too. How can we leave the farm? Where will we go, our family have lived here forever. If I cry Mum will be mad, she can't *stand* me doing that. It doesn't bother her when Susan cries. Maybe it's because she's little. We can't leave the farm, we're not 'done'.

'I've got bloody cobwebs everywhere!' says Bill.

'Yes, I'm done,' says Grandpa as he slowly walks out onto the verandah. I follow him and slip my fingers into his palm. 'We had a super Guy Fawkes here, all of us, didn't we?' I say.

He squeezes my hand, 'Yes, it was grand. It will be alright, Beverley.' The screen door bangs behind us and we walk towards the turkey run beneath the mango trees. Grandpa sighs and says, 'Yes, we are done.'

***

White ants used to fascinate me. After the rains, they'd fill the air, a fluttering mass of tiny fragile wings that fall off, and gather in soft piles blown against the walls while the wingless ants scurried away from bird's pecking beaks. I used to pity these defenceless, flightless creatures!

I hate them now! Grandpa and Nanna would say, 'Dislike. We don't hate in this house. And we don't say stupid either.' Sorry, but I hate them. They are horrid, deceitful, stupid crawling ants chewing up our home.

The farm is sold, to a family called Bromehead. Mum says Broomhead, and I silently agree, because they are sweeping us out of our home. We won't miss the gossamer wings, the Broomheads will sweep them up too.

Every day something else is gobbled up. I dread coming home from school. Today the cattle are gone. Will we chop off the chicken's and turkey's heads? Will I sit and watch that one more time? 'Gruesome child,' Mum says. Or will they be jammed into cages and carted away? I close my eyes. It's better not to look too closely. Bill and Mum's voices smother Grandpa's; the white ants are eating him up too. That I *can't* ignore.

People are coming and going, strangers mostly, and occasionally a friendly face who drinks tea. There's an unknown car parked out front. The adults are all chatting away. Susan is running around on her three-year-old busy feet. She finds Bluey, curled up in the ferns on the verandah. Bluey yowls.

'Beverley, quick—get her before that cat scratches her. Stupid thing lying there where she can get him!' *Mum, he's in Nanna's ferns, you should have shooed him out and fluffed up the flattened leaves. We don't say stupid.*

Susan's fingers grip Bluey's long ginger fur, he's thrashing around, and I try to pick Susan up. She hangs onto the cat and screams in protest. Bill's behind us, 'What have you done to her?'

'Nothing, Mum said to get her away from the cat, she won't …'

'You must have done *something*, she's screaming!'

Susan looks up at us, lets go of the cat, and hurries towards Bill's outstretched arms. He lifts her and wipes away her tears. 'Now, why are you crying?' She points sniffing towards the cat and me. 'Did Beverley upset you? Never mind, come along with me.' He frowns and walks away with Susan giggling in his arms.

The strangers are leaving. Suddenly, they put Loompi in the back seat, the engine kicks over and they start to drive away.

'Loompi!' I shout and dash towards the moving car. He's looking out the back window, barking. 'Loompi. Stop!' Dust puffs from the wheels. I can't catch up—my bare feet are chasing down our driveway. He's barking for me!

Hands grab at my shoulder. I spin around and fling myself at Mum. 'Stop it! Just stop it, right now.' She holds me away from her. 'What on earth will those people think of us? You with bare feet and carrying on like this!' Frantically, I look for Grandpa, but he can't come to me, he's coughing badly into his hankie. I know it's not from the dust. Mum walks towards Bill and Susan. Grandpa finally reaches me and pulls me close. 'I thought they'd told you, Loompi has a new home now.'

'But he's my dog, Bill said so!' Grandpa sighs and leads me away. The car and Loompi are long gone. 'Let's go and close up the chickens,' he says. We walk past the fruit trees, sprayed with special muti, across to the chicken runs. They are very posh, built with farm-made clay bricks. It's a family joke: we live in a mud house, and the chickens in a brick house.

Over the next few weeks, the animals are sold. One afternoon when I get home from school Noddy, Whoo, and Pansy's beds are empty. There are no wagging tails and barking, just silence. Mum tells me that a farmer came for some turkeys and offered to take the dogs too. No time to say goodbye. 'They will have a great time on the new farm,' she says. But I'm not convinced. Without their beds?

'But I thought farmers like big dogs better, why don't we have big dogs?'

'Yes they do but little dogs are good too. We did have big dogs, but they knocked you over and you cried! So, Dad had them destroyed!' Sorry Grandpa, I truly am. I must remember not to cry.

Down at the compound, things feel different too. Everyone's still there, going about normal daily chores, but their voices aren't as they should be. There's a sombreness. It hangs heavy with the smoke from cooking fires and even they seem to be dull and low. I leave and wander back towards the house. Grandpa's sitting on a stool under the mango trees, smoking. I join him. No need to close the gate, all the turkeys are gone and the ground's been swept clean of feathers and poop. Why did we even bother with that?

'Grandpa, we are leaving, but are the people in the compound staying?' There are a few feathers, white ones, caught in the fence. Those turkeys are the best!

'Yes, they will, Bromeheads will employ them.'

'Will they mill the mielies for them too?'

'Yes, that machine stays.' Grandpa looks up at the leaves. 'These trees have been here for as long as I can remember, just like the compound down there.' His head nods towards the path and beyond. 'My parents came here over 40 years ago, you know.' No, I didn't, but now I do. 'Madala was here then, lots in the compound will remember back then.' He sighs, 'They aren't happy, it's understandable, we've all been living here together for decades. It's change and uncertainty, that's what it is.'

I'm sad, they are sad, and it's all because of the white ants and terrs. I wonder if the Africans blame them too.

I don't want to leave. Only Grandpa sees me, sees my upset face, and they're all busy packing; I don't want to pack. It's too final. I can't ignore the empty spaces around me, the physical and emotional ones; everything familiar is going.

My feet decide to leave this sad place and run fast into the late winter sunshine, over the packed hard dirt, down narrow winding paths through tall dry grass that whispers in the breeze, dry, brittle, and dead. Dead like so much. My breath aches in my chest and three-sided devil thorns stab my bare feet. I stop and pull them out. It's past lunchtime now. I don't want to eat.

Where am I? I'm not sure. The sun's in my eyes; then squinting I see them. Graves. A sagging wire fence, crooked crosses, and names on stone. This is where Great Gran and her bunions are. We should have buried her walking stick and a tickie with her. Hope they leave the stick behind. The shorter dry grass snaps beneath my feet and I pass acacia trees with long grey thorns, hard and mean, and wander between the graves. Some are nameless, others with leaning rusted metal crosses and there's Great Gran's, an earth mound littered with dry leaves and perspex domes—splattered with the mud of three years!' rain—shielding bright plastic flowers. Soon the perspex will become opaque, clouding the flowers and memories.

It's peaceful here. I sit for a while on the edge of the grave. There's no headstone, nothing to say this is her. And over there is Uncle Sonny, who drank himself to death, nameless too in the bundu. Goodbye Great Gran, thanks for the tickies, and goodbye Uncle Sonny, even though I never met you. I'm almost nine years old.

***

We leave. Move to the Giant Mine a few miles away past the narrow bridge, so I no longer have to cycle there. Grandpa doesn't have to take me to and from school, the bus stops at our door. There's no more ice cream or singing out the window, no more Pekingese pack chasing our wheels, no mango trees to hide in, or sadza in the compound. I miss that. I wonder if they're happy with the new owners, hope so. I'll have to ask Mr Markee—he's still living there and riding his bicycle over that narrow bridge to work here. There's no farm to return to now.

It's done! This I'm beginning to understand.

The white ants are eating Grandpa. He's quiet. The house is filled with the sounds of Susan, Mum and Bill. Their noise is unfamiliar and dominant without the farm cries and space. I retreat to the outside and friends. Grandpa gets work at the Mine Club. I hear Mum say, 'Dad's drinking too much.' I close my ears. At night Grandpa's with me, at the table, reading in my room, but he's fading away like an old photograph. I try to understand.

***

Mum says, 'We have to stop in at the Farm, the Broomheads want to see me. Goodness, I hope they haven't looked up in the roof!'

Even before we park the car, Mum and I are horrified. Our lush front lawn, surrounded by flower beds, is gone. Ploughed up and planted with lucerne. We remain seated for a few minutes, looking. *How could they do this?*

'Remember how we planted the runners, Mum?' I say. She nods staring out the open window, her cigarette burning long ash.

'Yes, I was so excited to get those grass runners.' She flicks the ash out the window and I see her way back then, holding a box stuffed full of grass runners, their little roots begging for soil. She was so happy as she said, 'Look at these, isn't this wonderful; we are going to grow a lawn out front. It will be just beautiful!'

Madala the garden boy, (silly to say boy, as he was very old, but then all workers were called boys), shoffled up (dug up) the front garden's bare earth. Then, together with several boys, Mum and I carefully planted runners over the huge area. Every day Mandala watered them, his finger over the end of the hose, creating a fine spray and small rainbows that arched over the red earth and wilting green tufts that grew, gradually, into thick clumps. We sat, like pixies perched on mushrooms in fairy books, on the green patches talking to each other, sipping cool drinks and curling our bare toes into the grass. Then the patchwork merged creating a lush lawn bordered by flower beds and the golden shower hedge. We'd sometimes lie there at the end of a hot day, in cool bliss.

Now Mum hurries to the front door, speaks to someone and comes back. We leave kicking up dust, where our dogs used to bark, without looking back at the ugly Lucerne.

Mum says, 'Stupid people, what would you expect! Ignoramus's, there's plenty of land out the back for that stuff!'

'Mum, what's Madala going to do now?'

'Oh, I'm sure he will be fine sitting in the sun, smoking, and talking with his old friends.'

I'm not so sure about that. Grandpa gave him a few coins every month, rations of food including sugar and jam which he loves, and from time to time old clothes too. If there's no garden to water what will become of him?

It's all too hard. I understand now what Grandpa means about being 'done'.

Chapter 10
Water Scorpions and A New Port.

Life on the Giant Mine settles into a rhythm. Grandpa escapes to the Clubhouse. I catch the bus to school and back. In a way, the two of us are fleeing the house for different reasons. Grandpa, possibly to forget what he's lost, me to distance myself from that too, and the fact that Grandpa is fading away from us.

Bill and Mum go to work and Susan's home with a nanny. They're happy—they've got their own house—and only their voices fill the space where once other adult voices crowded together. Is it just because the house is smaller, with less yard, or has there been a shift that I don't understand?

Susan is now three and a half years old and into everything. She's endearing, with blonde wavy hair and blue eyes that captivate everyone, especially Bill. But she can be noisy, destructive, demanding, defiant, and then so sunny and funny too.

'She's got spirit!' Bill says, 'Because she nearly died. So we must not break her spirit!' I think 'spirit' is considered 'naughty' in *my* case. Why aren't *I* allowed 'spirit'? At other times laughing and hugging her, Mum says, 'Susan reminds me of the rhyme, you know the one, *There was a little girl who had a little curl right in the middle of her forehead. When she was good she was very very good, and when she was bad she was horrid!*' Even when she is horrid, Mum doesn't smack her.

Are Grandpa and I displaced in this family?

***

Grandpa buys me two guinea pigs, a concession for the loss of Noddy and Loompi. They're cute little creatures, tan and white, with twitching noses and bright eyes. They know my voice now and when I get home they rush towards the cage bars making little twittering noises.

This afternoon the cage is empty. No waiting wet noses and little eyes. They were here before I'd gone to the pool, found Grandpa and gotten a Fanta drink—orange and cold—and before I hunted water scorpions too.

'Mum, where are they?' She's standing very still, apron tied around her waist, pastry on the table for sausage rolls. It's Saturday. Outside a bus roars past. The African passengers are shouting at each other, they do that even if they are close together, their voices filtering on the warm wind through the back door. Inside it's quiet. Susan's quiet. 'Mum, where are my guinea pigs?'

'Susan, go and play, outside.' Mum's flour-covered hand leads her firmly towards the back door, 'Off you go,' she says, and we both watch her walk, without protest, down the back steps. Mum turns and says, 'They died. I came in here just now and they were dead, must have been the heat.' Her words rush out in one breath.

'But they were fine at lunchtime! I take good care of them, they have water… where are they?' My eyes search the kitchen for their little bodies.

'Mr Markee has buried them, he will show you where. He was going to take the cage away before you returned.' Mum turns her back and starts rolling out the pastry, fast and hard. Flour puffs around her hands and I gaze out the door to where Susan is playing in the late afternoon shade. She's singing to herself. An insidious thought snakes through my mind. The rhyme, *There was a little girl who had a …* Did Susan do something to them? She's always around the cage and trying to open it. Mum's eyes are on me. 'Take that look off your face! Susan didn't do anything!' She says. My thoughts have betrayed me; tears wobble at the rim of my eyes and I hurry outside as Grandpa's car pulls up.

***

The school bus drops me near my house. It's on a steep hill and I look back towards the low-level bridge that I used to cycle over from the farm. I'm still sad about leaving the farm, about Nanna, about the dogs, and now my guinea pigs are under a pile of red earth at the far end of the yard. I'll go and change the flowers in the jam jar at their grave today. I don't care that Mum thinks it's funny!

Grandpa's standing at the back door. He's smiling like mad. I haven't seen him smiling like this for ages. He steps aside. I can't believe my eyes!

'Grandpa!' I shriek 'Is that for me?'

'Yes, yes it is!'

I recall my words from months ago, 'If you win something in the Lottery, will you buy me a bicycle?'

Grandpa had looked down at my eager face and said, 'Yes, of course.' I'd leapt around, singing, 'We will win, we will win.' Grandpa had chased me away saying, 'Don't hold your breath!'

'I won 100 pounds in the lottery! You get a bicycle!'

My eyes travel over it, leaning against the wall. I can't touch it yet. Red and white, with straight handlebars, a shiny bell—and brakes!

Grandpa helps me onto the seat, 'You'll grow into it,' he says. Like I grow into my shoes stuffed with newspaper! And he gives me a push. I'm off around the house, around and around and around. It's a good day and as I cycle fast past him, I shout, 'Told you we'd win the lottery, Grandpa.'

***

School ends at 1 pm and after lunch, I vanish to wherever the kids are meeting up in the afternoon. It is so much easier than having to cycle from the farm. If it's hot we gather at the Club pool, a large, rectangular one plonked in the ground surrounded by bundu, with a pump that rarely works. The water gets progressively greener over the summer months.

We always do a water scorpion patrol before leaping in. They glide over the surface, stalking us. Flat brown creatures flexing their front pincers and trailing thin stinging tails that curve out of the water to attack; or they linger around the pool edge just on the water line, waiting to sneak up on us. We snatch them out by their tails and fling them onto the concrete surround, and before they dry out and fly away, we smash them with a rock. Their bodies are tough. We make sure they are dead.

Frogs also take up residence in the pool, along with small darting black bugs we call water dogs. We don't bother much with these. Flicking the frogs out is a waste of time, they hop right back in.

The paint, applied every winter, bubbles away from the pool's surface, and bursts and peels, like sunburnt skin. At the end of summer, the pool is drained. All wildlife and children are evicted, and the paint remains are scraped away. The fresh coat of paint dries and it's ready to refill for next summer.

Towards summer's end, the rivers begin to trickle and dry up. We explore the exposed banks and paddle in the slow-moving water. 'Don't go in the stagnant water, you'll catch bilharzia!' We are warned. Being mindful of the painful injections needed to cure this, we listen and hop from rock to rock, our arms winged out to balance and wade only in the deeper water. If we fall into still water we yell, 'You'll get bilharzia in your brain and go mad!' None of us ever did, go mad that is.

Over the seasons we wander through the bush and feast on whatever bush fruit is around. In the summer months, it's sour plums we look out for, bright orange or red fruits that we chew on with screwed-up faces because they are so sour, and then our dry mouths thirst for water.

During winter it's the snot apples, hard round five-sectioned fruits, about the size of golf balls but with a green furry outer. We break these open and chew endlessly on the 'snot' inside and eventually spit out the remnants. Or monkey bread, a hard long flat pod that is rusty brown and, when ripe, falls to the ground. They refuse to split open and we hit the hard outer casing to reveal the 'bread' inside, which we chew on.

We are a happy little gang of kids, barefoot and free, with too much imagination. But this creates a problem, actually two.

The first is there aren't enough kids on the mine to form separate gangs to hide out from or do battle with. We decide to form one gang and we hide from the other gang: the adults. We won't tell where our fort, gang HQ is, *ever*. The Africans know, they know everything through the bush telegraph, and if something dreadful happened to us, they'd raise the alarm. They only 'tell on us' if it's necessary. The adults use conventional telephones, so the exchange ladies know everything, even though they are not supposed to listen in and they always 'tell on us!'

Our second problem is that we need a new fort. Our current one, a lean-to made of bare branches, sits under a winter-naked thorn tree, surrounded by tall grass that rattles restlessly. November brings the big rains that will pour into our shelter.

We scout around the bush for a good location for our new fort, well away from the houses, from prying parents' eyes and from the mine works that we never go anywhere near.

This afternoon, George and Andy are so excited when we gather. They've found the perfect place, not far past our current fort and about half an hour's walk from where we live.

'It's an abandoned mine!' George announces proudly. He stares at our dismayed faces and flicks his blonde hair away from his eyes. 'What's wrong with you lot? It's great!'

'Man, it's so good!' says Andy hopping from one foot to the other.

Suddenly they seem taller, their skinny ten-year-old chests puff up with loud bravado. 'Come on, let's go!'

In a single file, we follow George and Andy along a winding bundu path, our feet leaving uneven small imprints in the red earth, into a world behind tall dead grass from which a bird suddenly takes flight. I jump and scan my surroundings. Grandpa says all the animals are hungry now, including us humans, before the rains arrive. It's getting hot. We are quiet. I shouldn't be going there and *know* it, the adults talk of mines and flooding in serious tones. 'Old mines cave in,' they say, whatever that means.

We arrive at the top of a large steep pile of rubble and from here we stare downwards. Cut into the rock face below, are three holes, all large enough to walk through. They stare up at me like black eyes.

'The middle hole is the way in,' George says. His skinny arm points and my eyes follow. 'The other two just meet up with that one.' He turns and looks at us, a wide grin showing off his too-large front teeth in a lean face.

'Did you two check it out?' asks Clive, raking his fingers through his thick dark hair and making it stick up. His skinny knees are scrabbed from falling over last week.

'Sure!' says Andy, 'There's another hole further in. We stopped there, 'cos we needed lamps.'

Today they are prepared. George and Andy open the sacks and hand out George's homemade lamps: jam jars, with lembu (cloth) pushed through a hole in the metal lid, tied in a knot, the other end hanging into paraffin. Two boxes of matches rattle in his hand. 'My dad won't miss this stuff,' he assures us.

I'm scared, they're scared, and none of us is going to admit it, but our quietness betrays us all. The boys have catapults and pockets full of rocks. 'My dad will sure belt me if he finds out!' says Andy and his words echo our thoughts.

I follow Andy down the rubble slope, my feet loosening rocks that clatter before me as we hurry after each other, down through the middle opening. From here we make our way further inside, along a slope towards another large hole. Now it's very dark. George lights the lamps, their flames smoke upward and waver. He holds one high and leans through the opening and says, 'Give me another one.' With a lamp in each hand, he crouches down and stretches his lean body into the blackness. Illuminated below is an earth ramp leading into what appears to be a large cavern. He jumps through the opening and runs down the soft dirt into the dark, lamps held high shouting, 'Come on guys!' His skinny body does a dance casting long shadows over the sand in the lamplight.

One after another we leap through the entrance, each of us clutching a lamp, shrieking and laughing away any fear. In the main cavern, we fall silent and hold the flames above our heads. Even if I stood on Andy's shoulders, I wouldn't reach the ceiling. To the right yawns a huge pit, its far section curves close to the stone wall. Sleeping bats hang over the hole, their wings folded as if in prayer. The stones we throw at them bounce off the rock face and vanish soundlessly into the abyss. To the left is another smaller portal and directly in front of us, across a flat expanse, the earth rises in a mound where blackness hangs beyond our flames. For a moment I wonder what lies lurking there, but the boys are excited about a hole in the ceiling above this mound. We stand on each other's backs, scrambling to get a look in and discover it's the entrance to a small cave, full of bats.

'This is Bat Cave,' announces George.

Andy's standing near the huge ground-level hole. He stretches his catapult, lets a stone fly and hits a sleeping bat. It falls silently into the blackness. 'And this one is bat grave,' he shouts.

It's the most awesome fort we have ever had!

Over the next few weeks, we strategically place lamps further into the mine to light as guides when we explore, then extinguish them as we retreat to the entrance.

We've been coming here for weeks now and today we find the bottom of the 'bat grave' abyss. Giggling we balance on old metal tracks and step over the remains of dead bats and finger larger bones that litter the ground. We are deep into the mine. The darkness is absolute beyond our lamps. I'm uncomfortable down here, and for the first time in my life, dead bones unnerve me. It's a place we decide not to frequent, and leave only two lamps.

Andy's brother, Adam, comes home from boarding school around that time. He's fifteen years old. Taller than all of us, showing shadows on his face, and his voice has deepened. Usually, we are restrained around Adam, but today we clamour around him, telling him about our new fort. He acts disinterested but finally agrees to see it. We march him, gun on his shoulder, through the bundu to our fort. Adam is impressed. He shoots at the hanging bats that silently plummet down 'bat grave'. We cheer, and the boys let loose with catapults. Some bats take flight and weave above, squeaking, as we dance wildly, creating grotesque shadows elongated by the glow of lamps, topped with small animal skulls as lampshades, the eye sockets spitting flames that lick and darken the white orbit bones; places where living eyes once blinked. Our shrieks echo off the walls. Several boys press themselves flat against the rock wall on the far side of the bat grave abyss and shuffle around the narrow ledge, their toes clinging to the edge knocking stones into the blackness. They are reckless, foolishly fearless, and I turn away. Perhaps we are too wild and free.

It's Saturday, raining, and we have hours to waste. A trip to the bottom of the bat grave is decided on, and we troop off, lighting our guide lamps as we go.

'We need more paraffin,' says George. 'Some of the jars are almost empty.'

We reach the bottom, balance on the metal tracks, and roam around searching for bones and skulls. I find larger ones, run my fingers over them and try to imagine what animal they belonged to… wild cats? Their surfaces aren't smooth like those I find in the dry river beds; these are pitted and chewed.

Andy shouts, 'Hey we need fire and food—just like cavemen!' He unscrews his lamp's lid, 'Check this out, man!' He pours the paraffin in a line, strikes a match, touches the wet ground and flames dash, leaping upwards, brilliant, smoking, and then they're gone. 'Do it again!' We shout. Eager fingers unscrew several lamps, pour out their contents and strike matches. Now multiple trails of flames flare, illuminating the cavern. We scream and jump over them, shoving and pushing each other like little heathens. Behind us live silent shadows flit. I don't see them but know they are there from their paw prints in the dirt. We fall around, the flames die and we are quiet, hushed by the blackness.

All the paraffin is gone. Only one lamp glows on the far side, its flame still, and small and the jar is empty. Suddenly the air is split with sound. A roaring that comes from deep within the mine. It rolls above us, around us, bouncing off the walls and echoing through the cavern. In the faint light, I grab at Andy's arm. The adult's words come back to me. 'Cave-ins in mines.' Is this a cave-in? Flooding from all the rains? No. The sound is high-pitched and rumbling, an animal snarl that fills my ears and makes us all scream in terror. Is it a big cat? Leopard? I've heard that sound before, when the leopards fought with baboons at night, at Auntie Ivys'. The far lamp goes out and I'm running towards where the light once was, grabbing at the others, shrieking and tripping in the darkness. There's a glow beyond, another lone guide lamp. Its faint flame breaks the blackness and I scramble, screaming, towards it. The cat is louder now, closer. Its roaring hounds me as I stumble along the lamp trail. My chest is tight, grit in my eyes and mouth. My throat can't shout now. I'm waiting for the pounce, the tearing claws. Will my bones be chewed like the ones I found?

I see daylight.

We rush towards it. Up the ramp, along the tunnel, out into the sharp sunshine and tumble into the dirt. Still, the roaring continues. We scramble on all fours, up the rocky incline, the stones, gleaming wet from the earlier rain, slip beneath us and we collapse at the top. My chest's heaving.

I turn and look back. Nothing is behind us. Only silence. Above, the sky is blue behind remnants of rain clouds. The late afternoon breeze, freshly washed, drifts warmly over my face. Wide-eyed and tear-streaked we stare at one another. Everyone seems OK. Finally, George says, 'That was a big cat for sure. I nearly shit my pants, worse than when my Dad's about to clobber me with his belt!' None of us laughs.

Scratched, filthy and trembling, we walk home, stopping briefly at the back tap of Andy's house to clean up. We will have to find a new fort, but there's a problem. We've left our lamps behind, evidence of our occupation.

'My brother will be home soon,' Andy says, looking at our worried faces, 'He will know what to do.' Finally, Adam arrives home. Away from the adults, with gabbling voices, we report our problems.

'You lot scared off by an itty bitty kitty?' he says scornfully. 'Man, you kill me.' With his gun over his shoulder, he leads the way through the bundu, along our well-worn path, past trees sprouting green. We are nervous, but we have Adam and his gun. He's going to show that cat who's the baas for sure.

At the top of the rocky slope, we lie flat and do a recce of the mine entrance. 'Stay here,' says Adam. He rolls over and with his gun in one hand starts to bum slide down towards the opening. Before he's halfway there a loud and rolling snarl reaches him and he 'puts foot' into reverse, his feet digging frantically into the loose stones. A moment later he tumbles over the top of the slope and falls back panting.

'Shit! That's a big cat for sure! Come on, let's get out of here.' No one says a word about the itty bitty kitty. We retreat along the winding path fringed with rattling grass that mocks us. The lowering sun is blinding. Adam looks over his shoulder, his gun pointing at the ground. 'Don't you lot *ever* go back there,' he says.

We just look at him.

'You hear me? Man, that thing will eat you for sure.'

Reluctantly, we all nod our heads.

'And forget about that stuff you left there, too!'

It was the best fort we ever had. Pity about the lamps and the skulls we lost.

Chapter 11
1967, On the Move Again

We are moving again. I don't want to.

Mum says, 'You'll like Hartley. We've got a lovely house.'

I reluctantly agree when I see it, but the best thing is the low-limbed flamboyant tree in the front yard, which is *perfect* for climbing. It's OK in another way too because I can easily visit my best friend, Sharon, who also lives in town. Her parents, Uncle Jack and Auntie Florrie, (even if you're not related all adult good friends are called Auntie and Uncle), become a more regular part of our lives. It was difficult for them to visit us on the farm with petrol rationing. 'That's all Smith's fault too,' Mum reminds us.

Sometimes, after school, I go to Sharon's house and we have lunch, avocados cut in half with vinegar dressing, which is awful. I show Sharon how to tip it out the dining room window and that works well until one day she gets it all over the glass. We almost have heart attacks until the cook boy comes in and silently cleans it off. He doesn't like avocados either!

Their house feels stiff to me. I always 'use my manners' here as Nanna would say. Uncle Jack and Auntie Florrie scare me a little. They are very strict. Posture is important to Auntie Florrie and on some afternoons she makes us balance a book on our heads. We parade back and forth with straight backs beneath her watchful eyes, and she tells Sharon that mine is perfect. Sharon also has to practice the piano *no matter what*, with no excuses allowed, and she attends swimming training. She's very good at butterfly. I just flop around like a wet cat and almost drown. There are no butterflies in me!

Uncle Jack has a nickname for Susan. When we arrive he calls out loudly, 'Where's the little sod?' That voice of his frightens me. I'd run off and hide if he was saying that about me. But Susan is fearless. She runs towards him laughing and shouting, 'I'm a little sod! You can't catch me, Uncle Jack.' And Uncle Jack laughs right back at her and says, 'You little sod!' While trying to grab her. She's got no fear and has spirit to spare. I think that maybe she's got 'spirit' because she nearly died.

Grandpa and I go grocery shopping and I spend ages mooning over the dolls in the toy section. It's November and new Christmas stock has arrived. I suddenly see her… the most *beautiful* doll. She's 18 inches tall in a pink dress with blonde hair piled into a bun on top of her head and she's all boxed up with a cellophane window. She's gazing out at me. Every trip to the store I rush in and stare at her and dream of owning her, and then suddenly she's not on the shelf anymore. I tell Grandpa and he says, coughing into his hankie, 'Well Beverley, all the dolls are for sale, so that's to be expected. Come on, ice cream time…'

The coughing worries me, I hear Mum and Grandpa every morning now. *Cough, cough, cough.* I can't recall if it was that bad on the farm. Or is it because the house we're in now is smaller and I can hear more? I'm sure it's the cigarettes though!

On Christmas morning I dash out to the tree in the corner of the glass-enclosed verandah. There's an oblong-wrapped box, halfway up the tree, stuffed between the branches. The name tag is obscured, but I can't reach it to peep.

We all gather around the tree and Bill starts handing out the parcels, reading the labels and calling each person's name. He's so slow. It's killing me, but I know I must keep quiet and wait. It's rude to be greedy. At last, he pulls the box from between the branches and reads my name. I knew it! Grandpa's watching me closely, a small smile on his face. Carefully, I unpick the paper. 'Oh hurry up!' says Mum. I don't, but suddenly *there she is*, looking at me through the clear cellophane lid. Her dress is patterned, not plain pink, but she's otherwise the same.

'Oh Grandpa, you got her for me!'

'It's not the one you liked, they'd sold her before my payday. But, they had this one out the back.'

'She's perfect!' I stare at her and then run over and fling my arms around his neck. I know I'm going to keep her forever.

Grandpa also has two dolls for Susan. They're smaller, about 12 inches high, and one dressed in pink and the other in blue. They are beautiful too.

***

It's Saturday and Uncle Jack and Aunty Florrie invite us over for something special. A professional photographer is coming to take photos of the family, and they have suggested we have some taken too.

Sharon and I are wearing similar dresses, one lemon and the other pale green; both of us have been scrubbed spotless and our hair has been brushed into submission. Sharon's upset because Auntie Florrie has had her fringe cut so short. Mine is short too but I've scraped it back in an Alice band. We pose on the front verandah with their pet dog, Butch, between us.

Uncle Jack says, 'Amazing Norma, the little sod's decent today, with that bow in her hair!' And for once Susan is not cheeky back. She's wearing a dress, even though she prefers shorts, and has even sat still long enough for Mum to fix a large bow on top of her head.

I hear, Aunty Florrie say, 'Pity about her teeth, Norma, but that won't spoil the photos I'm sure. She is very cute without them!'

'Poor child,' Mum says, 'All that medicine when she was a baby just ruined them. All six front ones came through rotten. Hopefully, the second teeth will be alright. I still can't believe she survived.'

'Who would have thought that would happen,' says Auntie Florrie. 'Small price to pay though.'

So that's why Susan has a gummy smile and so many missing teeth! Now I know that it's because she nearly died! Is that why we must not break her spirit, as Bill says?

It's March and Susan turns four years old and her spirit grows with this milestone even *more*. She is into everything, her little fingers fiddling, riffling through draws, undressing my dolls and she's even into Mum's makeup. *Nothing* is safe. And she is fast, in and out before anyone knows it, leaving a trail of destruction.

One afternoon Susan and I are playing under the flamboyant tree, which is now sprouting green from the rains, and Sharon cycles into the yard and says, 'Let's go for a ride.' I grab my lovely new bike and we are off. It starts to rain so I cycle home fast, but it's too late. Susan is cross with me for leaving her and has taken several of my *Noddy* books outside and left them open under the tree, and now they are soaking wet.

I shout at her, 'Carl gave these to me! Look what you've done!' But she runs off laughing and Mum comes out onto the verandah, 'Oh for goodness sake Beverley, it's just a few books. They will dry out,' she says. 'Anyway, aren't you a bit big for Noddy now? And don't yell at your sister!' Yell at her! All I want to do is hit her! But that's not allowed. I gather my books and take them into my room. Susan's singing away, quite happily. And yes, the books do dry out, but they now have wavy pages and covers that will never shut properly.

***

We are moving again. This time to Rusape, a town on the other side of Salisbury. It's something to do with Bill's new job. And I do not want to go. I like it here in Hartley.

Mum says, 'You'll like it, Rusape is just another country town like Hartley. Auntie Ivy lives there, so we will know someone. We can still go to Salisbury a few times a year for shopping.' But I don't care about any of that. I don't want to move. Hartley is home now, the school is close by, and so are my friends, I've just joined Brownies and I don't even mind having to go to church some Sundays.

Moving day arrives, and it's a sunny mild mid-winter morning. We pile all our koutunda (goods and chattels) into the station wagon, onto roof racks and squash Mr Markee into the very back surrounded by more stuff. Mum, Susan and I are in the rear seat, with bags under our feet and a cranky caged cat, which we recently acquired.

Auntie Florrie, Sharon, and Uncle Jack all wave as we pull out of the driveway, and Uncle Jack calls out, 'Bye little sod and family.' The pantechnicon lumbers off, belching black from its exhaust, and with my final glimpse at the flamboyant climbing tree, and its winter-bare branches, we are on our way.

The familiar towns of, Selous and Norton flash past the window and then we drive through busy Salisbury, with its wide streets, traffic, and pavements full of people. We stop at rest spots on the roadside. Winter brown surrounds us and we sit at concrete picnic tables, eat soggy sandwiches and sip lukewarm tea before stuffing ourselves back into the car. We look like a bunch of Africans on a bus. All we need are chickens in woven cages on the roof racks to complete the picture.

Beyond Salisbury, we are on the A3, and the towns are unfamiliar. There's Melford and Bromley and Marandellas, then Macheke and finally in Headlands, Bill says, 'Rusape next stop!'

'Thank goodness, I'm sure the cat needs to pee.' Mum says. We run into the bush to do that ourselves, but we can't let Felix out of his cage.

***

It's mid-afternoon when we arrive. Our rented house is just off the main street. It's small, the yard is barren, and we are exhausted. The pantech pulls up, reverses in and the boys fling open the rear doors and begin unloading.

While this is happening a khaki-clad boy wearing a white apron appears. He's smiling and carrying a huge cloth-covered tray which he sets down on a table near the neighbour's fence. He then brings a letter over to Mum. 'Afternoon tea, sandwiches,' he says pointing to the table. 'Medem says sorry not here, you have now.' And then he gestures to us to step over the two-strand wire fence and sit in the shade of our neighbour's garden.

Mum opens the letter and tears fill her eyes. 'Oh goodness,' she says, 'This note's from our neighbour apologising for not being here to greet us! We are to have tea and sandwiches and tell the boy if we need anything else. She will see us tomorrow! It's signed, Lyn Barlow.' She looks up smiling, 'Well I never, isn't that so thoughtful and kind!'

And that's how we came to sit in the shade of Lyn Barlow's garden, sip hot tea and eat fresh sandwiches. The boys unloaded under Mr Markee's watchful eye and he had the house sorted – quick smart!

The next morning I smell toast and tea. Mr Markee's in the kitchen, banging around, and for a moment I feel like we are still in Hartley. Suddenly I wonder, where did Mr Markee sleep last night? And then, where did he live when we left the Giant Mine and moved to Hartley? I realise that I don't know. He's always just around us, and on the farm I knew where his house was. I'll have to ask Mum when she's got the time. It's funny how we don't talk about this.

Chapter 12
We Are Poor, Grandpa's Sad, and There Are School Bullies

We are poor, not outwardly because Mum sews beautifully so we are well dressed, but financially, we are poor. And Rusape is cold, physically and emotionally. Our teeth chatter in the mornings, mist rises from our breaths and Mr Markee grumbles in the kitchen about the cold. The June days just don't warm up as they did in Hartley. We are all used to the milder mornings and warm winter days. Mum unpicks the grey padded lining of Bill's jacket and makes it into a little coat for Susan. 'I'll have to find a job too,' she says.

The house is awful, with an unloved garden. Susan and I have to share a bedroom and Grandpa has a small one at the front of the house. It's barren outside his window and inside his life; he's even sadder. The house is on Milton Street around the corner from the main street of town where we find the Spar Supermarket, which we walk to for groceries. There are small shops clustered on this street, with neat pavements, including two banks, Barclays and Standard.

'Considering the stance Britain has taken,' Bill says, 'I fail to see how and why Barclays has maintained its services here. One can understand Standard Bank, after all, it's been South African-based since 1862! *Goodness Bill uses big words.*

Houses line the street and opposite ours, there's a Mess. I find out that that's where single young men live. When the warmer months arrive, they get 'inebriated and are decidedly not salubrious,'

Bill says, as they party late into the night. Mum sometimes walks outside in her dressing gown, and shouts, 'Shut up you lot!' By this time she knows them all and they laugh and call out, 'Come on over and join us, Norma!' Some nights one of them blows mournful melodies on his trombone, but it sounds more like a cow in labour. I wonder if he's a bit like Whoo and howling at the full moon, or if he's just 'bubble-arse' (drunk) as Mum says? Mum shouts at him too, and he shouts back, 'This one's for you Norma…' And then serenades her with another mournful tune.

Bill strolls across an empty corner block, at the other end of the street, to his office at the District Commissioner's building and walks home every day for lunch and a short nap.

John Cowie, the primary school, is a short bicycle ride away. We finish at 1pm and students go home for lunch but have to return for sporting activities some afternoons. School is not going well and after a few days, I broach the subject at the dining table.

'Mum, they hardly speak English in the playground. I can't understand them and they won't let me join in their games.'

Mum looks up from her plate, 'Well, that's no surprise to me! They're speaking Afrikaans.' I've not heard Afrikaans spoken so much before, only the occasional greeting in the Post Office and Nanna muttering, 'I don't speak that language.' And Grandpa would say, 'Only because you can't pronounce the words!'

'But we speak English in class.'

'Yes, because that's the law, but in the playground they can speak whatever they like!' She sighs. 'Look, the farmers around here are mostly Afrikaans, not like at Hartley where there was a mixture of English and Afrikaans families. That's why we don't speak it.' *And also Nanna wouldn't because she couldn't.*

Bill lights a cigarette and places his knife and fork together. 'And, from what I can ascertain, the town is mostly Indian-dominated.'

'Aren't their saris beautiful? I just love their little shops too!' Mum says.

'Precisely the point, the Indians are the business people in town.'

I've seen Indian ladies around the town. They're graceful in their flowing bright saris and long glossy plaited hair that hangs far down their backs.

'But Mum, what am I going to do, they won't play with me. They just run off laughing!'

'Oh, not much I can do, you'll need to sort it out yourself.' Seeing the pleading look on my face she adds, 'There's no point in me talking to the Headmaster, he's not going to do anything.' She pushes her dining chair back, 'Rest time now, take Susan to your room and read. Be quiet.'

Grandpa gets up slowly, hugs me briefly, ruffles Susan's hair, and walks to his bedroom. He's vanishing before my eyes and only joins us for meals and to have a drink with Bill in the evenings. Everyone, in our house, smokes and drinks. Grandpa's doing more of both and I'm not supposed to know about his extra drinking, but I do because of all the crates of empty beer bottles in the pantry. We never throw them away because we pay a 'deposit' for each one and return them. I don't dare sneak a few to cash in for pennies.

In the evening, a beer is always close to his hand, along with cigarettes that tremble between his nicotine-stained fingers. Their stubs fill the ashtray and ash drifts over the edge, clumping in the condensation dripping from his pewter tankard. The smell lingers on his clothes. If Mum's been sitting with him, her lipstick-bleeding cigarette butts jumble in the ashtray too; red and tan fallen soldiers betraying her vacant seat.

In the mornings, Grandpa's hacking 'smoker's cough'—that's what Mum calls it—barks from his room. I don't dare say she's coughing like that too. It's frightening, he is slipping emotionally away from me. I need him, but he can't be with me. His spirit has left to live with Nanna.

Mum says, 'Dad's sad without Mum.' I see that she is too. It's in her brown eyes, on her face when she talks of Nanna, and in the way she looks at Grandpa when he's unaware.

We have left the places I love. We are in this cold town, poor, and the adults are busy with their daily lives. I miss the farm and Hartley, the mango and low-limbed flamboyant trees.

***

And the problems at school won't go away. I can't communicate, am shy and out of my comfort zone. The bullying gets worse and when the perpetrators realise that no one is going to reprimand them, it escalates even further and they grow bored with taunts and running away from me.

It's morning break time and some kids are giggling, watching me. They've done something, but what it is, I don't know. I open my lunchbox and see that my sandwich is gone and has been replaced by leaves and dirt. I look up. Their bunched bodies erupt into laughter. I close the lid, place it in my school case and push past them. At home time, the same group gathers and sniggers at me, and I find that my bicycle tyre's flat, again. I start pushing it home and their taunts in Afrikaans follow me. My polished shoes scuff at the dirt and I want to get away from this town. I'm so miserable.

At morning Assembly, my long hair is often pulled and muffled sniggering puts me on alert. They're tying knots in the ends of my hair. We get into trouble if we fidget so I'm forced to sit still. I try to sit away from this particular group, but they shift to sit behind me.

During most break times I retreat to the KG1 (Kindergarten) play area, which excludes older students, 'play' with the younger children. It's the only way to avoid bullies and the teachers don't stop me. There are nice children at the school, but they won't be friends with me. It's all about keeping in good with the bullies.

In the classroom, most children want to be the teacher's pet. Competition for the front seats is fierce, and the popular kids grab them. I'm pushed to the back and get into trouble for talking when all I'm doing is asking the child next to me what's written on the blackboard because I can't see. My grades fall.

Mum gets a job at the Spar Supermarket—around the corner from home—on the checkout. This provides the bullies with more ammunition. I'm now physically pushed around, punched and taunted with, 'You're curry lovers,' and 'My Mom's (they say Mom and not Mum) taking me shopping this arvie! I'll check out if your Mom's on the register!' Much laughter and mimicking of working on the grocery register and shouts of, 'Howzit curry lover kinder!' (How's that Indian loving child). Mum's being bullied too, by the townspeople. The Indians are the only ones who offer her a job even though she's a qualified bookkeeper and secretary with lots of experience.

We start socialising with Indian families, go to their functions, eat Indian food and Mum wears a sari when she goes out. She has two: one white and silver, and the other red and gold. They wrap around her and shimmer and she looks beautiful. But, when she puts a red dot between her eyes, that's it for me at school! No one dares be my friend now.

Today it's compulsory afternoon sports, and as I walk towards the school's playing fields stones hit my legs and chest. Kids are throwing stones at me. Their skinny arms arch back and forth launching them and their laughter mocks me as missiles sting my flesh. Stunned, I turn and run, 'Curry lover, curry lover!' They shout, and their words land harder than stones. 'Voetsak, curry lover. Hartloop curry lover. Hartloop!'

I don't tell anyone. The teachers were there. I understand this, but I don't have the words to describe it, yet.

Chapter 13
Grandpa's Gone, and We Don't Eat Nasturtium Leaves

There's a calendar stuck to the dining room wall, and each month has an animal picture. This month it's a hippo, head raised out of the water with its mouth wide open—huge teeth curve upwards—like the one in the Umfuli River. I wonder where they took this photo. Hippos are scary, they can run fast and kill you. They say you can't outrun a hippo.

I can't run away, today even though I'd like to. My finger traces over yesterday's date in a red-bordered square, Thursday 15th and at the top of the page in bold black, August 1968. Yesterday's date. Today is Friday. Grandpa died, yesterday. Thursday. I remember Nanna's calendar, the one with the English countryside.

Great Gran, Nanna, and now Grandpa are all gone. But where? I hope they're having tea and hot buttered bread together.

Grandpa's bedroom door, next to the front door, is closed. Only it's not his anymore, is it? The round battered brass knob turns in my hand and I push it open. His cigarettes are on the bedside table, and his pipe's leaning there too. Their stale familiar smell lingers, his voice lingers in my mind, and his smile lingers, but he's gone. The finality of this is known to me. I think I'll use the backdoor from now on.

It was only a few days ago that Mum, Susan, and Grandpa went to Salisbury and came back without him. Susan's fine, she's playing outside and chasing the new dog, Squibb, a compact black and tan Schipperke. It's Bill's dog. I don't want a dog of my own again. She doesn't understand. Mum's distraught. She hasn't said much, but her red-rimmed eyes say she's been crying, secretly.

I cry too, in the garden. The one person who always listened is gone. No one explains anything to me. Susan and I don't go to the funeral and his death isn't discussed around us. One day he's here and the next he's not, leaving a void in my life that can't be filled. The face that turned to me with understanding, the calm arm on my shoulder, the gentle hand on my hair, the person who loved me is gone. The red bicycle with its shiny bell, a Burmese coin and a bank note, signed by the men he served with in WWII, are a few treasured physical reminders of him. I keep the coin and note in a special box. They're things I can touch, and keep close in the memory closet of my mind. Now I begin to understand grief, it's an empty aching sobbing sad place in my body.

***

Weeks after Grandpa vanishes, Bill wanders in from work and says, 'Beverley, can I have that Burmese note you've got? I was talking to a chap at work who collects them. He said it would be a fine addition to his collection, because of the signatures.'

'No! Grandpa gave it to me, I don't want to give it away.' Bill's frowns at my refusal. I hurry to my room, unfold the note and examine the signatures. Then, carefully tuck it away in the box with the coin. It's safe. The following Saturday, bored and feeling sad, I open my treasure box and the note's gone! I run to Bill who is relaxing in the sitting room, 'Did you take my note?'

'You must have lost it,' he replies, drawing on his pipe and puffing smoke before my eyes.

I'm so mad that I almost shout, but instead say very fast, 'I didn't, it's special. I put it in my box! I know it was there. You took it for your friend!' Bill's face rearranges itself and he leans forward. I'm on shaky ground now.

'Not my fault you lost it!' He snaps back. 'Go to your room now!' His arm thrusts towards the door and I bolt. Bill's angry with me. He doesn't hit me, he shouts though, and I don't defy him. Grandpa's not here anymore; there's another shift in the dynamics of the house.

It's subtle to start with, but definite.

***

'We are moving,' says Mum. 'When you come home from school, go to the new house, alright?'

'What new house! Where?' I say staring at her as I stuff my lunchbox into my school case. Mum laughs and flicks her hand at the empty house next door, 'The Barlows moved away last week. So, just there!' She says, 'Off you go now!'

I get home from school and there we are, now living in the house next door. A hot lunch is waiting on the dining room table, and Mr Markee is singing in the kitchen. The furniture has been carried across the yard, over the two-strand wire fence and is now positioned in its new home. Grandpa's favourite chair, with the wide wooden polished armrests, is in the sitting room, safe. The matching chair is close by, a small table between them, on which there is a black ashtray with a round base and a metal screw-on lid with a plunger. When you press the plunger the metal plates spin and fall, dropping ash and butts into the container and then it snaps up shut. It's Grandpa's ashtray. I like his chair there because I can imagine him sitting in it, using that ashtray.

It's a larger house with an enclosed verandah and an established garden out front. Susan and I have separate bedrooms. Mr Markee has retrieved my newspaper-wrapped special things from under the floorboards, where I'd hidden them from Susan's litte fingers. He's clever. I hadn't told him about that, but he knows *everything* and has stored them in my wardrobe.

I relish my own space. I haven't had a chance to ask Mum where Mr Markee lives. Is it rude to ask him?

We've been in the house a few weeks now and Mum says, 'Bill, the yard needs a lot of work. We can't afford a gardener, can you get the convicts to come over?'

Bill lights his evening pipe. 'That can be arranged. How many days?'

'Oh, a week would get it all done. We only needed them for two days next door, the yard there is so barren!'

This morning the convicts are on their way. I watch them walking the short distance, from the prison around the corner, dressed in comic book uniforms—off-white baggy shirts and pants with brown arrows painted on them. They're talking and laughing. A smartly dressed guard is at the rear and the convict beside him is carrying his gun! I call out to Mum and together we peer through the gauze on the verandah and giggle.

'Well, I'll be!' says Mum as the convicts troop past us into the backyard. Mr Markee knows exactly what has to be done. He's out there telling the guard just what he wants! Mum walks down the back steps and stops before an old convict with steel wool grey hair and a bent back.

'You're in jail again!' She exclaims, wagging her finger at him, 'I remember you from over there, months ago!' Her arm waves towards the next-door house. 'What have you been up to now?'

The old man grins, most of his teeth are gone and the few remaining are nicotine-stained. 'Too cold, Medem, too cold. I steal at Spar, they lock me up. Very good!'

Mum shakes her head, 'Humba lapa kia?' (Go to your traditional home?)

'No kia, Medem.' His face folds in on itself with sadness that he quickly shrugs off, 'Jail warm. Tea and jam, veery good here.'

Mum walks over to Mr Markee and the guard. I see her hands fluttering around and then she hurries towards the kitchen.

'Beverley, grab that tatty blanket and give it to Mr Markee.'

I do so, and watch the old convict sit, lean back against the tree trunk and wrap the blanket around his body. Winter sun sifts through the leafless boughs and he sighs. Mr Markee leaves the kitchen carrying a large old jam tin, wrapped in a cloth, brimming with sweet milky tea—with at least eight spoons of sugar in there—and a huge wedge of bread slathered with strawberry jam. The old convict will get more at morning tea, with the rest of the crew and the guard.

Mum watches him for a few minutes from the kitchen window. 'He's far too old to work,' She sighs and turns away. 'It's so sad, they're displaced now, the war, kids going to cities and not returning, their old life is drifting away. Poor old man. Fancy having no kia!'

I have to agree with the last few words, some of the rest I understand, but don't really. And what's even more puzzling is Mum's attitude toward Africans. In one breath she's moaning about all the bad things they do, and then she does this. And there's Mr Markee whom she cares very much about too, and the old African, Sandy, who was with them in Ndola all those years ago. I suppose he's long dead now. Mum tells the story of how Grandpa asked Sandy to look after the Medem and Misses when he went to the war. Nanna got into a temper many times with Sandy and would fire him, but Sandy would say, 'I stay, the Bass said I must look after you. When he back, you fire me!'

When Mum talks about him it's in a voice that says she cares too. And she tells us, 'Sandy told Mum, If the skelems (bad people) come you shoot them before they get in here. Then call me, I come and pull them inside and then call police!'

And then sometimes I feel like she loves Susan much more than me. Does she? Oh, it's all so difficult and I hate this town called Rusape!

**

It's not long before our financial situation slaps Mum, Susan and me. Some nights we've been having sugar sprinkled on buttered bread; but Bill doesn't, he has lunch leftovers or nasturtium leaves on sandwiches for dinner. Mum and I collect these in the flourishing garden.

'Pick the small ones, they are the best, not bitter. The big ones are too tough,' she says pointing to those under the larger leaves. I get amongst them in the flower bed, and she bends to help. Bees hover over orange bell-shaped flowers and the afternoon sun warms our backs. I like collecting nasturtium leaves with her. We have crumbed brains for lunch at least once a week too, and that's on today's menu. I don't think anything of this until we finish eating.

Our chairs are scraping back from the dining table when Bill says, 'Wait!' His face contorts. He glares at Mum, inhales deeply, clenches his fist and hits the table rhythmically, 'I ... don't... ever... want... to ... see ... brains... on... this... table... again!' He jerks upright, his chair legs scraping on the wooden floor. We all sit silently. 'And no more bloody nasturtium leaves either!' He shouts and stalks out, his body is rigid, and stomps down the passage. We wait until the bedroom door slams. Mum's body loosens and a nervous laugh bubbles in her chest and I cover my mouth smothering giggles. Susan stares at us with wide blue eyes.

'Well, suppose we had better not suggest tripe then either!' She finally says. I liked crumbed brains and small nasturtium leaves on buttered bread! Tripe?! We've never had that and won't *now*, for sure. Nanna would be horrified at the thought of serving tripe or rabbit.

***

Mum has no idea what Bill earns, he gives her housekeeping every month and I hear her moaning to friends about it. 'He thinks it's a 'good allowance' for food and keep, but it's not!'

And then, just as it's beginning to feel like home, I return home early one Saturday afternoon and don't call out 'Hello', at the back door because I can hear Mum and Bill in the sitting room, arguing.

'I'm not financially supporting her,' Bill says.

'Honestly, Bill, it's not that much!' Mum's exasperated.

'I don't care, she's not my child, she has a father and I've got Susan to consider.'

'Oh, and do you consider me too? No, not really, isn't that the truth! You're aware her father sends a monthly cheque, it covers most of her expenses, but not all.'

'So, who has been picking up the shortfall then? You've not required additional funds before. Have your wages funded her? Is that it?'

'My Dad did, out of his pension.'

'Now, *I'm* required to pay. Is that what you're proposing? Because I will not.' His tone says the subject is closed.

'Look Bill, she's here…' Mum starts coughing. The same cough Grandpa had. It's frightening.

'Only because we inherited her when your parents died. They were very young, her father didn't consider that event when he left her with them. Did he?'

'Fine, I'll pay out of my wages and not from the 'housekeeping' you hand out so generously!' Mum's voice is rising, I can visualise her pursed lips.

'Her father's got custody. Send her to him. Susan doesn't like her—it will be quieter around here too. No more her antagonising my child.'

'Bill! They're sisters…'

Yes, she is my sister and I love her, even though we sometimes fight with each other.

This is horrid. I close my 'elephant ears' and tip-toe down the back steps. There are no climbing trees in this yard. Only tall jacarandas along the fence line—with trunks too round to hug. They soar skywards, and their branches pointing at the clouds are too hard to reach.

There is nowhere to hide. There is nowhere to go. I wish there were climbing trees here, with low horizontal boughs. When I complain to Mum about this she says, 'You're too big to be doing that now.'

Maybe we all need trees to climb? To hide amongst the leaves, to peep below, to stretch out on wide limbs and catch glimpses of the sky with its ever-shifting moods and clouds. A place where the mind can soar, where the body can relish in the texture of wood and the shift of the branches in the wind. Yes, *I like* to climb trees.

Maybe, I think, my father will arrive on a white horse and carry me away. Oh, but he can't because I'm too old for fairy tales, and climbing trees, and he has a wife now. What if she doesn't want me either? There's a huge pile of swept-up leaves. I burrow into them and fluff their brown crispness around me, close my eyes and breathe deeply. *Grandpa, are you there? Grandpa?* Stale cigarette smells. My one eye opens and focuses on two butts caught amongst the leaves, lipstick free. I stare at them.

It will be alright, Beverley. You're not done yet.

Grandpa? It's not alright. The beginning of leaf decay fills my throat. They cremated you—you're there with Nanna in a rose garden, defined by a two-name plaque—but think I'll visit with you now, for a while.

***

The shift in dynamics I became aware of weeks ago has now deepened. Grandpa's death has broken the barrier he created. He was the buffer that stabilised the relationships between us all. I have no protective arm around my shoulder. Susan is difficult or loving depending on who you are, and her mood. She's got everyone where she wants them. When the two of us are in a room and she wants me out, she screams and pounds me with shoes and toys. Her left-hand aim always hits its mark, hard. There's no anticipating this behaviour, but when she starts, Bill or Mum will rush in and I'm *always* the guilty one. They reason that if Susan is screaming, it has to be *my* fault. I am shouted at and sent to my room. Susan always has her way.

Eventually, I get tired of this and decide if she's going to scream and I'm going to get into trouble, I'll give her a reason to scream. So, when she starts yelling, I thump her and get sent to my room for something I've now done!

Besides, I know Bill doesn't want me here, so I don't care what I do now.

Chapter 14
The Bullies Meet Antoinette

It's Monday at school. The kids are all excited because there's a new girl in our class. They're clustering around vying for her attention. She has to be Afrikaans because she's so popular already. I notice how tall she is, has dark, thick, wavy hair, and a wide smile, and when the bell rings she walks confidently into class. I realise she's already wearing a bra! The teacher introduces her, with a name that declares her heritage! Antoinette Blankenberg. With a name like that, she will fit in easily. I retreat, hovering in the background, relieved that the attention is temporarily diverted from me. I know she won't be friends with a curry-lover rooinek! (Indian-loving Brit.). I hear her Dad is the new bank manager. 'Which is akin to being "God" as all the farmers owe the bank money,' Mum says.

By Friday, the novelty of the new girl has waned and now the bullies are around me chattering like monkeys. They push me down, their shoes are too close to my face, they are kicking dirt in my eyes and their hands paw me, rubbing my long hair into the ground. I struggle to get up. I can't. They're egging each other on, and their voices rise and fall over me. I don't understand their words, I don't understand them at all. Suddenly it all stops. Their hands move away, scuffed shoes shuffle, and I roll onto my back and look up. The sun's in my gritty eyes. I'm blinded. Someone's standing over me. They move and a shadow obliterates the sun.

'Get away!' Antoinette shouts. She grabs my hand and pulls me to my feet, glaring at the kids around us. Her arm links with mine and we walk away.

'Want to come to my house this arvie?' She says as if nothing has happened. I'm so shocked, that this girl is talking to me and inviting me over.

'Yes,' is all I can say.

***

Within weeks Mum is working at the bank and soon becomes Mr Blankenberg's secretary. Ant's parents are Auntie Lilly and Uncle Mike, and Mum's lost the stressed look she had. I like Auntie Lilly, she makes beautiful little dresses for our Barbie dolls and is kind to me.

I don't go anywhere without Ant. Why she's my friend I don't know, but I do know she doesn't like bullies and is not afraid of boys. The taunts have stopped. The bullies don't like it, but they have no choice but to leave me alone. They are wary of Ant, and her dad is, after all, the bank manager! I begin to make friends. One of them, Rodger, has a pet monkey he can't keep; his mother is angry with him for buying it from an African. I think it will be a great pet. So this afternoon, on a bush path, he gives me a vervet monkey.

'It's tame,' he says handing me a rope attached to a small dog collar around its hips. Deep brown eyes examine me from an oval black face fringed in soft grey fur that darkens over its small head. It quickly moves to settle on my shoulder, and with nimble paws begins to search through my hair. I walk home, and Susan is excited. 'I want to hold it,' she demands, following me into the sitting room.

'Put your arm out like this,' I say, showing her. She does and I pat her forearm. The monkey jumps and lands on her arm. Susan shrieks. Frightened, it leaps off and the rope slips from my fingers. It cavorts across the room latching onto the curtains where it hangs for a moment, and looks up. Susan shrieks again. Up the curtain, and onto the pelmet it goes, and sits there for a few seconds before scurrying the pelmet length, scattering Mum's precious china ornaments which smash around our feet. Now we are both screaming. The monkey launches itself at another curtain, climbs to the top and hangs there for a moment, before sprinting along that pelmet too, dislodging *more* ornaments. The polished timber floor is a mosaic of china.

Mr Markee appears in the doorway. His eyes widen and in a low voice, he says, 'Humba lapa, checha!' (Go there, quickly). His hands gesticulate to the far side of the room. We skirt the furniture and brush past him into the hallway, he follows us and slams the door. From the hallway, we hear more crashing. Mr Markee is breathing fast, glaring at us, 'Mai-wea, eish Missis,' he says. 'That one... it bite you!'

More smashing and we are all frightened of what will happen next. Me, for what is going to be said; Susan of the monkey; and Mr Markee because he's in charge of us. It goes quiet and Mr Markee cracks the door open. We see the money perched on the back of a chair, grooming itself.

'Humba, lapa.' (Go, that place) He points past the kitchen to the garden, and for once, we don't argue. A while later he emerges from the house carrying the monkey in an old pillowcase and vanishes up the laneway, shaking his head and muttering to himself. By the time Mum comes home from work, the sitting room has been restored to order and all her broken prized ornaments have been swept up and thrown out. Mr Markee is in the kitchen, still angry with us and scared. Susan and I are hiding in my bedroom and the house is quiet, far *too* quiet. Mum knows straight away that something's happened!

We can hear Mr Markee's voice, and Mum shouts, 'Beverley, get out here right now!' She sees me hovering in the sitting room doorway, chewing my lower lip.

'What were you thinking? A monkey, for goodness sake!' She glares at me, her arm waving towards the empty pelmets. 'My beautiful ornament collection, all smashed, I can't believe it, a damn monkey!'

This time I've truly done it. I'm trembling. Susan's nudges me from behind and her head pops up under my elbow. She looks up. 'Mummy, you should have seen it swinging on the curtains!' She says and giggles. 'Up it went and along the pelmet, you should have seen it!' Her fingers dance in the air mimicking the monkey. The tension leaves Mum's body and she starts to chuckle.

'Up the curtains, you say. Well, that must have been funny, like this?' Mum's fingers climb the air, 'You're lucky it didn't bite you, it could have rabies!' Susan laughs and runs into the room pointing to the curtains the monkey climbed, 'It didn't have rabies, it was just playing!'

Mum surveys the empty pelmets and with a dramatic sigh she says, 'Well, I suppose you can buy me ornaments for Christmas and birthdays for the next few years.' With her arm over Susan's shoulder, they walk away talking and joking. Briefly, I wonder what would have happened to me if Susan had stayed in the bedroom. I don't like the answer.

In the kitchen Mr Markee begins to whistle, he's still got his job, not that it ever was in jeopardy, and Susan's gotten me out of trouble. No one says a word to Bill and he doesn't notice the missing ornaments. I wonder what Mr Markee did with the monkey? Maybe I don't want to know.

***

Living with Susan is never dull. She's strong-willed, feisty, funny, lovable, challenging, and has her father *just* where she wants him. I love her. I don't know if she even *likes* me! Bill doesn't want me here. Maybe, if we stop fighting, Bill will change his mind, maybe not; I'm not his child. But it's hard to stop, no one listens to me.

One of Mum's big issues is Susan's hair. It's white-blonde, fairy floss fine and habitually knotted at the back. Sue brushes it *her way* which achieves nothing; Mum tries but Susan refuses to sit still and thrashes around shouting. One afternoon Mum's had enough of looking at Susan's unruly fluff and with brush in hand, she grabs her. Susan squirms free, darts out the back door and begins a circuit run of the house, arms flailing, bellowing. This is her usual tactic. Most times Mum gives chase and always fails to catch her. But today Mum dashes through the house, out the front door, and down the steps. As Susan careens past, eyes scrunched up, arms churning, yelling, Mum snags her and drags her inside, partially sits on her, brushes out the knots she can and cuts the rest off. She's finished. Susan's an angry tangle of arms and legs coated in hair, still shouting, on the floor. Mum's panting, satisfied.

Shoes are another thing Susan detests. Mum forces them onto her feet before she runs outside to play, where she removes them and buries them in the sandy soil of the rear lane. By the time we go to retrieve them, they've been dug up by African children and found a new home. Eventually Mum gives up and Susan roams barefoot, owning one pair of shoes—for best.

I have my battles with Susan; usually, I lose.

After school, I have to take her out with me and look after her. Sometimes to the swimming pool, or on errands to the corner store; Mum sends us to check if the magazines from England have arrived. She has a standing order for *Woman's Own* and a few others, it doesn't matter that they're months out of date. I find it strange that the magazines haven't heard about sanctions, they should have because they're British! Susan delights in telling, or *threatening* to tell tales. Anything that will get me into trouble with Bill: I walked too fast for her, didn't let her have a lolly, jumped off the high diving board, and didn't swim with her enough. There is always something, and our outings are fraught with blackmail.

Yesterday I was in trouble, again. Susan and I were going out on my bicycle. She was seated on the carrier and I was standing astride the bike; I'd looked back over my shoulder at her and said, 'Keep your feet sticking out, OK?' And pushed off, pedalled a few yards and was about to sit on the seat when suddenly, Susan's screaming. She'd turned her foot inwards catching her toes in the spokes, sending us sprawling into the dirt. That night she showed Bill her small toes, no blood, but bruised, saying, 'Beverley put my toes in the spokes and hurt me.' Drips of tears; I'm in trouble *again*. Now, she's on the carrier saying, 'Don't get my toes stuck again!'

I've had enough. I pedal a few feet and stop.

'You have to get off,' I say, 'Something's wrong with my bike.' Off she gets; I hop back on and pedal away, *fast*. She yells and throws herself down screaming in the sandy laneway; she will be fine, the house is right there, and Mr Markee will hear her – the whole laneway can hear her. The peaceful, no-tittle-tailing afternoon was worth all the shouting later.

Mr Markee also has his battles with Susan. He wins a few. This afternoon Susan was banging on the bank's Staff door, shouting and crying. 'Mum, I want my Mum.' Mum's called for by the security guard and hurries outside, 'What on earth's going on?'

'Mr Markee locked me out of the house!' Susan says sobbing and lifting her blood-smeared arms. Mum carries her home. Mr Markee is sweeping up the broken glass from the kitchen window.

'What happened?' asks Mum, through clenched teeth with Susan draped around her, still crying loudly.

'Medem, the picanin missis she in kitchen, she pulling all pots and food out, she no listen....eish Medem, I tell her to play outside. "No," she tell me.' Mr Markee throws the broom aside. 'I can do nothing, I lock kitchen door! Miss Susan so mad, she…' his fists smack together, 'the window, it broke …. eish!' Mr Markee's lean limbs gesticulate wildly to the window and smashed glass.

Mum washes Susan. There are small cuts that bled profusely making her look like she's been massacred. This time *she* is sent to her room! Bill's not home and Mr Markee is singing in the kitchen. No tales are told that night. The window was fixed the next day.

***

The bicycle Grandpa bought me provides freedom. There's a great spot to swim. The only thing is, it's out of town, a long hot ride away. Sarah and I cycle there very fast, past a cemetery, along the dirt road, and arrive sweating. We lean our bikes against a tree and run barefoot over the flat expanse of scorching rock, dodging biting ants and scaring the blue kop lizards lazing in the sun. They scuttle into the rock crevices and flick their tails with annoyance. There it is, the river, which is low now and flowing in shallow clear streams between rocks and boulders.

Water laps at small sandy beaches, and clumps of tall grass grow close to the banks. We squeeze between two boulders into a cavern, and from above, through a narrow crack, the sun spotlights the rock floor, and we stand as if on a stage. Our voices echo as we strip off our clothes, leaving only our panties on.

We shuffle out sideways between boulders and sprint to the water's edge, our feet burning on the rock, waving to a few fishermen who are casting fishing lines further down the river. The water is cool on our soles. We drop onto the sandy riverbed and lie back, look up at the cloudless sky and let our arms float in the shallow stream. Sarah rolls over.

I see them, the bruises her dress hides, up the top of her legs and on her back. Her Dad beats her in the bathroom with a belt. I don't like going to her house.

'My Mum said we mustn't come here anymore,' she says and rolls onto her back. 'I heard them talking, saying we might get raped.'

'My Mum told me to stay away from here too. I asked why and she said: "Because I say so." What's raped?'

'Don't know. Who cares, anyway they won't know we're here.'

'You're right, who cares!' I say.

We shouldn't be here.

We wallow, splash around, float and then sit on the rocks with our feet dangling in the water. When our panties and skin are dry we get dressed, wave to the fishermen and cycle home, although not so fast past the cemetery. I decide not to go there with Sarah again, even though the bruises on her legs are fading, and because neither of us knows what 'rape' is.

***

It's Saturday morning; Mum hangs up the phone and calls out, 'Right! No rain in Inyanga, just a bit of guti (fine misty rain) that will be gone soon. Mr Markee, picnic basket, please. Let's go!' He's grinning because it's a day off for him too. He can sit in the shade and drink lots of milky tea in his oversized enamel chipped cup, with six sugars, and eat slabs of bread, butter and jam. And then lie back, deftly roll a dagga joint, puff and doze. Just what he needs. Everyone's happy.

Within half an hour we are packed into the car with swimmers, towels, a thermos of hot water, food, and with the windows down we head out of town. It takes about an hour to drive up into the Inyanga Mountains, an area of rolling hills, valleys, rocky peaks and slopes of fruit, pine and wattle trees. It's also known for its unpredictable mists and rains. Rusape can be clear, dry and hot, while Inyanga is cold, misty and wet—even on the same day. Mum always calls the Montclair Hotel up there to check on the weather before we leave.

It's hot. Dry grass stretches away from the road. Mum and Bill are smoking in the front seats and flicking ash out the windows, and in the back, Susan and I are separated by the picnic basket. Today, we are in tune with each other. With a glance over the basket we start singing, 'The bear went over the mountain.' It's a monotonous song of five repeated lines that will drive Mum and Bill nuts—and they'll let us open the picnic basket to shut us up. It works; we get peanut butter biscuits. Susan grins at me. If we push it, we might get a Coke to share!

As we drive through the mountains, we wiggle out of our clothes and into our swimming costumes. Bill parks at the Inyangombe Falls and we leap out, leaving the car doors wide open and dash away. 'Hey, you two, come and help! No Mr Markee here!' Bill says. We ignore him and run towards the small sandy beach, dodging bikini-clad teens on towels, who shout at us for kicking up sand and stop abruptly at the water's edge of a large natural pool. Icy small waves ripple at our toes, and we gaze at the far side where the water darkens and butts up against an embankment of the craggy earth which is woven with tree roots and low-hanging branches cast shadows towards us. It's dark, scary and bottomless over there.

To our right, a waterfall tumbles over a long wide expanse of sloping rocks. Kids are sliding down on their bums, shrieking and laughing, or bumping along on tyre tubes into the pool. Sunlight blinks on the wet rocks, flowing water and shallow edges. To the left, the river winds away over rounded rocks and between fallen trees, and through the encroaching bush.

Our toes creep forward at the water's edge and we suck in our breath. It's freezing. Bitter, numbing, stupidly freezing, and Bilharzia-free; even those pesty microorganisms can't survive the cold streams of Inyanga. Susan turns and runs away. Then she streaks past me, skinny tanned legs pushing hard, shouting at the top of her voice, and throws herself into the pool. She surfaces spluttering, face contorted, and flings water towards me, and the spray partially obliterates her. She's shrieking. Her blonde hair sticks to her head, her teeth chatter between blue lips, and goosebumps dot her skin. I launch myself towards her and we flounder around giggling and numb. We can't stay in long and retreat to the beach to build sandcastles, the sun shining on our bent knobbed spines and tanned skin. Our hair dries; mine in its long plait, Susan's to a halo of blonde curls. Light reflects on the few remaining water drops, and her ice-blue eyes, so naughty and nice, rest on me. I do love her, even though she's a terror at times.

After lunch, Mum says, 'You can't swim on a full tummy, you have to stay out of the water.' We know this, it's the boring part of any swimming time and we annoy Mum until she relents and lets us back into the water.

Earlier, we had buried Coke bottles in the cold sand and Mum's walking to the spot at the water's edge. As she leans over to dig them up, Susan and I look at each other and Susan gestures to me with a pushing motion. I dart forward. My hands are on Mum's back. I push hard. She stumbles forward, loses balance, falls in, splashes around and rolls onto her back, spits water, and sees us clutching each other and laughing. We run and Mum chases us across the beach, past Bill dozing with a newspaper over his face, and we vanish into the bush…

'You little so-and-so's. Just wait till I get my hands on you both!' She calls out, but we can already see the anger dripping away as she begins to dry, and she starts to laugh. We peep out from behind the bushes.

'Mum, how about a cold Coke?' Susan says. Mum shakes her finger at her, 'You little sod!' Susan leaves our hiding place and I watch them stagger, giggling, towards Bill who peers out from under the newspaper, 'What's so darn funny?' They can't speak and he starts to chuckle with them. Susan's telling him, 'We pushed Mum in the water and...'

From a distance, I watch their fair heads bend together, their arms playfully pushing each other, the same mischief on their faces, the same wit that I don't share. Instead, I can hear Mum's voice in my mind: *For goodness sake don't be so serious, take that frown off your face you'll get wrinkles, and your hair's so brown, it looks better where the sun's bleached it. Don't worry about that Burmese note. Why are you so shy? What have you done to Susan, now? And, when the hot oil from the crispy potatoes spurted into my eye. I cried. They laughed.*

The view through my sun-shaded eyes is ugly. And uglier still, does Mum even *like* me? I shove that thought away. Was it always like this? I don't know. Was it Grandpa who shielded me? Oh, this is a cold reflection in the clear water at my feet. I shiver and drop the hand shading my eyes, better to be blinded. I shake my arms and look around.

People are lying on towels, eating, drinking, and talking with families, and small brown birds are stealing picnic crumbs. They're the type I used to watch building their cup-shaped nests in Grandpa's fruit trees where their featherless chicks with wide-open hungry beaks hatched and grew and flew. Yes, that's me, a little brown bird who is running forward for the crumbs.

Chapter 15
Holiday to Beira, & Beware the Dentist

Yards of dress fabric are tossed over the sewing table on the verandah. Bright, colourful cotton lengths: stripes, flowers, dots, swirls, abstracts. It's not what we usually wear. Mum's had a spend-up in the Indian shops and is singing along to records stacked on the player inside. The music is flowing through an open window to us. There's a pause, the next record falls, and the needle comes down. 'Bend me, shape me,' blares out and we start to dance. Susan's draped in a multi-striped cotton, Mum's wrapped in a length of bright orange swirls, and I've grabbed an outrageous purple flower-power print. We're singing loudly, badly, 'Bend me, shape me anyway you want me…' swinging our bodies about, and Mum says, 'Just what we need to help make holiday clothes!' And the next single falls, click. 'Picking up pebbles and throwing them into the sea…' and we fall around laughing, because that's where we are going—to the seaside. We've never been to the seaside together. Even better, it's to Beira, which isn't as far as Durban. And we're going for *three whole weeks* to a posh hotel near the beach, called The Estoril.

A small voice hovers at the edge of my thoughts. *We don't have much money. How can we afford a holiday? Holiday clothes?* I smooth out the frown from my brow before Mum sees it, and glance at her. She's folded up some of the material and her head is bent in thought. Her painted fingernail traces the fabric pattern of orange swirls and another record drops. Under her breath, she says, 'Thanks, Dad. We all need a holiday.' I pretend not to hear. Mum sometimes says things out loud that she'd rather catch back.

So with music playing, the early summer sun warming us, storks in the trees bothering Mum—they bring babies the fable says—we sew. Susan willingly tries on her holiday clothes, a rare event as we usually have to cajole her to 'try on' anything. We finish them as well as matching mop-hats. How good is that?

The trip is still a few weeks away, but who cares, anticipation is half the fun. For now, we are sewing, occasionally singing choruses out of tune, but in tune with each other for a while.

When the holiday morning arrives it's crisp and clear, promising to be hot. Bill secures suitcases on the roof racks and in the boot of our cream and green Vauxhall station wagon, which used to be Grandpa's car. He's in a good mood, grinning at Susan, who's dashing back and forth, doing nothing but making noise and choosing stuffed toys to take with her. Mr Markee is packing us lunch: a thermos, sandwiches, biscuits, and drinks. We are ready by 6am so we can arrive in Beira after lunch.

'No time to waste,' Bill says. Mr Markee agrees, nodding his head and waving us off, flashing his fake gold front tooth. He's on holiday as well. From us.

Within an hour we reach Christmas Pass, a dual carriageway that winds ribbon-like, hugging the cliff, down the steep mountainside into a valley. Dense bushes and trees stretch away from us in both directions, and in the distance miles of mountain ranges ripple through drifts of mists, their murky peaks etched against a blue sky. The carriageway ends in the valley, and flat-topped trees line the main street into the city of Umtali (now Mutare). We cross the border into Mozambique, drive through Machipanda and on towards the coast, windows down, listening to the LM radio station that plays all the popular music. Susan and I don't sing, 'The bear went over the mountain.' We are being good.

We arrive and are in awe. Hotel Estoril is enormous, a long, multistorey building that curves in and out like a wave, with a checkered façade of large blue and white squares. Behind it, flat grasslands stretch away and Bill mutters, 'It looks like a swamp. We're going to get eaten by mosquitoes.' But we don't care. Shops line the pavement under Hotel Estoril, holidaymakers stroll past and no one is in a rush. The foyer is grand, our rooms are grand, and the whole place is grand. *Thank you, Grandpa.*

Dressed in our new holiday clothes, we hurry out into the balmy afternoon to explore. We cross the road and walk through a caravan park, laid out in a grid of dirt roads, lined with trees, where caravans and tents are clustered in the shade. Mum points out small buildings and says, 'Those are chalets you can rent.' I'm glad we are at Hotel Estoril, and not here in the camping ground.

Bill's been told the beach is beyond the caravan park. We wander onto manicured lawns dotted with multicoloured umbrellas under which adults on deckchairs are watching their children in a rectangular pool. The pool is much bigger than the one back home. We dip our toes in. It's so *warm,* not bone-shatteringly cold like the Inyangombe Falls. On the far side, kids are roller skating in a Pavilion, their voices echo out into the bright afternoon sunshine. Susan and I run over to watch; we've never seen roller skating before. I wonder if we can do it? Bill calls us and we continue walking, past the tree-lined pool perimeter towards the trees along the beachfront. The sound of waves is louder now, and we can smell the ocean. Susan tugs on Mum's hand, her little face alive with anticipation, and she begins to skip.

'I think we should head towards the lighthouse,' Bill says, pointing to a red and white tower rising above the trees. We've never seen a lighthouse! It's so tall! The bright white sand of the beach greets us. We shade our eyes and watch waves churning back and forth, in awe of the sights and the sounds. To our right, at the water's edge, there's a shipwreck, aged to a rusted copper and burnt brown. Costume-clad bodies are lying on towels in its shade, sheltered from the wind. Waves rush into the far end that's ripped away and open to the ocean. Suddenly, Susan pulls away from Mum's hand and runs towards the water.

'Susan, stop!' Mum yells at her, but she keeps running, her feet leaving small prints in the flat sand. As she enters the water, a wave engulfs her and she's upended and goes tumbling over and over. The water retreats leaving her face down in the sand. She sits up in the shallows, hair plastered, and spitting sand, as another wave surges forward. Bill reaches her just in time to drag her backwards. She stands up, shakes herself and looks at the ocean in disbelief. 'It's salty. Yuck!' she says, pointing at the offending waves. We all laugh, then wander off along the beach where we discover that the evening drinks at beach bars are accompanied by free snacks of piri piri chicken wings, mussels in buckets, nuts, and crisp bacon rinds. And the Cokes are cold.

We spend the mornings at the beach. Mum and Bill lie on their towels and read, or use their book to cover their faces from the sun. We—beg them to build sandcastles and swim with us—and sometimes they do, but it's safer to let them lie on their towels and amuse ourselves. They are more relaxed then, and more likely to let us have money for ice creams, which are extra good from the kiosk near the pool. We have a yummy lunch at the restaurant in Hotel Estoril followed by the boring obligatory afternoon rest because according to Mum, 'We've had too much sun and it's hot'.

In the late afternoons and evenings, we go for long walks and find Johnny's, with its red and white checkered tablecloths and buckets of fresh prawns. It is so good because we *never* eat prawns at home. Bill shows us how to peel them, and laughs when we can't get the heads off. We also find beach bars with bands playing modern music that doesn't sound quite right. But who cares, Mum and Bill are enjoying their drinks and the free bar snacks. Susan and I aren't arguing, so no one is shouting at me.

I soon notice the people here are different too. Mum says, 'This is Portuguese Mozambique, so lots of the people are of Portuguese descent.' But there aren't only light-skinned Portuguese, there are Chinese too, whom we don't ever see at home, and others quite dark but not African.

'They're a mixed race of African and Portuguese,' Mum says when I ask her about them, 'Like our coloureds back home. Now stop looking and asking questions!' It's very strange, we aren't that far from home, but the people are different and speak different languages too. I'm fascinated.

The Chinese have shops like the Indians do in Rusape. 'Full of rubbish,' Bill says, and he refuses to go into them with us.

'Oh leave Bill alone, he's just being grumpy!' Mum says with a laugh and the three of us go and have a great time looking around. There are so many different toys for us to exclaim over and Mum has a great time looking at dresses and shoes. The shops have funny names too, like Yip Kuk and Ping Tah. That's where we think the best toys are. We are allowed to buy buckets, spades and one other item each. Susan chooses a small plastic tea set and I buy a music jewellery box. It's shiny red with a small ballerina who turns around to the wind-up music. We even see large intricately carved camphor laurel kists (linen chests) with big, polished brass locks. Mum opens one up and it smells just like ours at home. She whispers, 'Ours is far nicer!' And I agree.

Bill discovers that Hotel Estoril provides babysitters, so one night he says, 'We are going out to the Grand Hotel for dinner. You two are staying here.'

Susan and I object loudly but they ignore us, get dressed up, and a shy Portuguese girl arrives to babysit. She can't speak English and we have a boring night reading books.

We pretend to be asleep when they return so the babysitter isn't in trouble! They're bubble-arse (had too much to drink) and we can hear them laughing and talking in their room. Susan and I keep our heads under the blankets and giggle.

Some evenings the organ player at the Hotel Estoril can be boring, and Bill says, 'We are not going near that place of ill repute, the Moulin Rouge!' I wonder why and what he means. I'm not going to ask, because he gets angry if I ask too many questions. Bill has a saying, 'Children should be born at seven and sent straight to boarding school!' But I know that excludes Susan. And I'm 11 now. I wonder if that's where he wants me to go.

There's also a zoo called Mrs Trinidad's. We walk past a bored lioness lying behind bars but her cubs are out of the pen and we can pat them, like big kittens. A crocodile bakes in murky water, and monkeys with sad dark eyes beg through the wire. I don't like it but don't say so. It's the first zoo we've ever been to. The Boswell Wilkie circus comes to Rusape from South Africa every year, bringing lions in cages, chained elephants, and monkeys that look fine. But I'm not sure about that. Wouldn't animals like it better in the bundu?

There are in-ground trampolines near the beach and we beg Bill every day for coins to buy time. We spend hours jumping on the black mats which get very hot! Back home, there's one trampoline in town, at the Crocodile Motel. It's free but you have to wait your turn and if there are lots of kids around, it's boring. Recently Dr Strydom put a trampoline in his backyard and allows us kids to use it. 'Sensibly,' he says. He will know if we aren't being sensible because it's his surgery we will visit with any broken bones. His kids are at boarding school so we can jump all term long, but not in the holidays. Here, for a small fee, we can jump and jump without waiting, and this keeps us out of the adult's hair, too.

Late one afternoon, Susan and I wander away from Mum and Bill towards the shipwreck. It's huge and towers above us. There's no one else there. I peep inside one of the many gaping holes. The sun is low, streaming yellow through the pockmarked hull, crisscrossing the interior, and piercing the deepening shadows. *Dare I go inside?* The tide's lapping at its edges. Small waves flounce up the metal shell and there's sea spray on the wind and seagulls gathered on the sand. I'm curious and want to explore but Susan distracts me and I chase after her, laughing. She darts away, back towards Bill and I'm left alone, standing in the hull's lengthening shade. *Do I go in?* As I stand there, I experience a feeling of being watched. *Is someone there?* Only shadows, outside and inside. Waves swirl into the hull's open end, receding and returning, and seagulls are rising, wings battering, screeching, circling, settling, and small sand crabs are scurrying past white cuttlefish on the sand. *Am I alone?*

I turn and peep inside. Something's moving in the half-light, up high. Eyes suddenly meet mine. It's a man and he's staring at me. He's not wearing any clothes and his hand is moving rhythmically, body jerking, and spurting. I don't understand what's going on. He grins at me and I turn and run. Surf rushes around my ankles. I run as fast as I can, kicking up sand that stings the back of my leg. I'm confused, but I don't tell Mum.

And then the three weeks are over, and we head home, tanned, with our shoulders peeling. Away from Beira and Mrs Trinidad's zoo, along the narrow tar road, through the poverty of Mozambique, through Umtali in the valley, over Christmas Pass, where occasionally traffic has to give way to lions. Away from the mountains that stretch south along our border with Mozambique, through the swirling mist that evaporates suddenly, and then the way is clear to Rusape and we are home.

***

Beware the Dentist!

Our tans have begun to fade and we've been home for a few weeks. It's Friday and we've almost finished lunch. My fork reaches for the last of the bully beef hash that we all like. I think it's funny that Bill eats it, considering it comes from a rectangular tin that opens with a small key that twists and rolls a fine strip of metal back. Mr Markee then forks the stringy meat-like contents apart and adds them to fried onions and tomatoes which simmer together. Today this is served with mashed potato, carrots, and beans—sliced in the shade of a tree by Mr Markee. Thank goodness there's no cabbage. Bill's happy to eat hash, fake-looking meat, but he won't let us have fresh crumbed brains. It makes no sense.

'You need to be there at 2.30pm, all right?'

'Where, Mum?'

'Don't pretend you didn't hear me, 2.30pm. The dentist called and said you need more fillings. Be there!' Her finger is pointing at me. I rather like the red polish on it, nicer than the pink, but chips show sooner on red... 'And don't forget like last week. You hear me?'

'You're not taking me?'

'No, I have to go to work.' She's got that no-nonsense look. 'We've talked about this before. Just go.'

Go to the dentist *on my own*. No. Just the thought of riding my bicycle towards the surgery scares me enough, let alone walking in where he waits with large needles, silver things that clink around my teeth, sharp poking steel sticks and a foot-pumped drill that screeches and turns, its speed governed by how tired his leg is. I'm going to faint, for sure.

Mum had taken me there a few weeks ago. She'd had to. My tooth was aching so badly. 'He only comes here once a week from Umtali,' she said. 'I've taken the afternoon off work for your appointment.' We'd driven there in silence, my hands gripped the seat and Mum chain-smoked. Her high heels punched holes in the dirt as she hurried towards the surgery with me straggling behind. She'd stopped in the doorway, poked her head inside and said, 'Beverley's here,' and then pushed me into the antiseptic-smelling room before adding, 'Send me the account,' and hurried away.

Suddenly I was in the dentist's chair with his large hands in my mouth. After what seemed like never-ending pain and drilling I escaped into the afternoon sun. Mum was in the car reading a British women's magazine. Her standing order from England had arrived, so she was very happy. We drove away fast, raising dust, with cigarette butts being flicked out the window. *We could start a bushfire. Don't be so serious, Beverley.*

When Mum and Bill leave to go back to work I dutifully cycle off, without Susan, to the dentist. I know he's come from Umtali, over

Christmas Pass—wonder if he's ever seen lions there? Not going to see him today, so can't ask. That evening Mum says, 'You went to the dentist?'

'No. I forgot.' My face is red; fibbing isn't my forte.

'For goodness sake!' Mum is exasperated and conflicted. She won't go to the dentist for herself, let alone take me. She knows that I'm aware of this. We're at a stalemate. I wait for her to slap me, but she's not game to do that either because it will make her confront our shared knowledge. These thoughts play out on her features, and I wait, and watch as she reaches a decision and says, 'You'd better go next week!' But I don't, or the next, or the next… until Mum nabs me!

'I've got the afternoon off,' Mum says after lunch one day, 'Hop in the car.'

Susan and I do, gladly, because it's the school holidays and we are bored. With the windows down and the breeze in our faces, we drive off. Maybe we're going to the Crocodile Motel for a Brown Cow (ice cream and Coke) and a jump on the trampoline. Mum will sit in the shade with a Coke, reading and smoking, while we jump or swim. Sometimes we get surprises like that. But we haven't got our costumes or towels, and this is the wrong way. We pull up at the dentist's rooms. The door is open.

'Stay here Susan, I'll be back in a moment.' Susan's not getting out, she knows about this place too. 'Come on,' Mum says, grabs my hand, and walks me quickly towards the building. Her fingers tremble in mine. Her hands are clammy and she's fumbling in her handbag for cigarettes. She lets go of me and lights up, and from the doorway says, 'Send me the account.' Her hand on my back propels me into the room, away from the sunshine and thoughts of a Brown Cow.

A few evenings later, Bill's resting in the armchair, beer by his side, pipe in hand, because the news will be on TV in a few minutes. Susan and I are playing snakes and ladders on the new red carpet. Mum shifts in Grandpa's reupholstered chair and stubs out her cigarette.

'By the way, Bill, the dentist called the other day about Beverley's teeth. I didn't bother saying anything until I had everything sorted.' Bill coughs and Mum keeps talking. He won't interrupt in front of us because that's rude. Now I'm alert, not only to the dentist issue. *She's timed this just right. Bill likes to watch the news, without interruptions.*

'He said that Beverley needs root canal treatment to save a front tooth and quite a few fillings. He can't do the work here, so he wants her in Umtali.' Bill's one eyebrow is raised now, he wants to speak, but Mum's not taking a breath. 'So, not to worry Bill, I've got everything planned.' *As you said, she's my child, not yours.* 'Mike's given me petrol coupons. *I don't need yours.* Auntie Di and Uncle Colin are having her stay for a week and will take her twice a day to the dentist. Now isn't that kind of them?' *You don't have to lift a finger, Bill. And she will be gone for a week so Susan won't be annoyed by her.*

'The two of us will drive to Umtali on Sunday and I'll go and pick her up the following Sunday.' *You can consider Susan your child and stay here with her. And I'm not asking you to take us, there's no inconvenience for you.*

I'm fascinated by the way Mum's saying stuff, *but not* saying stuff. Bill's mad, but he won't say anything because Susan and I are sitting here. Mum's taken care of everything, hasn't she? So why is he angry? All this double talk. It's a bit like what Nanna and Mum did to Grandpa on the farm when they said the Umfuli River was in flood. But Grandpa knew what they were up to. Adults are strange. I just say what I'm thinking. I suppose that's why I get into trouble.

'This is the news,' says the TV announcer. And Mum's final words are, 'The rest of it Bill, including petrol costs, that's sorted too.' *That must mean you've called Dad and he's sending a cheque for petrol and the dentist.* And we watch the news, but gradually the words sink in. Dentist, Umtali, Auntie Di and Uncle Colin (whom I hardly know). A whole week. I leave the room and lie on my bed and cry. It's Thursday night.

The next morning I'm still snivelling, and at breakfast, Mum looks at me with raised eyebrows and I run to my room, crying *more* now.

I don't hear her come down the hallway, and suddenly her arms are around me. I snuggle into her and sob, 'I don't want to go!' She smooths my hair, and says, 'It's only for a week. You'll like Auntie Di.'

'It's not that, I'm scared.' Her body stiffens. She's scared of the dentist too! A small part of me takes comfort in that, but *I* still have to go.

From the dual carriageway of Christmas Pass, I gaze out the window. Wouldn't it be great if a lion plonked itself on the road and we couldn't get past for days? Mist smothers the valley below us, milky white and fluffy, and it's as if Umtali doesn't exist. But it does, and so does the dentist. The sun filters away the clouds and the small city emerges. We descend into the valley and drive down avenues of flat-topped trees. It's quiet. Sunday slumbers around us in neat houses with neat lawns and neat hedges. I can't stop crying, silently. Mum's now irritated with my tear-stained face. I don't understand why I can't stop, but in a memory tucked away, I know this has happened before when Dad was taking me away for a holiday. Grandpa was there, and it was alright, in the end. Mum glances at me, suddenly pulls over and stops under the trees lining the street. The engine's vibrating, and my stomach is churning.

'Beverley, stop it, just stop it right now! We're near Auntie Di's house. What on earth will she think of me dropping off a snivelling child?' A large hankie is thrust into my hand, 'Wipe your face!' I wipe my cheeks, blink rapidly trying to suck up the tears, and sniff. Mum glares at me. Sniffing is rude. She pulls away from the curb and our destination is around the corner. After a cup of tea, Mum gets up and says, 'See you next Sunday, thanks so much both of you.' And she is gone.

Auntie Di and Uncle Colin are tall and lean, not cuddling types, and they are around Grandpa's age. I'm not too sure where they fit into the family. But they are real Auntie and Uncle relatives. Their only daughter has grown up and left home so I use her room. It's a teenager's room. Some of her ornaments are on the dressing table and a few clothes are in the cupboard. I don't fiddle with them, just look. The house is quiet. A wind-up clock on the living room mantelpiece ticks rhythmically, the furniture is the sit-up straight sort, and the dining room table gleams with polish. Even the house boy is quiet. There is no singing in the kitchen, banging pots or spontaneously cooking sponge cakes in this house. But they are kind to me, in a stiff sort of way.

The week is traumatic. Twice a day Auntie Di drives silent me to the dentist. She thinks I'm alright, but I can't speak from fear. The dentist pokes around clinking silver mirrors on my teeth, umms and jabs me with needles and then drills. The root canal is the worst. Then we go home and the numbness, an awful tingling creeping feeling, wears off just in time for the afternoon visit. I chew dinner slowly, not fast like Mum and I eat. By the end of six days, my body is aching from clenching onto the car seat and dentist's chair. My jaw struggles to open, and my gums are on fire from all the injections. There is nothing left of me, I'm a silent aching wreck. Mum returns on Sunday. She smiles and chats away with my hosts as they sip tea.

'Beverley was so good, not a complaint out of her,' says Auntie Di. *Only because I was so terrified I couldn't speak.*

'An absolute pleasure to have at the table, such manners,' Uncle Colin says. *I wasn't going to let Nanna down, and my mouth was so sore I didn't want to speak or eat much anyway.*

On impulse, I hug Auntie Di goodbye. She smooths my hair and smiles at me. 'You were very brave,' she says. There's a softness in her eyes and I think she understands, a little. *This is how Grandpa used to look at me. Suddenly I feel him around me and feel better.*

Chapter 16
Dad's Coming To See Me and I Don't Understand Animosity

Sunlight filters through the flyscreen on the verandah. The half wall is protecting us from the early winter breeze and Susan's running around outside with Squibb; she loves that dog like I loved Noddy. Dress fabric is laid out on the wooden sewing table. Mum's hands are deftly smoothing it and bringing the selvedge edges together. How elegant are her hands and ever-painted nails? The pattern pieces, fragile around the edges with many pinholes, are sorted and flattened ready to use.

'I've had a letter from your father,' Mum says placing pattern pieces on the material. Pins lie on the scratched table surface. She picks one up, stabs the pattern and material and weaves the pin in and out. That's another scratch on the table for sure. I wait, anxiety fills me. We don't talk about my father. I occasionally overhear things about him, and it's always related to money.

'He's coming to pick you up for a holiday.' *He's coming here! Daddy's coming to see me. No. I'll call him Dad, I'm bigger now. I'll be twelve in November.* The breeze lifts a flimsy pattern piece and it floats to the floor. I snatch it up. Mum straightens and reaches into the pocket of the apron tied around her waist, unfolds a letter and reads.

'Frances and I will collect Beverley on the first Saturday of the school holidays and take her to Umtali. We will all stay there with Frances's parents for a week.' She looks up at me, her face for once neutral, but her pin-stabbing is saying something else. I feel sick and excited. My thoughts scratch around like dogs chasing fleas on their backs. Oh, those dogs are gone, the farm's gone too. That was the last place I saw Dad, about six years ago. *'Grandpa, guess what Daddy's coming'* and *I'm hopping from one foot to the other in my mind.* 'Yes, child,' *he says.*

'So, what do you think?' Says Mum stuffing the letter into her apron pocket.

What do I think? You want me to talk about Dad when I haven't for years. I can't answer, everything's jumbled up in my mind. Mum's not looking at me, she's staring out at the rose bushes—she loves them—so I say, 'OK.'

'That's all you've got to say? OK?' She's irritated. My shoulder shrugs towards my ear. This is too hard and the funny wiggles in my tummy are worse. I don't want to think. Won't think now. Slowly, I position a pattern piece on the material and say, 'Here alright?' Mum nods, and I pin it down, carefully. Mum places a piece now. 'We can squeeze this one in here and have enough material left over for summer shorts for Susan,' she says. Bill's outside now with Susan. He's *her* father. *Mine* is coming to see *me*. Pity there isn't enough material for shorts for me too, then we would all match; occasionally. I like this fabric.

Once alone, the impending visit intrudes and my initial excitement fades. I'm scared. Scared of everything: of Dad who I don't know, of meeting Frances, of going away with them, of doing the wrong things. What if they don't like me? Panic gushes through and over me. Why are they suddenly coming after all these years? Why? Churning waters and rapids tumble in my mind, gathering mud. It's murky and it feels as if there are hidden boulders. I feel sick! My face is wet. I wipe it with my hands and tears I hadn't felt fall are on my skin. My breath shudders and there's an unseen hand on my shoulder. *You have to go. Your father has custody of you. I know Grandpa.*

And it's easy to ignore the letter. Mum hasn't mentioned it again. School holidays have started and this morning I'm thinking of going over to Ant's house. Mum hurries past me towards the front door on her way to work and says, 'Your father will be here tomorrow at lunchtime. Pack some clothes, there's a suitcase on top of the wardrobe.' Her heels click across the veranda, and the screen door bangs. She's gone.

Thoughts scurry around in my mind. They're coming, tomorrow,. Saturday? Yes, that's tomorrow. *I know that just keep quiet, will you?* I take a deep breath. You knew this was going to happen, didn't you? It's like going to the dentist, no escaping.

In the main bedroom, I stand on a stool and pull down an old blue suitcase, dust drifts around me and I sneeze. I suppose I'd better take it outside and clean it. Mr Markee will help me. He knows my Dad. Wonder if I could ask him questions? Better not, he might tell Mum.

The next morning Bill takes Susan out. 'Rather not be here!' he says. *No, because I'm not your child. Am I?*

They arrive. The four of us are seated in the sitting room. Mr Markee has set a tea tray down and Mum's poured steaming, rich, fragrant tea. The conversation is stilted and Mum is blowing smoke nonchalantly towards the ceiling. Dad and Frances are clutching cups on saucers, and Dad coughs. I'm trying not to stare at them. My Dad's here, he's like I remember him, but this time I couldn't rush up and hug him, have him pick me up or swing me around. I'm older now. He has Frances too.

'Oh, sorry Denny,' says Mum stubbing out a cigarette, 'I'd forgotten you don't like smoking.' She sighs, 'Well, that's something you will have in common with Beverley, she hates it too.' *She's a serious child.* Dad says nothing. Mum smiles at Frances, taking in her simple dress, sensible shoes and dark-set hair. I've looked at her too. She's so different to Mum. Frances is plump, and she's wearing little makeup. There's no nail polish or perfume, either. She's plain looking. Frances watches Mum back with dark eyes set in a round face and compressed lipstick-touched lips.

'Dennis and I are taking Bevlee to my parent's house,' she says. The teacup rattles in its saucer as she puts it down. Mum's eyebrow arches and her fingers drift towards the cigarettes lying on the timber armrest beside her, they stop mid-air and drop away. She says, 'Are they retired?'

'No, my father is a Methodist Missionary, his work will never be done.' Mum looks away and I sense her amusement. Her face always gives away her thoughts. She's thinking, *a Minister! You're kidding!* Now, she reaches for the cigarette packet.

'Well, I'm sure it will be wonderful for you all to visit. I won't keep you as any longer.' She looks directly at my father, 'Denny, Beverley's suitcase is on the verandah, you can pick it up on your way out.' Mum uncoils from the armchair. She's tall and looks down at Frances who's shifting forward to stand.

'Thank you, Norma, for the tea. Dennis and I will take care of Bevlee.' She takes Dad's hand and they walk across the room, both limping slightly to the left in unison, away from the cloying atmosphere into the fresh air. Mum's heels tap on the wooden floor as she follows them out, her measured tones tell me she's amused, 'Be good, Bev..er..ley.' There's no goodbye embrace. We drive away and out the rear window, I can see Mum. She's not waving, her face is obscured by cigarette smoke and I can imagine the laughter bubbling inside her. She has a wicked, irreverent sense of humour.

Silence. I don't know what to say. We drive for miles without a word. In later years I learnt that this was normal. They can drive for hours without talking. We can't in our house! It feels uncomfortable.

But now I've got time to think. Isn't funny how Dad has changed his name to Dennis, or did Frances change it for him? Like Betty did with Carl, who will always be Carl to me, but Carlos to her. Why did they do that? Did it change the person? Maybe. Come to think of it I don't like my name. Beverley. It makes me feel like I'm always in trouble. Is it the way Mum shouts it when she's cross, or mutters it under her breath in exasperation? No, I don't like my name. I'd rather be called Bev. Is that how Carl and Denny felt? This is confusing but distracting at the same time.

Suddenly I recognise where we are and say, 'Oh, we are on Christmas

Pass,' as we reach the dual carriageway. 'We came this way to Beira a few months ago…' Silence. Their heads don't move at all, it's as if I've not spoken. I feel awkward, everyone at home, even Mr Markee is always talking and arguing and carrying on about something.

'There are no clouds in the valley today,' I offer. Frances looks over her shoulder,

'Lovely clear day. My father says it's beautiful to see the clouds from up here on the Pass.'

'Yes, it is, and there were clouds on the mountains over there,' I say pointing to the far ranges that are clear-cut against today's sky, 'when we came here for the dentist a few months ago.'

'Dennis, do you think we will be there soon?' Dad nods his head.

The long back seat is empty without Susan jumping around and being annoying. I miss her. Then, suddenly I understand. Don't mention my family, just as at home we don't talk about Dad. So what *do* I talk about? The dentist should have been alright to say, but he's not. Best to say nothing for now.

Grandad and Granny Wright, that's what I'm told to call Frances's parents, ask me about my school, my subjects and what I do afterwards for sports. There's nothing about my family. Just about me. Grandad Wright asks if I read the Bible, and I say no. He peers at me over his glasses, with his bushy grey eyebrows raised. I imagine him saying, 'What, you don't!' Instead, later that day he gives me a Bible of my own, with a written message. My name and his, Grandad Wright, the date. That's special. *Is he saying I'm part of the family?* I like it when people do that, write my name and theirs. Carl used to do that.

We say prayers before every meal, but not the sort Grandpa used to say, 'Little fishes lick the dishes, all say Amen.' And Nanna would say 'Eric!' sharply, but always with a smile. No. We are serious about grace and are 'grateful' for what we have. We go to church on Sunday, twice, and it's boring. The seats are hard and I don't understand the sermon even though I concentrate. I'm frightened Grandad Wright will ask me Bible questions later, as he does to Frances. And he does. When I can't answer Frances gives me hints and soon gets Grandad Wright talking about the Bible with her.

No one smokes, drinks or talks out of turn here. Frances is quiet in their house, but we go for walks and she chats with me. We laugh and talk about what we like to do. She makes all her dresses and cooks too, so we have something in common. I'm careful not to mention Mum and I sew together.

Dad is quiet, he's always watching but says very little. Is he watching me with Frances? Yes, I think so. He does ask me if I still collect stamps, which I do, and about school as well. I don't say anything bad, even when he comments that my grades have changed. I think they're alright, I'm now in the middle ranking for class grades, around 15th or 16th out of 30 kids. One year the Spanish flu was bad and we all hoped to catch it so we didn't have to do exams! Some kids *did* get sick, but I didn't and came ninth in the class that time.

The three of us are at a cafe in town having a special morning tea before leaving tomorrow, Saturday. Thank goodness there's no Sunday Church. It's a beautiful room with large windows looking out onto trees, and tables set with white tablecloths and waiters quietly serving us tea, scones, jam, and cream. I'm allowed a chocolate milkshake.

'Apparently you have to go to boarding school next year?' Dad says. The treat's ruined. I feel sick. Just the thought of going to boarding school is enough to make me want to throw up.

'Yes,' I finally say and lose control of my decision to say nothing bad. 'I don't want to go, I'm so scared, I just don't want to go.' My forefingers trace lines in the condensation on the glass and I watch the milk bubbles popping on top of my milkshake. Dad nods his head, 'It is frightening, I know,' and he looks directly at Frances. She tilts her head sideways in thought and then says, 'I went to boarding school and it wasn't nice, so I understand. The children were unkind.' She nods to her permanently bent crippled leg, 'I couldn't run like them.'

This opened the floodgates. I tell them how awful school was until

Antoinette arrived and how most of my class will be going to boarding school. Even now I don't mention Mum or anyone at home. Dad listens, and when I finally run out of words, his face is expressionless as he says, 'Finish your milkshake. Beverley.' I've ruined the outing and they must think I'm an awful child now. Why didn't I just keep quiet?

***

Unlike other trips over the mountain pass, this time it's through swirls of mist with Dad and Frances, in silence. But it's comfortable now. In Rusape, Dad parks on the street in front of the house. He and Frances come inside, perch on the couch and sip on the obligatory tea, poured through Nanna's silver strainer. I resist quoting 'MIF' (milk in first) which is what she used to say. Frances is sitting close to Dad. I feel anxious for her, she's been kind to me and her body language—which I sort of understand now—says she's not enjoying this tea or Mum's company. So I sit next to her, our shoulders close. They can't wait to leave. I don't understand the tension. It's all very confusing. And then they are gone. No hugs, no tearful goodbyes, no 'see you soon'. Nothing. Just 'Goodbye, Beverley.'

I wonder if it will be another six years before I see Dad again, or maybe never. Was I a disappointment? I'm good at that. I think I'll miss them though. They are so different from everyone here. He's *my* Dad. Susan's got her own Dad. I want mine too. There's no one I can talk to. And why did Dad and Mum get a divorce? I've thought about this a lot recently and I want to ask Mum about it. Maybe it will help me to understand all these confusing attitudes.

'Thank goodness that's over with!' Mum says. 'Bill and Susan will be back soon.' She turns towards the house. It's now or never. 'Mum,' I say, 'Why did you and Dad get a divorce?' She stops, and looks at me with her lips pinched together, 'Ask your father.' Cigarette smoke drifts, and she walks away leaving me in the front yard. At the base of the front steps, she glances back. 'Well, are you coming inside? We're having roast chicken for lunch.' No one asks about my trip. Did anyone even realise I was gone for a week? Yes, one person does, Mr Markee. He comes to my bedroom door while I'm unpacking and says, 'Missis you back! Good, I make cake.'

Mr Markee makes the best sponge cake without measuring anything. He simply throws together handfuls of flour, and sugar and pours milk and other ingredients into the bowl, mixes, bakes, and serves a light, fluffy cake with jam between the layers. And he dusts it with icing sugar. I guess he knew not to serve it to our guests. He's grinning, flashing his fake gold tooth, which he's moved again, and gathers up my dirty washing. I bet Susan's been bothering him too.

Chapter 17
Another Holiday and Dad's Letter

Weeks pass and this Saturday afternoon, as I lean my bicycle against the side wall of the house, I hear, 'Holiday, holiday....we're going on holiday!' It's Susan and she's circling, arms outstretched like an aeroplane, around Mum in the front yard. Mum's laughing at her and swats her playfully with a rolled-up magazine as she runs towards me.

'Holiday, I knew before you,' she chirps hopping up and down.

'Holiday?' I ask 'Where, when....?' I'm so surprised, another holiday?

'Oh for goodness sake Beverley, stop frowning, you'll get lines,' says Mum, 'You're just too serious!'

Mum and Susan chortle. Yes, I'm not funny like them. I don't have the same wacky sense of humour they do. I'm just more practical; but I can be fun *too*, if they let me.

'We are going on a big boat,' says Susan, 'To Cape Town. Knew before you!' She drags out the final three words in a sing-song voice and runs into the house shouting, 'Let's find the holiday clothes!'

'Hey, Mum!' I say starting to laugh. 'More like we need to make her more clothes, and buy her shoes, she's only got one pair! Nothing will...' But Mum suddenly snaps round to face me, 'Oh for God's sake child! Do you always have to be so sensible? Honestly!' She turns away and calls out to Susan, 'I've put the holiday clothes in the spare cupboard.' *I doubt the Beira clothes still fit her, her slops (thongs) are worn out. And that's a fact. So what's so wrong with being sensible?*

***

The cruise is with Lloyd Triestino liners. They haul cargo and also have berths for a few passengers on the Beira to Cape Town return trip. We're booked on the *Europa* there and the *Africa* on the way back. After loading cargo, the hold is closed which creates a seawater swimming pool that provides us with hours of splashing around. Meals are served by Italian waiters, who speak broken English, in a small dining room with wooden tables. One of them always asks us if we've had enough to eat. His Italian accent makes T's and O's sound so funny, 'Tommy touching table?' We all laugh with him.

We dock in Cape Town where Auntie Hazel, Mum's first cousin, and Uncle Roy book us into a posh hotel at Sea Point, right opposite the beach. It's full of holidaymakers, local and international, with fascinating accents that we strain to hear and understand. Some don't even speak English! We *oooh* over the ladies who perch on bar stools holding long black cigarette holders, wearing elegant clothes, shoes, and handbags, the likes of which we never see at home. Their hair is set high in curls or waves, sleek and stiff around their shoulders. They're on the arms of men with smoothly combed hair in dinner jackets. The men all wear ties and gleaming leather shoes. No men in shorts and pulled-up socks, nor barefoot kids are running around here. No mothers in homemade dresses, either. But Mum looks lovely in the evening. No one will know her dress was homemade.

Meals are in the dining room, with white tablecloths and serviettes. Nanna would so approve. Waiters with swift hands move away plates and pour cool water into our glasses and tea for Mum and Bill. We speak in quiet voices, in harmony with the other guests. This creates a polite hum above the tinkle of silver on china. The knives, forks and spoons are in their correct place and have to be used in the correct order. Bill shows us how to tip our soup bowls away from our bodies, not towards us as we do at home, and he demonstrates how to eat a fish called sole. Silly name that! But it's a tasty fish, and if you do it Bill's way there's no bones!

Auntie Hazel's home is large, immaculate, and perched on the cliff side at Bantry Bay, with sweeping views over the Atlantic Ocean and Robin Island, where the adults say that 'awful man, Mandela,' is in prison. For his whole life with 'hard labour'. I can't imagine that. The island looks peaceful from here. No one says why they locked him up, but they make him sound bad, so I don't ask about that, or ask about the joke Auntie Hazel and her maid share. The maid, who has worked for her for years, is old with wavy grey hair and a curved back. She arrives and Auntie Hazel says with a naughty look on her face, 'What bus did you get today?'

The maid puts down her bag, changes her shoes, chuckles, and replies, 'The white bus!' And they both laugh! 'You fooled them again! One day you'll get caught.'

'What they do with an old lady like me! I tell them, listen here boy, I'm old enough to be your Granny! Get away.' More laughter as she waves her closed umbrella around. I'm baffled. It's a bit like, 'That Mandela man.'

Behind the house, Lion Mountain crouches like a lion's head rising above the city. Beyond it sits Table Mountain, large, rectangular, bold, and frequently wearing a white cloud tablecloth that drifts over its edges. On clear days, it stands grey and flat-topped against the sky, and we can see cable cars moving up and down the mountainside.

When Auntie Hazel and Uncle Roy visited us in Rhodesia they always brought us gifts, thoughtful things that we couldn't buy for ourselves, either because they were too expensive or unavailable due to sanctions. Mum sheds a layer of restraint when they come to stay. Now I realise that they are very wealthy and have paid for the hotel and all our food! Amazing what I hear! Bill was puffing on his pipe, complaining about something minor, and Mum said, 'Well, you didn't pay for this expensive hotel, Hazel did!' *That got him for sure! Mum wouldn't have said that back home. Bill scowls at her. Mum is having a good time and ignores him.*

On warm evenings, we gather at Auntie Hazel's home for drinks, nibble snacks, and the adults laugh a lot. Neil, their only son, joins us. He's close to Mum's age, and the three of them share a fast-paced wit and affection for each other. Uncle Roy and Bill sip beers and chuckle at their antics. Susan loves the joking, even though she doesn't understand it all, and Bill even joins in and has Uncle Roy to talk to. When the five adults are socialising, attention is diverted from our small family and its daily issues. Susan's not bored and stops taunting or throwing things at me, so I stop thumping her! Mum is happier than she's been for ages with all the boring daily rituals gone. Here she's vibrant and outrageously witty. She adores these cousins and shows a side of herself that only peeps out at home.

Bill relaxes, he's not paying for anything, and chats easily with Uncle Roy. It's one of their conversations I overhear that makes me think about Bill more. They're discussing food coupons and rationing. What's that? I lie on the carpet 'reading' my comic book. They are enjoying their beers, and smoking pipes—I like the smell of them.

'Dreadfully inconvenient, this rationing in Rhodesia rather reminds me of war times in Britain…' Bill says and continues talking in his funny British accent. My concentration wanders until he says, 'My brother went down with a ship… I was serving…' And I hear Roy say, '… caused a bit of an issue here, sending men to fight for the King. Some Afrikaners were more aligned with Germany.' Pipe smoke drifts over me, and in the background, Mum laughs, light and full of bubbles. She's with Neil in the dining room.

Now I get it, the same war Grandpa was in. But Mum was a small child then, about four years old. Bill was in the war? How old is he? Now I'm not bad at maths, so if Bill was in the war he must have been about 20 years old. Mum was about four. Take four away from 20. Sixteen. Bill's 16 years older than Mum. No wonder he's got grey sideburns and Dad's got none.

Most mornings Mum and Bill are happy to recline on chairs by the hotel pool and leave us to our own devices. So we swim, float on rubber tubes, or cross the road and run on the beach, build sandcastles, find shells, and watch colourful anemones open and close in a tidal rock cave.

The Atlantic Ocean sweeps past this coast and it's freezing. Hardly anyone swims. We watch bronzed bikini-clad ladies dip into the icy waves and retreat, their skin goose bumped, to bake on their beach towels. They're all fully aware of the young men watching them from behind sunglasses.

The days fly by and soon we are on the return liner to Beira and then home to Rusape. It's been exciting and I realise Susan and I are nice to each other away from home, and Bill, well, he's old!

***

Weeks later Mum's in the sitting room, it's warm outside and the breeze drifts through the room cooling it. As I wander past on the verandah she calls out, 'Beverley, come here.' Sunlight through a side window draws lines on the polished floor and small dust motes drift aimlessly about. Mum's sitting in Grandpa's favourite chair. The room's been redecorated since Grandpa died. The lounge suite's old upholstery has been ripped away and replaced with a textured soft grey-fleck fabric. The wide wooden arms of the two armchairs gleam richly against this soft background and they stand, with the settee, around a new red rug. Grey and off-white curtains finish the room. Mum's made it modern, but I can still visualise Grandpa sitting in his chair.

I plop myself down. Mum leans over and pulls a letter from the depths of her knitting basket, which always stands near her chair, just like Nanna's used to. A lit cigarette balances in the ashtray, slender smoke drifts upwards and the tip burns low. Paper rustles between her fingers and she glances up at me, 'I've had another letter from your father.' She waves pages before my face, 'He says "We think Beverley should come and live with us. She can go to high school in Bulawayo and come back to you for the holidays."' I stare at her. They want me to go and live there!

Mum's slender fingers, tipped with pink nails, carefully lift the cigarette, and she taps it on the ashtray. Slowly, watching me, she moves it to her lips. Her eyes narrow slightly. I can't speak, nothing wants to come out of my mouth. I *don't* want to go, my heart thumps and I realise I want Mum to say, *no Beverley, don't go, stay here, we love you.* My toes scrunch into the carpet pile and I look straight at Mum willing her to hug me and say, 'Stay'.

'What do you want to do?' Mum finally asks.

'I don't know,' I mumble. I feel like I'm watching a film and this isn't real.

Mum stubs out her cigarette. The lipstick-stained filter falls against its friends in the ashtray. 'Well, it's not a hard decision is it?' She snaps. 'You were sitting right next to "her" when they brought you back from Umtali. It made me sick! Sick to see you next to her!' The words hiss from her perfect lips.

I'm stunned. You didn't hug me, you didn't ask how the trip went, how I felt. No one said I shouldn't like Frances. Wasn't I supposed to? She's Dad's wife. You don't even like Dad. They'd been kind to me, talked to me, and asked me questions.

'Mum, I'm sorry.' I want to run to her, but she's angry. Deep down a memory flutters of another time when I'd flung myself at her. It ended badly.

'So you should be! All cozy with that woman! Anyway, your father has custody of you, you know.' Yes, I *do* know. Mum stuffs the offending letter deep into her knitting basket. 'If he wants to take you he can. They're asking if you want to go. So do you?' In a flash, I realise that Mum's not going to say, 'Beverley, stay here, we want you here,' and I feel as if I've been stabbed. My longing for those words thunders deep within and reverberates in my ears. Say it *please*, say it, *stay!* She doesn't.

'OK, I'll go,' I say and slowly walk out onto the verandah and down the steps into the front garden. Above me, there is a promise of rain. Angry grey flat-bottomed clouds are gathering on the horizon, marching forward with deep rumbling in the distance, and the sky darkens. Nothing can stop them, *nothing*. I start counting the rose bushes, even though I know there are 80 of them, all planted under Mum's loving eyes. I'd watched as she instructed the garden boy just where she wanted each hole. He dug hole after hole, and she inspected every one to ensure it was perfect. Then he planted Flora Bunda roses that are nurtured, watered, pruned and admired by everyone. Beautiful colours. Beware those aphids!

Slowly, I sort through my life and acknowledge the reality that this is Bill, Mum and Susan's home. It doesn't include me. My bare toe stubs at the dry ground that's begging for water. With one last look at the pampered roses, I emotionally turn away for a moment from everyone in the house.

Do I go to Dad and Frances in Bulawayo? May as well. Maybe it will be OK there, and they have asked me too. If they didn't want me they wouldn't have asked. Would they? But why? They don't have any children, is that it? Oh, this is all too hard. *Grandpa! What do I do?* The first drops of rain fall, thunder crashes overhead, and I run inside. The rain-fresh air follows me, blowing away my anxious thoughts, for a while.

Chapter 18
Operations and Decisions.

Susan's crying in the middle of the night *every* night now. Loudly. She begs for the pain in her legs to stop. We are all awake. Mum and Bill don't know what's wrong and the Doctor is mystified. She's not being naughty. Bill gives her Aspirin and sits smoothing her hair back and talking in a low voice until she falls asleep. After weeks and weeks of this, Mum and Susan return from another visit to Dr Strydom's. 'It's her tonsils!' Mum says sounding happy. 'Can you believe it, they're so rotten and infected that they're poisoning her and causing all the leg pains. Easy to fix, he's taking them out next week! Hers and Beverley's.'

'Mum! Why me too?' I'm horrified at the thought.

'Well, you get sore throats sometimes and anyway you can keep Susan company.'

There's no further discussion. Once, Mum, has her say, that's it. The subject is closed, even if I did have a point of view. Children do as they are told!

"Next week" arrives far too quickly. Mum tries to make us feel happy about the "little tonsils and adenoids op." She buys us each a fluffy toy and says, 'It's nothing to worry about and you'll get to eat lots of jelly and ice cream.' She smiles when she says such things, trying to make it sound like a treat. Susan thinks it is. I don't. My toy, a lean-looking grey and white plush cat, is sitting upright on my bedside cabinet, staring at me with dark eyes. It's not trusting either!

And now Susan and I are lying between starched white sheets, in a room on our own, with tiled floors. Everything smells of a hospital. The nurse says, 'Lights out now, and no talking.' She flicks off the glaring ceiling light and we're left in darkness, except for a sliver of light under the door. Susan's quiet for a bit and then she starts whispering to me. I whisper back. She's afraid because she's only five years old, all alone in a strange bed, clutching her new stuffed toy. I've left mine at home.

The next morning they wheel Susan away. She's crying and as they leave the room she starts screaming, 'No! I want to go home. Mum, Mum …' and she tries to get off the trolley. I can't go to her. Her voice echoes down the corridor and grows fainter as they take her further away. I'm terrified for her and myself. Then people dressed in white appear and wheel me away, down that same corridor. I clench my fists tight and my fingernails dig into my palms. It's painful but doesn't distract me from the urge to leap up and run away. But I can't anyway. Fear is pushing my body into the thin mattress against my back. The lights above me blink, and to the whine of turning wheels, we move through huge doors into a room that smells even more of the hospital. I stare at the ceiling. Different lights here. I'm so scared that my neck won't move, but peripheral vision tells me people are moving around me. Quietly. Then, eyes above a mask stare into mine and a voice says, 'Breathe in deeply.' I close my eyes as a black object moves towards my face. Something hard and stinky is covering my nose. Now I move. I reach up and grapple with this thing on my face. Hands pull my arms down, hold them hard and I hear a firm command, 'Breath in deeply. Stop struggling.' My eyes are open, there's a bright light above me and my legs are bouncing up and down. They won't stop bouncing, running, running towards the mango trees, but I shouldn't be. There's no sun.

The next thing I know is that I'm awake. Vomiting. The water and jelly the nurse encourages me to swallow razor blades its way down and back up again. I cry. The nurse moves away and Susan says, 'What's wrong with you?' I look sideways. She's sitting up in bed near me, eating jelly and ice cream. 'This jelly is good,' she says and pops another spoonful of wobbly red stuff into her mouth. I vomit again, into a bowl beside me. That night, I'm still unable to keep anything down. A nurse is leaning over me. The lights are low and she says, 'I'm going to give you an injection.' She rolls me over and jabs me in the bum. It is the most painful injection I've ever had. I stop vomiting and fall asleep.

Two days later Susan's playing outside with friends, still eating ice cream and jelly which Mr Markee dishes out on demand. He brings mine to my bedroom and mutters, 'Eish... picinin missis!' Shakes his head and hovers in the doorway for a few moments. I'm so sick.

Mum says we are going to Doctor Strydom's today for a check-up. The Doctor puts his horrible stick on our tongues and looks down our throats. Susan's bored and wants out of here, and so do I. But the Doctor and Mum are talking about us as if we have no ears. Adults do that. Assume we don't hear. Sometimes I don't, because it's not interesting, but then I hear my name.

'… but we had issues with Beverley. Unfortunately, she haemorrhaged during the operation, and we had to administer further ether. Her excessive vomiting can be attributed to that.' Mum nods her head. I shift in the chair. My bum's still sore where the nurse jabbed me. They chat and after a few more comments, we leave.

***

A few weeks later, after lunch, when we are supposed to be resting, Mum comes into my bedroom and sits down. She's wearing her 'serious' face. I wait. After a few moments, she says, 'Your father has written to me.' I stiffen and sit up straight. 'He's booked you on the overnight train from Salisbury to Bulawayo in early January, about a week before school starts. You'll be going to Eveline Girls High which is in town. I remember it. It's a lovely school.' Now she's smiling, almost to herself. 'We lived in town, on Main Street. Mum, Dad, and me.' There's a tone in her voice she uses sometimes when talking about Grandpa and Nanna. It's sort of dreamy, sad, and soft. Like a loving memory, her face reflects that. We sit quietly for a while. Me with gathering tears and Mum with thoughts of her parents. Her brown eyes meet mine and she sees my watery eyes.

'Don't start carrying on! You said you wanted to go,' she says. I blink. I haven't felt like this since Dad took me from the farm to Durban years ago. Does she remember? Is that why she's cross now?

'Anyway, you've been on a train before with your father. So this will be the same. He's booked a coupe which means there will be only one other lady with you.' I realise that I'm going on the train alone, tears tip onto my cheeks, and Mum gets up. From the doorway, she looks back and says, 'It'll be fun, new school and friends, you'll see!' Ant appears beside her. 'Hello Auntie Norma,' she says, walks in, and hands me a brown paper bag. 'Here, Mum's made you a new Barbie doll dress.'

I uncurl the turned-over bag edge and peep inside. It's pink! An evening dress with a fitted strapless bodice and chiffon gathered skirt, all fully lined with soft satin. My fingers stray over the fabric. I examine the fine stitching and small press studs at the back. It's beautiful. Ant's dark eyes are on me and she's ginning. 'Thought you'd like it!' I reach for the blonde Barbie doll that Granny in South Africa sent me years ago, and undress her. The new evening dress slips up over her legs and does up. It's a perfect fit. Once she's standing up in her jam jar on my dressing table, with the skirt floating around her, we sit back and admire her.

'I'm going to Bulawayo in January.' Ant doesn't take her eyes off the doll. 'That's when I'm going to boarding school,' she says. 'Suppose we will have to leave our dolls at home.' We sit for a few moments. We don't play with these dolls, they stand on our dressing tables in clothes Auntie Lilly or we have made using leftover fabrics from grown-up dresses. Suddenly Ant laughs, it's a deep full sound and she turns to me. 'Oh, who cares about next year! Come on, let's go swimming at the Crocodile Motel. Mum will take us for sure!' I grab my swimmers, a towel, and we hurry outside and cycle to her house. Auntie Lilly takes us to the motel, buys us Brown Cows and we swim all afternoon. Mum didn't suggest I take Susan with me.

That night I lie on my bed and gaze at the dressed doll. I think about after Christmas; that's when I have to get on the train, alone. I don't think I want to now. But, going to boarding school is even *more* scary. Well, that's over two months away and there's my 12th birthday in November before then. Ant's right, who cares about next year? I won't think beyond now, and with that decision made, I find a book to read and life feels normal again.

Chapter 19
Christmas 1969 and I Leave Mum.

The Christmas cake's baking this hot Saturday afternoon.

'It's ready,' Mum says and opens the oven door, bends, and with gloved hands lifts the tin out placing it on the counter. She sighs, half smiles to herself and breathes in deeply. I do the same. Together, without speaking, we visualise another cake, another kitchen—the farm—with its black wood stove and pock-marked wooden table. Mum's wearing the same apron around her waist, but it's faded now. This cake is in the same tin lined with layers of brown paper. Familiar Christmas aromas waft around us.

Mum takes a knitting needle from her apron pocket and begins to poke holes into the cake. Methodically, slowly in and out, in circles starting from the edge. Suddenly she's stabbing them randomly all over and finishing with a final thrust into the middle. She drops the knitting needle on the table, rests her palms flat on either side of the cake for a few moments, before unscrewing the lid of a bottle of brandy. Slowly, she pours it over the dark bumpy surface. A rich fruity fragrance fills the room with the promise of turkey and pudding with coins and charms hidden within, and voices from years gone by are there in my mind.

'That's it for now,' she says as she unties her apron, drops it on the bench beside the cake and walks away. Her soft brown eyes meet mine. There's something there I don't understand but don't know what to ask. The illusion is gone.

A few weeks later, with Julie Andrews singing 'High on a Hill…' in the background, Mum spreads apricot jam all over the cake, rolls out the marzipan until it's a thin sheet, carefully lifts and lays it over the jam, and smooths all creases with her fingers right down to the bottom edge. It's as neat as a well-made bed. She trims away the leftovers and then it's ready to ice. With icing-sugared hands on her hips, she steps back and examines her work, lips compressed in thought, and eyes full of anticipation.

Mum loves Christmas and birthdays. Deftly, she mixes the Royal Icing—that's the brand name on the packet—it's beaten up and slathered on, snow white, and with the flat of a bread knife, she quickly taps up and down all over the cake top, lifting the stiff icing into peaks, which will harden into little sharp mountains. Around the outer edge, she smooths the icing and wraps it in a red and silver paper cake frill, securing the ends with pins. We carefully sift through the ornaments: a green snow-scattered tree, a street lamp, a girl on a sleigh, a house, and best of all—a smiling Santa. We position them between the snow mountains of icing, and they're set into place. When the cake is cut, the ornament bases will be encrusted with hard icing and a hint of marzipan and jam that will remain until next year, when we will melt it off with hot water.

Bill and Mr Markee drag a freshly cut pine Christmas tree into the sitting room and push its base into a bucket of sand. It's standing up straight, woody, and fragrant. Grandpa's precious tree lights are tucked between the branches, blinking on and off, just like they do every year, even though he's not here. The same brittle decorative balls hang amongst the green, and Susan has fun putting them up, but they're only as high as her lean arms can reach. When she gets bored and runs outside, Mum moves a few up higher and drapes tinsel over the branches.

It's a strange Christmas. Our second one in this town without extended family. It's just the four of us now and we have different visitors around for tea. But it's not the same, and it never will be again. I'm sad when the tree lights are taken down and put away in their box. Everything keeps changing, no matter how much I wish it wouldn't.

***

Today is Saturday, a hot day in January 1970, great for swimming and jumping off the high diving board with Ant. But that's not going to happen. Grandpa's two-tone cream and green Vauxhall station wagon is parked in the shade of the jacaranda trees. The purple carpet of flowers beneath them is gone, and now the branches are lush with green leaves swaying in the heat. I am alone, and there's no avoiding today for me.

Mr Markee appears in the doorway of my bedroom and grunts as he lifts the large off-white, hard shell suitcase with its silver locks snapped shut. Mum's had it for years. I wonder if she had it when she lived with my father, but that's not a question to ask. Almost everything I own is in it. All my life apart from my *Noddy* and other Enid Blyton books—I'm too old for them now—and a few keepsakes in drawers. Did I ever live in this room?

'Beverley, hurry up.' Mum's calling down the hallway. 'We have to get going, everyone's in the car. Come on!' I look around my bedroom. Doors and drawers yawn open, and my special things are packed away on top of the cupboard safe from Susan's little fingers. She won't be able to climb up there. The curtain moves and flaps goodbye. I walk through the door, down the hallway and avoid the creaky floorboard, it's funny how one keeps to habits, past the kitchen and Mr Markee, out the screen backdoor that bangs behind me, into the sunshine. Mum's standing by the car beckoning me to hurry up. Bill's got the engine running and Susan's cavorting around, shoeless with half-brushed hair, in the backseat. Mum and I get in, slam the doors a bit too hard. She tosses Susan's shoes over her shoulder at us and says, 'Right, let's get going. We don't want to be late getting to Anne and Peter's.'

We leave Rusape. Through the front window, over Mum's shoulder, the tar road ribbons and hovers in the heat, almost as if it's alive. Mum adjusts the radio dial and Martin Locke's upbeat voice crackles above the engine, and he says, 'With Lyons Maid, you're laughing!'

Lyons Maid ice cream is sold all over the country in stores, and from ice cream carts with a clanging bell pedalled by uniformed Africans. Now Martin's talking about the top Lyons Maid record hit of the week. We are all quiet; this is our favourite Saturday radio show, except for Bill, who likes cricket. Finally, we hear, 'Once again the Lyons Maid Number one hit is from The Beatles, "Abbey Road"… and the slow melodious words, "Something in the way she moves…" soar above the engine noise, above the wind blowing our hair, above the sounds of the wheels on the tar. Mum says, 'That's about six weeks now at the top!' And we try to sing along, very badly. Bill half grins at us and flicks cigarette ash out the window, remnants of which drift back in over us.

Hits of the Week has ended. Our journey has ended. We are in Salisbury at Mum's first cousin, Aunty Anne's house, sitting very upright in a polished sitting room overlooking a lush garden. I'm next to Mum, who told us very firmly as we pull up, 'to behave'. Susan's intimidated for a while and then escapes into the garden with Aunty Anne's two girls who are close to her age.

'I've organised an early dinner,' Aunty Anne says, 'It's only a 30-minute drive to the station from here. The train leaves at 9pm?'

'Yes, Beverley's booked in a coupe.' And turning to me she says, 'You'll enjoy the journey. It's so lovely listening to the wheels going round and falling asleep.' My eyes fill with tears. Her look says, *don't start now!* I've been crying for days on and off. Mum's had enough of it. Fear renders me silent.

The sun sets as we eat dinner. Outside, crickets tentatively begin to screech as the cicadas fall silent. Our knives and forks barely clink on the bone china, and starched serviettes lie on our laps. Soft adult conversations surround me. Nanna would've been pleased. This is our last dinner together for three months. I excuse myself and vanish to the bathroom.

All too quickly, we leave, and Bill pulls up outside Salisbury Railway Station's imposing two-storey building. Exterior lights illuminate a series of large façade windows with curved tops painted white, stark against reddish bricks, and we hurry past stately columns supporting the verandah roof. Crowds are moving with us through a walkway and onto a large platform. Above me, metal beams support a massive curved roof, and then I see the train: long, two-tone tan and red carriages with polished windows, waiting. The doors at each carriage end bang as people board and move down the internal corridors searching for their allocated compartments. Voices ebb and flow.

Mum calls out to a porter, and my suitcase is loaded onto a flat long trolley with other cases on their way to the guard's van, where they will stay for the journey. Mum grabs my hand and pushes through the crowd, 'Your father will sort out your suitcase in Bulawayo. Come on, we've only got a few minutes left.' Mum hurries up the metal steps into a carriage. I follow her. She's already in the doorway of a compartment talking to a lady, '… so could you just make sure Beverley finds her father when you get to Bulawayo? …' She turns to me, 'Here, in you go. This is nice, a first-class coupe, only the two of you in here! So much better than sharing with four or six people.'

I hover in the doorway of the narrow room and peep inside. Polished timber-clad walls surround a green leather bench seat. In the corner is a storage unit and below that a round metal plate, which when pulled down, reveals a small basin and tap. The whistle sounds, 'That's the final one, you'll be off soon,' says Mum, and gesturing down to her right, says, 'Look, the toilet is just next door, so you won't get lost!' With a brief hug, she turns away and says, 'Quick, come into the corridor and you'll see us through the window.'

I watch her pull open the exit door and she's gone, down the stairs we climbed minutes ago. *Bang*; the door slams behind her. I jump. From the window, I look down at them amongst people waving and blowing kisses. Susan is holding Bill's hand, her arm swinging back and forth because she's impatient to leave. My cheeks are wet. The train jerks, nameless parting fingers touch, goodbyes are called out, and the train moves, slowly at first. Below me, massive black wheels are turning, steam hisses clouds of white from the front ones, and the *huff huff huff* builds momentum tugging us away from the crowds. My family gets smaller and smaller as the train goes faster and faster, and I watch the three of them walk away. And I see another figure, Grandpa, who stood years ago and waved to me and Daddy as we left Gadzema. I wave to him again.

Now, they have all melted away with time and the departing crowds, beneath the stark platform lights. I lean out of the window until I can't see the station anymore. They're gone. So fast, *so final*. I'm alone with a hint of Mum's Youth Dew, the memory of Grandpa's pipe, the sounds of wheels click-clacking and compartment doors closing. Above me, a moth flutters against a tubular light and beyond that, house windows wink as we steam through the dark suburbs and leave the city, and soon the night sky with its pinpricks of light embraces us. Even the stars aren't alone. The air is cool on my face. A hand touches my shoulder.

'Come inside with me,' says a soft voice and I glance up into a woman's face. She's younger than Mum. I follow her into the coupe and she closes the door quietly. The porter has made our beds. White sheets and blue blankets are neatly tucked together and before climbing onto the top bunk bed I clean my teeth in the shiny metal basin, complete with a little tap and slow trickle of water. My travelling companion then changes into her pyjamas, cleans her teeth and gets into bed. 'Shall we read our books for a while?' She asks and I agree.

The train sways gently from side to side. It lulls me and ignites a memory of doing this before, years ago, with Dad. We'd had a coupe too. He'd come to the farm and had taken me to Bulawayo and back, on the train a few times. On one trip he'd borrowed two of my 18-inch dolls for a friend to dress and enter a competition at the Bulawayo Trade Show. One, a blonde, was dressed as a bride and the dark-haired one was a Flamenco dancer in a beautiful red dress with a lacy black mantilla. That one won an award at the Trade Show! Dad had returned them wearing their lovely new clothes.

Now, I glance down at the metal sink cover, where Dad had stood them for a while so I could admire them, before putting them carefully away. I can visualise them now, packed away in Rusape and stored on top of the cupboard. Rusape is getting further and further away. I wonder if they are home yet? I click off the light by my head, squeeze my eyes tight, and mumble, 'Good night, sleep tight, don't let the bed bugs bite. *Goodnight Grandpa.*' A soft laugh reaches me from the bunk below.

Chapter 20
Life Changes and I'm Dumb.

The train pulls slowly into Bulawayo station at 7.30 the next morning. Somewhere during the night, the stream engine was changed over to a diesel one, so there is no hissing and billows of steam to announce our arrival, but rather we glide towards the platform and I lean out of the window. There's a man crouched at the platform edge tapping the passing wheels with a metal rod. *Tap… tap…* and from long ago a voice, *my* voice, asks 'Daddy, why's he hitting the wheels?'

'Why? He's checking for punctures!' Daddy replied.

'Punctures! Trains get flat tyres?' And Daddy's answer was to laugh.

The train halts, and carriage doors are flung open. I lean out the window. There they are, walking hand in hand towards me, limping slightly in unison to the left. It strikes me that both their disabilities are on the same side. I half-wave, grab my overnight bag and hurry to the exit door. Several passengers are in front of me. I wait, they are slow, and finally, my shoulder's in the open doorway. I stare down the steps I climbed last night. *Was it only last night?*

They're waiting, and for a few moments, I can't move. Fear grips me. I don't know these people. A voice from behind prompts me. I hurry down the steps backwards, my feet find the pavement and I turn around. People are bustling, hugging, and chatting, but we stand as statues, the three of us, a mirror of each other's uncertainty on our faces. The enormity of my arrival momentarily hangs in the air and my legs ache to run away and climb trees.

Dad half smiles at me, it's slightly lopsided, and he tilts his head. Suddenly I see him, from a few months ago, from years ago and a small bubble rises in me, and I smile back. Frances blinks and as if leaving a trance says, 'Goodness Bevlee, you are brave to come all this way on your own!' She glances up at my father. 'Come on Dennis, let's get going.' Dad turns and leads us along the platform, greeting workers he knows, and we stop at the guard's van where men are unloading suitcases. Dad signals a porter, his eyes run over the stacked suitcases and without asking me, he points and says, 'That one.' For a moment I'm puzzled. *How did he know it was mine?* Frances has noticed, she's frowning slightly. It's *Mum's* old suitcase. It's older than me! The porter heaves it onto his trolley and follows us as we join the crowds hurrying along the platform, past dark brick walls, large cream-painted arched windows, and through a huge curved walkway out to the car park and into the brilliant morning light. I blink rapidly, and hurry after Dad and Frances, making their way between parked vehicles, many with doors and boots open, until we stop beside a blue and white Cortina station wagon, rather like Grandpa's Vauxhall. I'm glad it's not green and cream like that was.

My vision has shrunk from the hustle beyond us to these people who are now my parents. Dad opens the door and climbs in. He's dressed in a light green open-necked short-sleeved shirt, plain beige shorts and matching knee-high socks. The left one has slipped halfway down his crippled leg. Nothing like the safari suits in light blue with matching cravats and socks that Bill wears. Frances sits sideways on her seat, swivels around, and maneuvers her permanently bent left leg into the car. The heel strap of her left sandal has slipped down. She closes the door, shifts the skirt of her A-line apricot-printed cotton dress, and straightens it above her knees. She glances back at me and nods as if to say, *yes she's here,* and looks away. I notice she's wearing hardly any makeup and pale lipstick, and her short dark hair is neatly set. No clicking high heels here or the latest dresses copied from 'on appro' clothing, or magazines, and no lingering ash and cigarette stubs either.

I glance back at the station. It's as impressive as Salisbury's, with a two-storey façade of red brick, a shaded wide verandah, and street-level cream arched windows mirroring those on the platform. A line of taxis waits, bicycles weave in and out past people spilling towards cars with porters following them. Above all of this, a clear cloudless sky, vast and uncluttered, promises a hot day. I shiver. I hope they will like me. They *have* to. I can't go back to Rusape.

We drive in silence through the wide, quiet Sunday streets. Seated in the centre of the back seat, I have a perfect view and my eyes dart from side to side. We pass beautiful shops with fashionably clad mannequins, furniture, shoes, and more and it reminds me of Salisbury. The quiet unnerves me. Car travel is never quiet with Mum, Bill, and Susan, so I search my thoughts for something to say and finally blurt out, 'Dad, I saw the man checking for punctures.'

Dad chuckles, 'So you remember that, punctures?' I think it's all a big fib on his part but I'm not sure.

'Yes, you told me that when we came here with my dolls in new dresses.' I hurry on, 'And we went to Durban, saw Granny and you ate curry.' Frances smiles at me over her shoulder. 'Your father still loves curry—very hot!'

'To make him cry. That's what he told me.' We all laugh and my thoughts run away from me. 'I packed those dolls away from Susan. She gets into all my stuff. Sometimes she breaks things and I hate it!' Silence.

'Mum says she doesn't mean it, but I think she does it to make me angry.' The two heads in front of me don't move. What have I done? Maybe I shouldn't talk about Mum and Susan. Perhaps they dislike Mum as much as she does them. Frantically I sift around for something unrelated to home and say, 'The Beatles were top of the charts yesterday.'

'Really,' says Frances glancing back at me. 'We don't always hear that program, we go into town shopping some Saturdays. I like Jim Reeves.' *Jim Reeves, who is he?* I subside into an unfamiliar silence. There's no radio, only the sound of the engine filling the car, and

I gaze out the window. Wide streets give way to houses and then scrubby green bush.

'Nearly there,' says Dad. Nearly where? My new home with my new parents in Bulawayo. I wish Susan was in the back seat trying to tickle with me.

'That's the Umgusa River,' Dad says pointing from the bridge we are on, 'We turn off just here to Woodville.' Woodville, that's where I'm going to live now. I roll the name around in my brain. There are no houses and I realise that there haven't been any for a few miles now. The bundu stretches away in both directions, long grass and thorn bushes line the tarred straight road. We pass a lone building, *Redman's Garage*, says the sign on it, go round a few more corners and *now* there are houses, stretched apart on large blocks of land. But there are no street lights, and it's quiet. Near the end of a dead-end street, Dad swings right onto a large circular driveway. Dust kicks up behind us. The front yard is huge. Stunted palm trees with brilliant blooming bougainvillea vines between them line the driveway, and a small house sits on the gracious curve.

'That tree gives us loads of fruit,' Dad says as we pass a massive avocado tree on our way around the corner of the house and stop near the back door. An old African man walks towards us and past him scurries a corgi barking. It's just like my Noddy, but this one's got a long tail that's swishing back and forth.

'Remember Lady,' says Dad opening the boot, 'and Lenid.'

Lenid? I look from him to the cavorting dog. They are so familiar. Lenid's face cracks into a wide smile and he nods at me. I know him! He's from the farm and Lady is one of Noddy's puppies! I remember them from six years ago. Lady's tail is long because Nanna had died and she was the one who chopped off the pup's tails! Mum couldn't do it, she screwed up her face and shook her head at the thought. I reach down and run my palm slowly over Lady's tan back. She feels like Noddy did and I glance up at Dad, who is watching me with a smile.

'Dennis, I'm making coffee,' Frances calls out the kitchen window. Dad and I walk towards the back door with the corgi at my ankles. I feel Grandpa's hand on my shoulder and hear him say. '*You'll be alright, Beverley.*'

Dad shows me to my room. The house is small. The yard is huge. 'Two and a quarter acres,' Dad says. My bedroom is one of the smallest I've ever had. A bed with a plain old yellow chenille bedspread, a small cupboard, and a tiny table with a chair, to do my homework at. I can hear Mum saying, 'Looks rather missionary to me!' There's one other bedroom, a sitting room, a dining room, and a tiny kitchen with a window overlooking the long backyard. At the far end are two small dwellings which must be where Lenid and the garden boy live. I'll have to visit Lenid's wife, Mai, and his daughter, Beauty. I wonder what they will have with sadza tonight?

Dad opens the cupboard and a few wooden coat hangers huddle in the corner. 'Unpack your things and put the suitcase under your bed,' he says. I hover in the doorway as he walks away. No Mr Markee is bustling into the room to help me, and Lenid isn't coming down the hallway either. Slowly I turn and open the suitcase, its silver locks snap open and I begin to take things out. This is something I've never done on my own, and I long for Mr Markee's deft fingers and rapid movements that had all my things put away in minutes. I struggle with the wooden coat hangers and worry over what to put in which drawers. I can't get to sleep that night. It's so quiet without Susan. And I'm lonely.

***

The next morning, Frances announces that we are going into town. Dad's gone to work so I'm alone with a stranger. She grabs her handbag, slips on her shoes, and I follow her out the back door. Her limp is obvious from the back. Her hip is off-centre and the strap of her sandal on her left foot has slipped again and is sitting on her dry cracked heel.

'I can't drive a car because of this stiff leg,' she says, 'So Dennis bought me a scooter.' She unlocks a large rear two-door compartment and puts her handbag inside. 'It's very economical on petrol too! Come on, hop in.' It's like nothing I've ever seen before. A funny pale blue vehicle with one wheel under the front doorless half-bubble cab, and two rear wheels under the huge metal box that sits behind the cab. There's enough room on the bench seat for us to sit side by side. The engine kicks over and Frances says, 'Hold on.'

I grab a small side rail curved at my hip and we take off up the driveway. The wind whips past us and we bounce off the dirt driveway onto the tar that ends just beyond our house, turn left, and roar past houses set far back from front fences. Frances eventually stops at a junction. 'This is the corner of Seventh Avenue, where we live, and Cooper Street,' her voice rises above the tinny idling engine. 'The bus stop is just there, see?' She gestures to a lone sign at the T-section. 'That's where you'll get the 7.15am bus from, and if you miss it you'll have to run up to Drayton Avenue and catch it on the way out.' *Bus? I have to catch a bus!* I swallow. The last bus I caught was a small school one. It stopped at our door and took us Giant Mine kids into Hartley. *How do I catch a city bus?* Tears gather and I wipe them away quickly.

'Oh, the wind makes my eyes water too,' Frances says, changing gears and we take off up Cooper Street and turn another corner. Above the noise and wind, I hear her say, 'This is Drayton Avenue, see, there's the other bus stop.' We pass another lone sign and bounce along the tar road, the wind rushing past us and snatching any chance of conversation. My eyes water even more. It's a long nine miles to the city.

'This is the City Hall, it takes up the whole block, the bus stop is just around that corner,' she says when we arrive and park. Magnificent gardens and manicured green lawns surround a large off-white building. Vendors line both sides of the pavement where we are parked and distract me from the 'bus' issue. I'm fascinated. Men showing off hand-crafted stone and wood carvings, call out to passersby. Women are sitting straight-backed among their crocheted doilies and huge bedspreads, their hands moving rapidly on their next item, all while chatting with one another. Other sellers hover over buckets of flowers, crowded together in a riot of colour. People wander the length of the block, browsing, selecting, bargaining, and buying under the shade of the tree-lined street. It's so *busy* compared to Rusape. But I don't say that!

We cross the street and move into the shade under a red and white sign, *Hassamal's—We Uniform the Nation*—and step through a large wooden doorway into a cool shop of dark polished wood floors with a matching counter that runs the width of the interior. An Indian man is behind the cash register, adults and children mill around waiting, whilst several Indian assistants hurry back and forth behind the counter, bending and reaching for items. Snippets of conversation reach me, 'Two shirts, three socks, shorts for Milton High, yes we have shoes…' The activity is overwhelming. This reminds me of the 'special shopping' trips we used to take to Salisbury years ago. I stand very still.

'Bevlee, come on it's our turn,' says Frances. I hurry forward and sit on a now-empty stool.

'Shoes, what size are you?' she says.

'Three.' A pair of lace brown shoes appear. I try them on. They are horrid, narrow-fitting, pointed, and they squish my toes. Grandpa would have bought me Clarkes shoes.

'They're fine,' says Frances. 'What do we need for summer—Eveline Girls High?' *So that's the name of the school I'm going to, now I remember Mum saying that.*

We leave clutching parcels containing the horrible shoes, three pairs of white socks, and two summer uniform dresses—insipid blue, a double collar in cream, front buttons, side zip, and waist skirt—ugly 1940s style. Sports skirt, shirt, swimming costume, and bathing cap. I hate sports. A 'boater' which we are told must be worn squarely on top of the head and not balanced on the back. And the final item: three pairs of thick, pale green, waist-high knickers. 'They're regulation', the Indian tells us!

Back at the scooter, Frances unlocks the rear doors and we put our parcels inside. She secures the lock and looks down at me. Her head tips sideways in thought and she says, 'I'm going to take you to Gordon's Supermarket, I want you to meet my dearest friend, Hester.' I follow her along the pavement, past the fragrant flowers in drums with a few bees flitting over them. Frances glances over her shoulder, 'I think we have earned an ice cream too!'

That's how I'm introduced to Eskimo Hut, a lone building with open serving windows under an awning that serves the *best* ice cream ever, on the northern edge of town, near the Trade Fair Grounds. We park in the shade and lick ice cream cones, fast, before they melt. And for a while, I concentrate on the drips and not on school.

***

Later in the week, Frances says, 'Bevlee, your washing is piling up. You need to do it.' *Do my washing? Mr Markee does that for us all.* I saw Lenid doing some this morning and hanging it out on the line. Mine's still in the washing basket that she's pointing at.

'There's Sunlight soap in the kitchen, put it back there when you're finished.' She walks away, leaving me staring at my pile of dirty washing in the bathroom. 'Oh and I think it would be a good idea to wash your school clothes too and get them all ironed this afternoon.' *Ironed?* I have to do that too; I don't know *how* to iron. Panic fills me.

I ask Lenid for the soap. He hands me the still-wet bar and shakes his head. In the bathroom, my dirty washing confronts me. I'm not sure how to do this. Slowly, I put the plug into the bath and turn the taps on. Frances is sewing in the sitting room. I can hear the steady sound of her old-fashioned Singer machine, with its manual handle. No wasting electricity here. Dad's sorting his stamps. I glance over my shoulder and Lenid is behind me, holding two buckets that he puts next to the bath, props a broom in the doorway, and kneels beside the bath. Quickly, he grabs the soap from my hand, rubs it on a dress, rubs some more, swishes, and moves on to the next item.

'Lenid, I'm supposed to do this,' I whisper. He glances sideways at me kneeling beside him and hands me the soap, nods and I follow his actions. The sewing machine stops. Lenid, with agility belying his age, is up and out of the bathroom, snatches the broom, and is sweeping the hallway by the time Frances appears. She looks down at me, 'Are you nearly done, I'm making some tea?' *Am I nearly done? No idea.* I nod my head. 'Well, hang it out and come and join us.'

Her uneven gait takes her towards the kitchen. Lenid stops sweeping, hurries towards me, pulls out the plug, and in a low voice says. 'Rinse now, do this.' He picks up my dress and vigorously twists it, squeezing out the dirty water and dropping it into a bucket. I watch him wring out each item as the dirty water swirls down the plug hole. He runs the rinse water into the bath. We work together, and soon I've got two buckets full of washed, rinsed, and wrung clothes.

Carrying the buckets, I walk past Frances in the kitchen, past drying sheets, and put my load down. Lenid's other washing is pegged out. I look at how he's done it and start to hang my rather wet clothes up. Lenid appears at my side carrying scraps of veggies in a pot destined for the compost heap at the far end of the backyard. Hidden behind the sheets, he wrings out my items, shakes them hard, and pegs them up.

'Thanks, Lenid,' I say quietly and he shakes his head from side to side again and mutters 'Eish miss! This my job, not for you!' And walks away carrying the veggie peels. My back's aching, my hands are sore and the ironing still has to be done. I don't understand why Lenid isn't allowed to do things for me too. Maybe I'm not part of this family, more like a boarder in the house. I hear Mum's voice, scathing, 'Oh for goodness sake, do your washing!' I'm so *alone*.

Later that afternoon, Lenid is ironing. I watch him. First, he dips his fingers into a large bowl of water, flicks it over the clothes, and rolls them up. I've seen Mr Markee do this. Soon he has a pile of rolled items on the counter and he grabs a school dress, flicks water, and rolls. I join him and soon I have my pile of rolled-up water-sprinkled clothes. He flicks water on the metal plate of the iron. It sizzles. He smiles at me and nods, unrolls Dad's shirt and runs the iron over it. Steam rises from the dampness, evaporates, and the wrinkles are gone. He continues for a few more garments and then beckons me to stand next to him and unrolls my school dress.

It's complicated, a skirt, and a shirt-like bodice with a double collar. The iron glides, steams and it's done and on a hanger. I watch. He hears a sound, moves adroitly aside, and thrusts the iron into my hand. I reach for a dress. Frances appears in the doorway, walks past me, and turns on the kettle. Lenid is now peeling vegetables for the evening meal. She glances at me and walks away. Lenid's soon back at my side, his hand covers mine that's holding the iron and pulls it upwards. I've nearly burnt my dress!

'Too slow,' he says and runs the hot iron quickly back and forth. 'You do.' And I do. But, at every chance he gets, Lenid irons for me. This cat-and-mouse game with Frances continues for years. I pick up my underwear and begin to fold it. Lenid shakes his head and takes it from my hands. 'Must iron! Bad flies make big sore.'

'Oh Lenid, I'd forgotten about Putzi fly, not good hey!' I recall having a sore on my arm long ago. Mum had put a plaster on it and one afternoon the plaster began to wiggle. I'd run screaming with fright through the house until Nanna stopped me, pulled the plaster off, and out popped a worm! 'There, the Putzi fly's gone now!' she'd said, 'Don't know how you got that, we iron all our clothes.' For years I didn't understand what she meant, but now I do. The fly lays eggs on clothing hung out to dry, and only the heat of ironing kills them.

***

Late on a Sunday afternoon, I see Lenid, Mai, and Beauty pass the side of the house on bicycles. Lenid has Beauty balancing on his carrier and Mai is proudly cycling behind him. It's Lenid's day off so they must have been to church. This is the first opportunity I've had to visit his family. I wait for a while and then wander to the far end of the acreage where two small houses hug the rear wire fence. John and his family live in one and Lenid's in the other. Mai has a fire burning and a huge black pot of water is heating. Beside it, John's wife, Charity, with her small son tied on her back, is stirring a bean stew. I watch Mai start adding powdery white mealie meal to the water in a black pot, while she stirs and stirs with a huge wooden spoon.

'I remember you from the farm,' I say to her. She grins at me, still stirring.

'Ah yah, picinin missis with bad dog!' I agree and we both laugh.

'You brought Beauty to see my Nanna.' When a baby was born, the mafazis from the compound would dress up in their Sunday best and gather together at our kitchen door to introduce Nanna to the new member of the community. It was a joyous occasion and I loved seeing them, so proud and happy. Nanna would greet them and always said how lovely the baby was. I thought all the babies were just too cute. Mai had come with her new little girl. Nanna had moved the shawl from the baby's face and exclaimed, 'Oh she's beautiful.' The name stuck and now Beauty is about seven years old, and still lovely.

Resting on my haunches, with the fire cracking, sadza in the pot, and beans simmering, I feel like I'm home on the farm. Familiar voices surround me and Beauty shows me her little doll and says she's learning to read at school. Mai's English is still not great, but we can easily talk together. She tells me that John, the garden boy, is from Malawi too, and that it's 'very good' because they have 'family' with them. I can't quite get how they are related, but it's not important. What *is* important is that they have like-minded people living with them.

Charity's very shy and I have trouble getting her to speak to me. Her baby boy, tied on her back is fast asleep, his curly little head lolling to one side. Mai tells me he's about nine months old.

When we were in Umtali last year, I recall Dad saying something about Lenid not being happy on the farm, and how he and Mai just didn't settle, even after all the years he'd been in Rhodesia and on the farm. Mai is a lot younger than Lenid and he had married her on a trip home to Malawi. That was when Dad asked them to come to Bulawayo with him. I decide I'll have to ask Dad about all of this again.

Mai points to the sadza. I take a small chunk, roll it hot between my fingers, and dip it into the stew. This is so good, but it's almost dark and I realise I've been there for hours. Frances is standing at the stove when I come in the back door. Without turning, she says, 'You're not to go down the back again like that!' I'm surprised and, without thinking, ask her why. She spins around and says, 'Because it's not acceptable behaviour! Don't let me see you down there again!'

I stand as if turned to stone. She's cross and I don't understand *why* at all. Mum's never said anything like this, but then again, we have been gone from the farm for years and Mr Markee is like family. We laugh and talk with him all the time. Occasionally he even gets cross with us kids and Mum would usually take his side.

Frances has turned her attention back to the stove. I've only been here a week and have made her angry a few times now, mainly because I keep forgetting to turn the lights off. I dare not ask why again. The pressure cooker begins to hiss and cuts off my thoughts. I glance at the stove. Three, three-cornered pots are clustered in a circle on one plate, simmering away. Another pot of rice is boiling and the pressure cooker's hissing louder now.

'Right, that's the sound, it's done,' Frances says. She lifts the heavy cooker and hurries to stand it in the kitchen sink. 'It's exploded on me a few times.' She nods towards a brown stain on the ceiling above the stove and giggles. 'Dennis had to get the ladder and clean it off! But, I've got it mastered now, no more stew on the ceiling.' She scoops rice onto a plate, hands it to me and then adds vegetables, including the dreaded cabbage, and beckons me to follow her. From the pressure cooker, she spoons out rich steaming and fragrant stew. I breathe it in. Cooking meals is also all new to me. Mr Markee serves ours in tureens on the table. How it gets into them has nothing to do with us. Her voice interrupts my thoughts as I hold the plate. 'We will drop you off tomorrow for school. This plate is your father's, take it to him.' As I turn she adds, 'You'll get the bus back after school.' As if in a dream I walk into the sitting room with my thoughts dashing wildly around.

Get a bus back! I'm terrified, my heart pounds in my chest, steam rises from the plate, tears threaten my eyes and I blink fast. I don't know *how* to catch a bus. Where's the bus stop to come back? How do I get there? The bicarb green cabbage smells awful. Panic grips me and my legs ache to race outside, and carry me up the huge avocado tree to hide amongst the hard green leaves.

Dad takes his plate, from my hands without a word. Back in the kitchen, the stew is now resting on two more plates. 'School finishes at 1pm and the bus goes at 1.15.' Frances says and takes her plate and I follow her. 'You'll have to walk fast because if you miss it the next one isn't until 5.15.' The plate is hot on my lap. Nanna would be horrified to see us eating on our laps. *Yes, Nanna, that's because Dad's got a jigsaw on the dining table.* Finally, I find my voice, it sounds strange, distant from me. 'Where's the bus stop?'

'Around the corner from the street sellers you saw the other day,' Frances says.

How do I find them? Can I find them? Cabbage! I want to be sick and can't speak.

***

Monday morning's light filters through the curtains. Today I start high school. I'm mute with fright. Dad's going to work this afternoon and the three of us drive into town, in silence. This I'm getting used to, the silence that is. But all the other rules are still rattling around in my brain. I've never had so many to remember. *Don't open the fridge without asking. Don't just help yourself to food. Don't sing in the bath. Don't leave lights on in empty rooms.* I've done that a few times. *Don't speak when the TV is on, especially during the news. Only wash your hair once a week. Do your own washing and ironing, apart from the sheets and towels. Polish your shoes, make your bed and dust your room.* But Lenid sneaked in on Saturday morning and made my bed. I could see he'd done it because the bottom sheet was nice and smooth but Frances pulled the top sheet back so I had to do it myself. When I was alone with Lenid I told him that Frances knew he had made my bed. He smiled, his weathered face scrunching up and there was a twinkle in his eyes. 'Next time she not know,' he said, 'I make not too good!' And we quietly laughed together.

So many rules. Dad and Frances are very different to Mum and Bill. There's no smoking in this house, not a drop of alcohol, no empty beer bottles in crates – that Sue and I used pinch to get deposit money and buy sweets—no going to the pub or club and no loud modern music on the record player. There's *none* of that. We go to church on Sunday nights and say grace at meals. Suddenly I snap back to reality.

The car has stopped. Frances turns, 'The school is a block back there,' she says pointing to her left. 'It's over the road, just cross at the robo (traffic lights) on the corner.' *Cross the road at a robo alone! I've never done that in my life, there are no robos in Rusape.* I blink rapidly sucking up tears. Frances and Dad are oblivious to my mounting panic. Dad points to his right and says, 'The bus stop is two blocks that way and then you just walk through the City Hall car park. The buses will all be lined up there. Look for the one marked Woodville.' My chest's tight. I don't know how to catch a city bus and I've never walked city streets on my own. What if I get lost? I got lost in Salisbury once with my friend, Sharon. Mum hit me when she finally found us. Panic rises in me and I manage to say, 'I don't know how to get there.'

'Just follow all the other girls. The buses park along the entire block, around the corner from the street sellers,' Frances says. 'Remember it goes at 1.15 and the next one isn't until 5.15—so walk fast.'

'Off you go,' Dad says.

'The fare is eleven pence. You've got a shilling. Make sure you bring the penny change home.'

'Yes, Frances,' I mumble and get out.

The car pulls away and I stand glued to the pavement. I think I'm going to throw up. If I do everyone everyone will think I'm stupid! Groups of girls dressed like me—with boaters balanced on the back of their heads—walk past laughing and chatting. I follow them with my boater on straight like I was told to wear it. As a group, we cross the scary wide road and walk through an open corner gate where girls wearing brown skirts with boaters squarely on their heads, are directing everyone up the steps and into the large red brick hall, with a huge portico flanked by two tall off-white pillars each side. They spot us Form One new girls easily and sit us in lines on the floor at the very front of the Hall. Behind me, the chatter of students rises as the Hall fills and eventually almost a thousand girls are seated. My stomach is turning over and over. So much noise and so many people. I feel ill.

Mrs Burke, the Headmistress, walks onto the stage, her back is straight like Nanna's. There's immediate silence and stillness. I can't concentrate. The Hall is enormous; teachers are seated on the stage and Mrs Burke is talking and talking and talking. I gaze at the high ceiling, the large polished wooden boards on the wall, with words in gold—I can't make out what they are all about. Out the large windows, I see trees nearby and wonder if they are good for climbing. My rising nausea settles as I watch the leaves. Suddenly there's movement behind me. Everyone is standing except for us new girls. Silently the older students file out.

One by one names are called out. These girls gather in groups and are escorted out of the hall in lines by older girls in brown skirts. 'Prefects,' a girl whispers near me, 'My sister said to look out for them! She's in Form Four.'

My name hasn't been called. The group is shrinking. Do they know I'm here? Nausea returns. *What do I do?* Voices are echoing now in the almost empty hall and finally, I hear my name, 'Beverley Walker.' My knees are stiff from sitting cross-legged for so long. I hurry to my feet. Just a few students remain. Fright sits on my shoulders as we troop out in single file towards an imposing arch of another red brick building behind the hall. So many girls, such large buildings and I still have to find my way to the bus stop. It's overwhelming. I mustn't cry.

And now there are more rules to learn. By 1pm I'm exhausted. All morning I've struggled to concentrate. My fear of getting to the bus stop and finding the bus has gotten worse with each passing hour. The final bell for the day rings and students rush from classrooms along the half-walled corridors and spill out through the main entrance. I hurry after them. Past the Hall, out the corner gate, across the road and suddenly I'm past where Dad dropped me off. Which way do I go? I'm fine in the bush, but here, with all this noise and clutter of bodies and cars, I'm lost. I panic and stop and gaze around. Frances's words, 'You'd better hurry,' echo in my mind. I quickly follow girls walking in the direction Dad pointed, along the pavement, across the wide road and through a busy car park… and there they are.

Huge metal buses line the entire block, with engines running. The noise fills my ears and I watch students jostle and climb up the metal stairs. They all know where they are going. *I don't.* I'm shaking with fear. My school case is heavy, and it's so hot. I hurry down the block, weaving between bodies and squinting at the signs above the bus windows. Suddenly at the far end, I see the sign I'm seeking. At the top of the steps I drop a shilling into the driver's hand and say, 'Woodville.' A brown penny lands in my palm and I slump into the nearest seat. My heart's pounding, the bus jerks and pulls away from the curb. *I just* made it. Above the roaring and rattling, I become aware of the voices behind me. I peep over my shoulder, past a few Africans. Some girls are clustered at the rear, their hats and suitcases lying on empty seats. They know each other well. I shrink down in my seat. The horrid shoes are pinching my toes and my heels are blistered and sore. '*They should have bought Clarkes!*' Grandpa says.

The bus jerks to a stop at Seventh Avenue. I get off and it roars away, trailing a dirty plume of diesel smoke, and from the back window faces look down at me. Slowly I walk the long straight street towards home and down the dirt driveway. Lady comes running to meet me and I crouch and rub her ears, just like I did with Noddy. I long for the farm, things would be so easy with Grandpa to help me. But he's gone. I straighten my shoulders, pick up my suitcase, already full of homework, and walk around to the rear of the house, through the back door, sit on the kitchen floor and begin to remove my shoes. I carefully peel off my socks and examine my raw heels.

Frances appears and looks down at me, 'Have you got the penny?' Her palm extends outwards. I stand up, reach into my pocket and place the change into her hand. 'Dennis is in the sitting room, I'll be there soon and you can tell us about your day.' She passes me a tea towel and I take my hot lunch plate from her. It's 2pm but I'm not hungry. Boiled cabbage lies limp beside peas, carrots, rice and stewed meat. I have to eat it all. I must be good.

In the sitting room Dad's in his favourite chair with a large brown cardboard box beside him—filled with stamp albums—drinking coffee. He puts his cup down and after a few minutes of questions asks, 'What stream are you in?'

I look up from the plate on my lap, 'Form 1D2.' The smile leaves his face. What is it I see there? Disappointment? I can't disappoint them. All week I've tried hard to do everything right so they will want me to stay.

'Did you say 1D2?' Frances asks.

'Yes.' I don't understand the look on their faces. We had all been chatting until now. I eat my lunch, take the plate to the kitchen, and stare out of the window. Beauty's playing way down the back, and Mai is digging in the veggie patch. Slowly a thought comes. There were only a few girls left in the hall. The last class I heard being called was 1E. I'm in 1D2, one stream before 1E, that's the last group, the *dumbest* group! I'm one stream up from the bottom! I'm dumb. Later that afternoon, just before Dad leaves for work, I'm about to walk into the sitting room when I hear his voice and stop.

'1D2! Her primary school reports were very average. I didn't think she was that stupid though.' I turn, hurry to my bedroom, and open my school case. We've been given two hours of homework, and it's only the first day. It's difficult to concentrate. I had better wash my uniform, and hang it on the line too, and not leave any unnecessary lights on tonight. I've disappointed them enough today. Now I'm going to bother Frances with my raw heels.

Lenid follows me out to the washing line, and I tell him I'm not allowed to visit again. He looks at me sadly, shakes his head, and mutters, 'Eeeish!' That sound says so much and I realise he understands why more than I do. I just don't get it! I wonder what Grandpa would say.

***

Every morning I'm up early to walk to the bus stop on Seventh Avenue. Frances loves her sleep and on several mornings has overslept, which means I do too. That's this morning, again, and I run out the door, through the bush to Drayton Avenue, hoping to catch the bus on its outbound trip. I dart over the road, puffing, red-faced, and drop my school case onto the ground. Has the bus been past already? There's no way to tell. A car pulls up beside me with its window winds down.

'I'm Mr Murray,' says the driver, 'You're Dennis's daughter, aren't you?'

'Yes.'

'We live over the road from you. Get in, you've missed the bus.' I hesitate and then see a girl in the back seat wearing the same uniform as me. 'This is Sheridan, another neighbour,' he says as I open the door. Sheridan looks me up and down and then gazes out the window. She's older and I'm intimidated by her immediately. No one speaks. This is another silent ride! We pull up at a side street that's unfamiliar to me. Sheridan opens her door, 'Thank you, Mr Murray,' she says.

I copy her, 'Thank you, Mr Murray.'

'I'll ask Mrs Murray to see Frances this afternoon. Be at our house by 7.15 and wait beside the car. See you in the morning.' I close the door, softly, and he drives off. Sheridan walks away. I follow her.

We are at the rear of the school and walk past the boarding hostels towards the main classroom blocks. She's still ignoring me.

That was how I got a lift to school for the next five years. A silent ride that I was very grateful for. There was no running up the street in the rain, missing the morning inbound bus or dashing through the bush to Drayton Avenue. For a monthly lottery ticket, Mr Murray puts up with us sleeping through alarms and pulls up at our front door hooting his horn. Frances would race out in her dressing gown, hair sticking up, to apologise. 'Mr Murray, so sorry we slept in!' I'd be out the door, hair half done, shoelaces trailing and clutching a peanut butter sandwich for morning tea with toothpaste still in my mouth. Sheridan would just look at me; bored. Mr Murray would say nothing, change gears and off we'd go. In the rear view mirror, I'd glimpse Frances, standing in the driveway, waving. Mr Murray's straight-faced demeanour never varied, just the tone of the car's hooter did. I like to think he was roaring with laughter on the inside! Sheridan never said more than 10 sentences to me in the few years we travelled together. I was in awe of her. She was so beautiful and confident. I think she saw me as a mouse.

***

I *love* school. It's a surprise to me. Life is structured, straightforward, and busy. For the first time in my life, I get to sit at the front of the class because it's not cool as it was in primary school. Now it's cool to sit at the back where they all think that the teachers can't see them passing notes, doodling in their books, whispering, and shuffling around on the hard seats. But what they don't realise is that's exactly where the teachers focus their attention, their eyes skim over us in the front rows. The front row is the place to be, for sure!

A whole new exciting world has become mine to explore. The information on the blackboard is easy to see. We hurry from classroom to classroom along wide half-walled corridors or almost run from the Home Economics Block to the Music Room and Science Labs. The library has more books than I've ever imagined, and the teachers answer my questions and the test marks in my books are the highest I've ever achieved. There are only two blights in my school life and both scare me.

Music is one of them. The teacher, Mrs Dawes, has purple hair piled high on her head which makes her look six feet tall. She's straight-backed, corseted and has ears that hear every instrument note or voice that's out of tune. She can also find the one girl miming—that's me—amongst 30-plus students. I only sound good with bathroom acoustics where I'm not allowed to sing anymore. The music sheets with all their lines and squiggles confuse me. Mrs Dawes scares me to death and I feel like vomiting as we hurry to her music room. On one occasion I almost threw up and was sent to 'sick bay' for observation. That was nice.

The other blight in my life is sport. The two sport teachers are young, recently graduated from Teachers College, fit, toned, and on a mission to get us all participating in sports. And they know all the tricks students get up to, because it was only about four years ago that they left school and have all the knowledge of how to 'get around teachers'. I decide this is not fair as they have insider information. But these ladies are not to be messed with. We are required to sign up for two afternoons of sport a week, which means I have to hang around until the 5.15pm bus and get home around 6pm. After a few weeks of trying to hit the tennis ball and missing dismally, failing at sprinting, and hovering at the edge of the swimming pool, and waiting around for the bus, I make a decision. With no money to spend, I quit. Not officially, of course, I just don't turn up to afternoon sport. I'm shocked to get away with it.

My sport report comments over the years read, *Beverley, tries hard when she attends.* They just accepted that I was a hopeless case who dutifully enrolled, turned up a few times, and then vanished. Later I realised there was an almost tacit agreement to overlook my non-attendance of afternoon sports, possibly because I was achieving high marks in every other subject.

But, I still had to suffer swimming during the morning school curriculum, and I dreaded stripping off and changing into a swimming costume. My response was to perfect the art of forgery and so I wrote my excuse notes. Anything from, *Please excuse Beverley as she has a cold, sore throat, periods* – which I never had –and sign it with Frances's cramped signature. I even make sure to fold the notes up and scrunch them into my pocket. They are never questioned. Girls with notes are sent to hit tennis balls against a wall. We don't bother and sit in the shade with our backs to the wall, and chat.

***

Where my school life is simple, my home life is not. Dad barely speaks to me when the three of us are sitting together. Rather, he talks directly to Frances and asks questions about me, as if I'm not there. When he leaves for work, he kisses Frances's cheek and says, 'Goodbye Mrs Walker.' It's a little joke between them and makes Frances smile, and then he walks out. There's no goodbye for me. However, if we meet in the hallway he will hug me briefly. Or if Frances is visiting the neighbour he will chat away until she returns. I'm baffled by this.

There are also the items in and on the polished dark timber sideboard that drew my attention in the first few days. A large crystal basket engraved with an unusual pattern, a white china fruit bowl with a green budgie in the centre, a cane basket with a centre handle holding six knives and a large dinner service behind the glass doors. One afternoon, when Dad passes me in the hallway, I see an opportunity. Frances is singing in the kitchen, busy cooking, and I say, 'Dad, that crystal basket has a pattern I've seen before.' He stares at it for a moment.

'I suppose you have, your mother has the matching lamp. Wedding gifts.'

I knew it!

'That budgie fruit bowl, the wooden one, and the dinner set down there behind the glass doors, are all from then too.' No one ever speaks about Mum and suddenly Dad is telling me all this. Frances is still singing. My silence prompts him and he continues, 'I've still got some photos too, from when your mother was a child. Have to find them one day for you.'

'Dad, why did you and Mum get a divorce?' Dad's lips do the same as Mum's did when I asked her.

'Ask your mother.' And with that, he walks away. I stare at him retreating. *I can't believe it!. Photos of my mother, here! I dare not ask where they are now. This is all very confusing.*

My attention returns to the sideboard. The bowls need dusting and the crystal one has screwdrivers lying in it. These I carefully remove and put them into the top drawer stuffed with more of Dad's tools and wipe away the dust. The afternoon sun comes through the window, touches the crystal and I imagine the lamp lit beside it. Beautiful! Why has Frances kept these things? She walks past this sideboard all the time, past The Past that no one talks openly about, past these undusted things. Dad sits at the table nearby doing his jigsaw and these bowls are beside him. I don't understand *at all*. I decide that I'll dust them from now on. And, I do that for years, and constantly remove Dad's tools from the crystal basket, each time, hoping it's not scratched.

Life settles into a pattern, and I try to adapt: don't leave a light on, don't just open the fridge—ask first, don't ask for money, don't talk when the TV shows are on—especially the news. Do my washing and ironing, only stay in my room if I'm reading or doing homework and sing properly at church on Sunday nights. That's the worst of it all. Sunday nights on a hard bench looking up at the minister in an almost empty church. At least no one asks me what the service is about, because I wouldn't know. If I can just manage all of these rules then everything might be alright, and they will let me stay.

Chapter 21
All Over a Penny and a Cent!

Monday at school has been great. Not only are the Easter holidays getting closer, but we also received our test results from the previous week. Dad and Frances will be so pleased, I'm *not* stupid after all! Sharply defined A's and B's sit at the top of my test papers—except for Music with a C minus!

In a few weeks, I'm catching the 9pm train to Salisbury where Dad says Mum will pick me up at 7.30am. I'm so excited, my feet are itching to leave, and the freedom of home will be mine soon. But for now, I want to show Dad and Frances my A's and B's. Dad will get up just after I get home—he's going to work around 3.30—I'll show them my results, together. I can't wait.

This is the best week *ever*, good marks and I'm going home too. I almost run to the bus stop. All the buses are idling, except ours. It's bonnet is open and two Africans in mechanic overalls are peering at the engine, shaking their heads while the driver is saying, 'No, get on!'

I retreat to the shade. The ice cream vendor, with his cart under the trees behind me, is ringing his bell. It's so enticing. I watch him. His cool box is open, cold air steaming, and he's selling penny cools to a crowd of school kid. It's hot and I'm thirsty. My blistered heels are throbbing. They haven't healed up all term and every day I put gauze and plasters on, and watery blood has stained my socks again today. I look down and wiggle my squashed toes. Two small, bare, black, feet are near my horrid shoes; the owner's toes are wiggling too. From the corner of my eye, I watch her, she's only about eight years old, scruffy, and all her attention is on my shoes. Shoes, I'd gladly take off right now and give her.

Her foot slides closer to mine. I don't move, so aware of how important shoes are to Africans. Some mornings, I watch children running down our street with their shoes strung around their necks, held by laces tied together. Their bare feet pound the hard tar and bush paths for miles to school, only then do they put their shoes on. How lucky I am to get a lift to school and wear my shoes—even though they are dreadful—and not have to run for miles. But maybe they are happier than me, are they? Her toes, with small chipped nails and cracked skin rest on my shoe tip. If only she knew how *sore* my heels are. The bus engine roars to life. We both jump.

'Money missis?' She begs, her cream upturned palm reaching towards me. I shake my head, climb the bus steps, buy my ticket and a brown penny drops into my palm. I glance back. She's staring up at me. The ice cream vendor's ringing his bell. I hesitate and then, on impulse, flip the coin into the air towards her. It spins over and over, mesmerising us both. Face alight, she leaps forward snatching it mid-air, turns and runs towards the cart, her bare soles flashing over the green grass. The bus pulls away, she waves—it's been a great day!

Frances is in the kitchen, the kettle's boiling as she hums away to herself. I sit on the floor, take off my shoes, and socks and peel away the plasters.

'Those blisters will heal over the holidays, but we will put plasters on when you come back to be safe.' She pours the milk—it's awful powdered milk that we make up with water in a jug every night—into Dad's coffee, and returns it to the old 1950s-style fridge. I wonder if it's been here since Mum's days too.

'I've got a surprise for you and Dad when he gets up!' I say intently examining my heels. Frances's feet are now beside me. The skin on her bent left shin is so dry, and her heels are cracked. They must be painful.

'Oh I like surprises,' she says. Her hand is stretched towards me. 'Change, Bevlee?'

The thought of the test papers with their A's and B's has pushed the penny change to the back of my mind. Without thinking, I smile at her and blurt out, 'I gave it to a picanin – she was begging.'

'What!' All trace of a smile is gone, her lips compress.

'Sorry, she was thirsty,' I say.

'Thirsty!' Her voice rises to a high pitch. 'More like you were and bought a penny cool!'

'No, honestly I *didn't*. I'm sorry, really, I didn't!' My words tumble over each other in the face of her anger.

'So you should be, wasting money! And don't lie to me either!' Hands clenched, she snaps, 'I can't stand liars!' Her words are clipped and sharp. I scoot backwards on my bum on the cold cement. Frances is *very* angry, I've not seen her like this before. I'm scared.

Lenid's shadow falls over me. I've scooted back so far that I'm blocking the back door. Lady is nudging my elbow.

'Medem?' His voice is deep and calm. I look up into his inscrutable face. Frances stares at him, blinks rapidly, turns and leaves the kitchen, her body is rigid with anger and heads towards their bedroom. Her uneven gait is more pronounced than usual as her bare feet slap on the parquetry flooring.

'Eeish.' Lenid's word gushes long and low between his teeth. His hand reaches out for mine, and I take it and allow him to pull me to my feet. *Lie? I didn't lie.* Grandpa always said to tell the truth. Mum says there are little white lies that don't hurt. It was a penny, it's not a lot of money is it? Grandpa used to give me pennies all the time and I kept them on a string threaded through their centre holes. He used to play a trick on me sometimes. 'Beverley, where's the rabbit?' He would ask, handing me a penny. I always knew the answer, but to play along I'd examine the penny hard before exclaiming, 'It's gone down the hole!' We would both laugh. It was a silly joke but a funny one. It's not working for me now.

I don't know what to do. Yes, Frances has been cross with me before over little things like leaving the lights on, not making my bed or doing my washing when she's told me to. But this anger is different and it's frightening. Quietly, I make my way towards my bedroom. The main bedroom door is open, I can hear Frances talking. I pause.

'Dennis, she lied. I'm telling you it's a lie. She didn't give a cent to a beggar. You know I can't stand liars.' She's still so angry and must have told Dad everything in a few moments.

'Calm down Frances, you shouldn't be upsetting yourself like this. Not now.'

'It's all that child's fault…' This is awful. I hurry into my bedroom and leave the door slightly open. My hands tremble as I take off my uniform and change. I decide that it's best to stay here and do some homework. I'm a bit envious of the kids running barefoot down the bush paths!

They have lunch without me. Good, I can't eat anyway. Dad will soon leave for work, so I decide to go into the sitting room while he's still home. Maybe he will understand. I'll act like everything is normal, show them my test results and hope that will help. Yes, that's what I'll do.

'Hi, Dad.' He doesn't look up from his stamps. 'I've got a surprise for you and Frances.' Neither of them acknowledge me. Did they not hear me?

'It's about school.' Silence. I watch them both. Yes, they've heard me. Gradually, I realise they are ignoring me. Neither of them is even looking at me. Frances has her body deliberately turned away. Dad's absorbed in his stamps. *Now what do I do?* Sit down and be ignored or retreat to my room. After a few moments, I turn, run through the kitchen, out the back door and around the corner to the large avocado tree. I scramble up onto a horizontal bough and sit amongst the leaves, trembling. No adult has *ever* behaved like this towards me. Mum shouted and hit me, Bill raised his voice and Grandpa was loving all the time, no matter *what* I did. All over a penny. The day is ruined now.

From my perch, I watch Mai digging their veggie patch. Beauty is chasing a ball around and John's watering fruit trees. My trembling stops. John's wife walks past, she's going out, with their baby tied to her back, and he's fast asleep. She smiles shyly up at me. Mai, Beauty and I chat easily but I make sure Frances doesn't see or hear us. I don't understand why I'm not supposed to visit them. On the farm I roamed down to the compound and talked to everybody. Mum did get cross when I smelt of smoke, but that was all. The car door slams and jars my thoughts. Dad is going to work. The engine turns, the car rolls past slowly and Dad can see me. He turns his face away. My eyes follow the car up the driveway. Small puffs of dust rise and then it turns onto the tar road. He's gone.

I'm alone with an angry Frances. So alone.

Dad ignores me until Wednesday afternoon. Frances only lasts until I get home on Tuesday afternoon and I sit on the kitchen floor to take off my shoes.

'What was the surprise from school you mentioned yesterday?' She asks. She loves to chat. My pride gets the better of me and after a moment, I say, 'Oh, in Assembly Mrs Burke announced that they are going to change the school uniform next year.' It's not a lie, because that did happen. It's just not what I was *going* to say. A white lie, as Mum would say.

'Oh no!' She's frowning now. 'I was hoping yours would last two years and then I'd sell them second-hand!' *Yes, I know, it's a waste of money.*

'But then again the way you're growing they probably wouldn't have. But they could have sold.'

'Yes, I think you're right,' I say and get up. 'Lunch looks good.'

Frances smiles at me. It's as if nothing had happened. It was nice to keep my marks to myself. The surprise was spoilt anyway.

***

On the 17th of February 1970, our currency will change from pounds, shillings and pence to dollars and cents. People are curious to see what the new money looks like, and how prices change, and all agree that doing the maths will be much easier.

The big discussion between Dad and Frances is over my bus fare! They decide, after doing all the calculations to do with rounding up and down the half cent, that it will be 10 cents. On the day of the changeover, the bus driver disagrees. He wants 11 cents. I argue with him. So every day, I pay 10 cents because that's all the money I have and he threatens to put me off the bus at Redman's Garage, a very long walk from home. Frances won't have any of it and says it's 10 cents and that's that.

I'm beside myself. With blistered heels, the walk from Redman's Garage will be torturous, hot and long. This standoff persists for a few weeks, and then one lunchtime, when I climb up the steps of the bus, Frances is sitting in one of the front seats. I recall that her scooter's in town for a service. The one-cent argument is on again. After a few moments, she opens her bag and calls out, 'Bevlee, here's another five cents.' The driver gives me the change and I drop it into her palm but don't sit next to her, as I normally would. Instead, I'm so angry that I walk past her and sit several seats away. She doesn't look back the entire trip and I walk down Seventh Avenue well behind her, go inside, and retreat to my room. I can hear her moving around in the kitchen. No singing. After a while she calls out, 'Bevlee, come and have a peanut butter sandwich.' And I do and we act like nothing happened. That's the sort of thing Mum does, act like nothing's happened when she's been mad.

***

Late March arrives and I'll be leaving in a week to go home to Mum. Home, where exactly is that? It's taken me almost three months to get used to this 'home' and the fact that every move I make is monitored. I feel stifled. For a while, it felt like Frances held the key to everything. Now after three months, I *know* it for sure. Dad defers to her on all issues concerning me. So far I've managed to follow most of the rules most of the time. But being in Form 1D2 was a huge disappointment to them. They think I'm stupid. Am I? I don't know. Nothing is connecting us. There's no common ground. I'm a child with no 'past' to talk about, and no memories that don't involve my mother. It's as if I'm a boarder.

The Saturday Lyons Maid's hits of the week have finished, and I leave my room. Dad's gone to work. Frances is sitting on the couch, listening to Jim Reeves and gazing out the window. She doesn't see me in the doorway. There's a faraway look on her face, like she's daydreaming. She's very still, hands resting in her lap. The window picture frames the bougainvillea-clad trellises along the driveway with their profusion of green leaves and red blooms. Everything is still. It reminds me of a photograph. Jim Reeves's smooth voice stops. The record player's arm lifts, glides back to its resting spot and the album slowly stops turning. Frances sighs, looks down into her lap, and then sees me. I feel guilty like I've intruded.

'Bevlee, you finished listening to the hits?'

'Yes.' I hesitate and glance out the window at the picture-framed blooms and a thought comes to me. 'Frances, would it be alright for me to see your wedding photos?' Her brown eyes look directly at me, the left eyelid that droops slightly is wide open now and thoughts show on her face that I don't recognise *Should I have said that? I'm sorry I did.*

Suddenly she shifts forward on the couch, gets to her feet and says, 'I think that's a lovely idea, come with me.' In their bedroom, she points to several drawers built into the bedframe. 'I'm sure they're in that one there, can you pull it open for me, I don't want to get down and sit on the floor.' I kneel on the parquetry flooring and pull the drawer open. Frances has been into these drawers before, I've seen her sitting on the floor with her stiff leg in front of her and she's able to lean over sideways and pull them open. This one is heavy so I guess that's why she's asked me to do this. She perches on the edge of the bed and peers down.

'There it is, under that big brown envelope, bring it with you,' She gets up and leaves the room. I lift the book, there's a wide slender box underneath it. The lid, broken at the corners, has moved. I glance over my shoulder, lift the lid and read, *Our Wedding* in gold script on a patterned cream background. I open it. This is the album Dad was talking about! Mum's in a wedding dress standing with a much younger Dad. I flip another page. Oh, Grandpa's looking at me, Mum's standing next to him, smiling. I drop the cover, replace the lid, and scramble to my feet. I shouldn't have done that. My face feels hot when I walk into the sitting room and my hands shake slightly as I pass her their *Wedding Album*. I won't ask Frances the question that neither parent will answer.

'We haven't had this out for a few years now,' she says softly. I sit next to her, our shoulders almost touching. She flips the pages and there she is in a black and white photo, smiling, looking like a doll, wearing a wide gathered skirt, gloves, and a short veil held in place with a tiara, and surrounded by little flower girls. Her forefinger, its nail bitten short, traces over the photo. I'm concentrating on the little girls, one of whom could have been me. A small curl of something twists inside me. It's not envy, more sadness. They had a wedding with little girls.

'The flower girls were all from St Gabriel's, that's where I worked,' she says, 'I can still recall all their names, such a shame most of their parents never came to visit them.' Her face is thoughtful, 'We used to bring these girls here for weekends sometimes.' Her finger traces over the photo and she shakes her head, 'But it was too sad taking them back to the orphanage afterwards. Some cried.' *Orphanage! St Gabriel's is an orphanage!* The curl inside me runs away.

'You know parents occasionally turned up when the children were 16 or so and about to start working. They only wanted them back to get their wages from them.' She flips the page and leaves that sadness behind. Now here is Dad smiling, standing next to her. He still looks the same. I think he's handsome in his suit, he's handsome in the other suit too with Mum, only younger and thinner. There are family photos with Grandad and Granny Wright and Frances points to her brothers and sister.

'Where's Dad's family?' Frances laughs, it's not the happy one she usually has, rather it's slightly sarcastic. 'Oh just ask your father about that! He will say, "Do you know it's further from Ladysmith to

Bulawayo than it is from Bulawayo to Ladysmith!" None of his family has ever come up here to Rhodesia to visit him.' The pages turn and there they are at the beach with waves breaking around their ankles. Dad has his arm around her waist and they're laughing.

'We went to visit his family at Ladysmith on our way to Durban as part of our honeymoon,' she says. 'This is at the beach there.' I recognise the beach. 'A photographer followed us around and took these lovely photos.' She draws out the word lovely.

Yes, photographers followed Mum and me on Durban's beach too and we have some great photos. But I mustn't say that. 'I remember Dad taking me to South Africa twice. We stayed with Uncle Duncan, Auntie Shelia and Cindy in Ladysmith and visited Granny in Durban.'

Frances glances up at me, 'If we go again, I'll see if you can come with us.' For a moment I'm excited but realise that it will mean I don't visit Mum. I don't want to miss going home to Mum. But, Frances is chatting about the photos and doesn't see the worry on my face. She closes the album and turns to me, 'How about we make some lunch and then finish sewing the dress you've been working on?'

'And can we have apples and custard tonight?' I ask. She smiles at me. This is our favourite dessert. I'm slowly getting to know Frances.

Dad's not as easy, but if I sit next to him with my collection of stamps, he will talk for hours and hours about stamps while we soak the paper off the back of used ones, chat about the new releases and all things 'stamp-related'. Some of the albums are old and have Mum's distinctive handwriting heading the pages. Pity I can't ask Mum if she liked doing the writing. It's beautiful, like her. Dad prefers to type the headings on an old typewriter.

Thank goodness I like sewing, even if the manual sewing machine drives me crazy. I never say a word about the high-end electric one Mum has, or how she upgrades it regularly or that tacking is something I left behind years ago. I just do as I'm told.

Chapter 22
I Don't Want to Go On the Bus Trip.

They are waiting for me at Salisbury station. The train pulls in and I spot them from a distance—Mum's roller-set blonde hair, it's longer than when I left—Susan is swinging Bill's hand back and forth and I wave like mad out of the window. Mum waves back. She looks as excited as I am. My heart is racing and as the train stops I hurry down the steps and throw myself at her. She hugs me briefly and then holds me away, 'Goodness, Beverley you've grown and put on weight!'

'Too much apples and custard!' I say laughing, and the smile leaves her face. *So stupid, that's what I am. Don't talk about Bulawayo!*

Susan's pulling on Bill's arm, 'I want to go. You promised milkshakes!' She darts away as I try to hug her. 'You can't catch me,' she sings and ducks behind Bill who's trying to walk towards the guard's van.

A few hours later, filled with milkshakes, tea and cake we start the drive home to Rusape—it's funny how no one mentions petrol rationing here. Lyons Maid's Number 1 for the week, 'Raindrops Keep Falling on My Head,' soars above the engine. Mum and Bill are smoking, flicking ash out the window that blows into the backseat. Susan is trying to tickle me and I feel like hanging my head out and singing at the top of my voice. Instead, I wiggle in my seat and hum along to the radio with a sense of total freedom. The green bundu blurs past as the car chews up the miles of tar simmering before us.

Bill parks under the jacaranda tree, all the blooms are gone, and the branches are thick with fine green fronds that will soon turn yellow and scatter over the yard. Mr Markee has my suitcase out of the boot and is grinning at me and I laugh. He's got two fake gold front teeth today.

He hardly *ever* grins like that; it's his special welcome home for me.

I'm surprised when Mum starts unpacking my suitcase, Mr Markee usually does that, and she's putting everything into piles, dresses, skirts, tops, shorts, and nothing is going into the drawers.

'What have you got these for?' She asks waving a handful of wooden coat hangers in my face labelled, *Walker* in black. Frances had added them with strict instructions to 'bring them back'. *What do I say?*

'I thought I may need them…'

'For goodness sake, we have coat hangers here too you know!' Mum tosses them aside and I snatch them up.

'I have to take them back.'

'She put them in there, didn't she?' Mum laughs. This is so confusing. It's fine for Mum to mention the other house, but not me? She's in a good mood and I don't want to make her angry. So I laugh, 'Yes.' I don't like poking fun at Frances because she did help me pack. Shoved in the corner of the almost empty case are the awful unspoken 'necessary items': sanitary pads. Quickly I pick them up.

'I haven't needed these yet.' Mum doesn't like this subject. She picks up a dress. 'This is new,' she says examining it. 'No zig-zagging. Goodness, you've turned every raw edge, so much work!' There's no way am I saying anything about the old hand-turned sewing machine Frances has with no zig-zag or buttonhole features. Mum prides herself on having high-quality sewing machines and she will laugh herself to death if I describe the one I used. Or she might say something horrible. I'm not sure. We enjoyed making this dress, choosing the material and pattern, cutting it out and finally modelling it when it was finished. Even Dad said it was nice.

'Oh Mum, sewing at school is driving me nuts!' She looks up from the dress and raises her eyebrow. I hurry on, 'They make us pin, tact, and press everything. It's so boring.' I roll my eyes towards the ceiling. Mum starts to laugh, 'So silly when you know how to sew. Everything is clean I see,' she says, and starts putting items back into the suitcase. 'I've got something so exciting to tell you!' Packing, holiday, are we going on a family holiday? Why didn't Susan spill about it? She can't keep secrets. *Ever!*

'We're going on a holiday!' I say almost hopping from one foot to the other, 'Beira?'

'No, to Durban.' I throw my arms around her waist. It's so slender, and I hug her. Her hands flutter over my back, Youth Dew fragrance envelops me and it's all so wonderful. I'm *home* and going on *holiday.*

'It's with the Lions Club, on a bus, all the way to Durban and back. Three weeks. You'll stop along the way at towns and stay with Lions Club members, or camp. It's going to be so much fun.' I step away from her. *You.* The word hangs in my mind. *You.* Mum looks away, 'There are about 30 kids and a few adults to look after you all. Best of all, Antoinette is going too!'

My body is rigid, and my tears wobble like an over-full cup of water, just before it spills.

'But, I just got here.' Tears fall slowly. 'I haven't been home for months. I've missed you so much!' I lean forward, perfume lingers between us. Mum steps back.

'Oh, don't start that now.' She says smoothing her dress. 'You'll have a great time. It will be fun. 'Just then the sound of breaking china reaches us. Susan's shouting, Mr Markee's voice joins hers. Mum hurries from the room. Their voices echo down the hallway. Susan's been annoying Mr Markee again in the kitchen. Mum's angry, shouting. Bill hurries to join them. Bill says what we are all used to hearing, 'Norma, don't smack the child. You'll break her spirit!' And I know what Mum will say, *spirit, break her spirit! Never.* But it was alright for me to be smacked with hairbrushes, wooden spoons, and coat hangers. Maybe I needed *more* spirit? Mum takes a lot more notice of Bill. I wonder if she's a bit afraid of him. She only smacks Susan if he's out.

The Lions Club bus tour leaves early the next morning. Everyone's excited. Except me. My eyes are red-rimmed, sore and my head is aching. Antoinette grabs my hand, pulls me onto the bus, and doesn't comment, but the look on her face tells me she understands. She's been at boarding school. If I look out the window I know I'll cry, so I push Antoinette into the seat first and she hangs out the window and waves goodbye.

Mum was right. The excitement of all the children is contagious and after a few hours the anxiety of leaving seeps away. By Day Two things are really fun. The bus is old and noisy. The adults are funny, not strict or shouting at us to behave. We sing songs, eat chips and stop at Lions Clubs along the way, where people fuss over us. We sleep in large halls, in tents and park chalets. And laugh a lot. The bus breaks down at regular intervals causing the adults stress that they don't show us. Some nights we arrive late at our stop and are greeted by smiling faces and warm food. It's freezing in some towns.

In Durban, we go to North Beach and I point out the building where my Granny lives and say I haven't seen her for six years. One of the chaperones decides to see if Granny's home. She is and when she opens the door, I say, 'Granny, it's me, Beverley.' Her eyes grow huge and she pulls me into her ample bust and hugs me hard. 'Oh Beverley, Beverley,' she says over and over again. 'This is such a surprise! Denny didn't tell me you were coming to visit.' She looks past me, 'Where's he? Frances?'

'I'm not with them…' A voice behind me says, 'I'm Janet, from the Lions Club in Rusape. We've brought a group of children on a trip to South Africa. Beverley pointed out your building and we thought it would be nice for you to see her. So here we are!'

'Denny didn't mention this to me. I spoke to him last week. He said Beverley was going to Norma's for the holidays.' Janet is smiling but there's a tension in her body and I realise that Dad doesn't know I'm here. Mum didn't *tell* him. Now, he thinks I'm in Rusape. I shouldn't be in South Africa *or* at Granny's. Is the Lions Club in trouble too?

Granny asks us in and we visit for a while. She asks how Mum is, and talks about Dad and Frances, and I feel free to chat about both families. I even tell her about how bratty Susan is but that I do love her. And too soon we are at the door.

'Granny…' I'm worried. She takes my hand. 'Remember when you and Norma visited, you were about six years old?' I nod. 'That was a wonderful surprise too. Maybe we should just keep this special time to ourselves, for now. Give my love to your mother. She can talk to Denny first.' Her gaze rests on Janet and I feel her relax. Mum's going to be so cross.

The three weeks go so fast. Crowds are waiting for the bus and Mum's there with Aunty Lilly. Antoinette and I rush towards them, our words tumbling out about what a great time we had and all the places we went to. We wander towards the cars, dragging our suitcases. All around, people are hugging, laughing, opening cars doors, engines start and dust puffs as people drive away.

'See, I told you you'd have a super time!'

'We did, Mum.' For the last few days, I've been thinking of when to tell her about Granny. It has to be now before we get home to Bill and Susan. Aunty Lilly's asking Ant all about the trip and I blurt out, 'And guess what Mum, I saw Granny in Durban. She sends her love.' Mum's happy face is suddenly gone. But with everyone around us, Aunty Lilly chatting and Ant standing next to me, she doesn't say anything. But she's angry.

'Granny said it was about six years ago we were last there. I remember that. Granny says the visits are special to her.' Mum half smiles and her features soften. 'I love her,' she says quietly, 'I'm sure she was surprised, and even recognised you.' Her fingers tremble as she lights a cigarette, inhales deeply and exhales. 'Come on, let's go home.' I wonder what she will say to Dad.

***

It's Saturday, an April afternoon, and Bill's waiting for us in the car. Susan's gathering up stuffed toys to take with her on the trip to Salisbury. I'm in my room, crying. It's empty of me already. I didn't even get a chance to put out the special things that I packed away on top of the cupboard.

'Stop this nonsense right now!' Mum says from the doorway.

'Come on Bill's waiting for us.' But I can't. It's the same as when I left in January. The thought of leaving reduced me to tears days ago. Mum's had enough. I rush towards her, seeking her arms. She holds me away.

'This needs to stop. Go and get in the car.' She turns and walks down the hallway. 'At least we are not going to Anne's. She commented on your miserable face last time we were there.' I follow her, stepping deliberately on the squeaky floorboard, out into the cool air and over the falling jacaranda leaves.

Salisbury station is cold tonight and I shiver. Mum hurries me into a first-class compartment and tells the three ladies already there my father will be waiting for me in Bulawayo. With a brief hug and kiss, she's gone, down the corridor, down the steps and onto the platform where Bill and Susan are waving at me. I hang out the window. A whistle sounds, the train jerks and massive wheels turn, turn, and turn, gathering speed, taking me further and further away until the station is a speck in the distance. It's the top bunk for me tonight.

***

At Bulawayo Station, early morning shadows darken the platform, and Dad and Frances are waiting for me. We drive home through the Sunday quiet city streets, through the suburbs, through the bundu stretch of road, over the Umgusa Bridge and take the right turn off to Woodville. This is all so familiar to me now, but not the chatting between Dad and Frances. Normally we drive in silence. It's relaxing to listen to them. Frances giggles a few times and I gaze out of the window enjoying the atmosphere. Lady rushes out the backdoor, her long tan tail slapping our legs, and Dad carries my suitcase inside. Lenid's gone to church. Frances follows us into my room and perches on the edge of my bed.

'Mrs Walker. Coffee!' says Dad. Frances smiles at him and doesn't get up. 'I'm going to sit here for a minute, with Bevlee.' I'm kneeling on the floor with the case open and look up at Dad. He's going to demand his coffee again for sure. He doesn't. He's smiling, turns and walks away. I watch his uneven retreating gait and am surprised. *Coffee, now* is what he should be saying!

'Did you do any sewing during the holidays?'

'No, there wasn't much time,' I say piling the freshly Mr Markee-washed and pressed clothes (I'm going to miss him) on the bed beside her with the coat hangers.

'No time?' She picks up the coat hangers. 'These aren't the ones I sent with you. Yours had *Walker* written on them.' She glares at the offending items. 'I told you to bring them back.' Between going on the bus trip and then having to leave home again, I'd forgotten all about the *Walker* hangers. Mr Markee's used them. *What am I going to say?* She's waiting and frowning.

'I'm sorry, must have picked these up by mistake. I'll look for them next holiday.' Frances is not happy. She was until now. I've ruined it. Dad will be told, and he won't talk to me for days, again. Suddenly she sighs, shifts forward on the bed and stands up. 'Oh it's alright, I suppose it's not easy for you to pack up all your clothes and things when you're not used to it.'

Relief washes over me and I get up from the floor. Frances smiles at me. 'Let's have some morning tea and toast, you must be hungry,' she says and leaves the room, humming softly to herself. I've been let off the hook! Everyone seems to be *too* happy. It's rather strange. But they don't know I've been on a bus trip. I don't want to ruin it. Hopefully, Mum will call and say something soon.

The sitting room smells of toast, coffee and tea and the sun's casting light over the polished parquetry floor. Dad puts down his coffee and sits back in his chair. 'Beverley, your mother called me at work yesterday.' Frances looks over the rim of her cup at him, her lips compressed and it's obvious she doesn't know. Dad was on night shift so he's had no time to tell her. He lifts a stamp book from the box beside his chair and rests it on his lap.

'She informed me that you went to Durban with the Lions Club.

On a bus trip for three weeks.' Frances's eyes widen, even the lazy eyelid. Dad opens his stamp book. 'I informed her that in future we are to be asked beforehand. Not told *after* the event.' *Is that because you have custody of me?* His voice is flat and emotionless and his face is white. Is it from anger or tiredness? I don't know. His cup rattles in the saucer as he lifts it. It's empty. If Frances wasn't sitting here, I'd ask him the divorce question that's plaguing me.

'Coffee, Mrs Walker.' Frances gets up, retrieves his cup and walks towards the kitchen. 'You saw Granny too, I'm told.' This is my opening. 'Yes, she was so happy to see me. One of the Lions ladies took me there. I remembered the building. It was super to see her, she was almost crying and hugging me...' I must stop babbling, right now. Dad's features soften, his lips quiver, 'I'm sure she was pleased to see you.'

'So you enjoyed the trip?' Frances says as she comes back with a steaming cup of coffee.

'Yes, it was fun.' I cough a few times; my throat is scratchy.

'I hope you're not getting sick. Dennis, are you going to have a sleep just now?' Dad nods his head, turns a page in the stamp book and reaches for his coffee. Frances's lips decompress and she starts to hum. I wonder if we will have apples and custard tonight. Maybe I shouldn't have too much and try to lose some weight.

On Monday morning, the first day of Term Two, we oversleep. I dash out the door wearing the winter uniform that includes disgusting thick stockings secured to a suspender belt. It's useless for warmth as the morning wind whips up my skirt raising goose bumps on my thighs, and I hurry over the road hoping that Mr Murray will not be in his car, waiting. He's not. My head is aching and my throat's sore. I'm getting sick. Frances will not be pleased. Between this, the coat hangers and the trip to South Africa it hasn't been a great start to my return.

Chapter 23
I'm Not Dumb After All And There's A Baby.

Term Two starts in the same way Term One ended, with morning Roll Call in our form room where 30 girls are banging desk lids, laughing and talking. Our Form Mistress arrives and there's immediate silence.

She opens the Roll. Calls out our names and gets to me.

'Beverley Walker?'

'Here.'

'Mrs Burke wants to see you in her office, now.'

'*Woooh!* You're in trouble,' filters from the back of the room. Mrs Renehan shifts her gaze towards the voices and they fall silent. But I can hear them shuffling in their seats and imagine quick notes being scribbled and passed.

'Off you go.'

My chair scrapes back, it sounds so loud on the wooden floor, and I'm trembling. *What have I done wrong?* Thoughts whirl through my mind. All my work was handed in on time, with no days off, no detention, or late arrivals. Fear grips me. I take the path across the quadrangle, staying off the lawn, and hesitate on the open verandah outside the office. Girls who are sent here usually return with red eyes and quivering grins. The school secretary spots me and beckons, 'Come in Beverley.' Goodness, I hate my full name, it makes me feel like I'm in trouble all the time. 'Mrs Burke and Mrs Watson are waiting for you. Just knock and go in.'

Mrs Watson, the Deputy Head, is also here! I must *really* be in trouble. For a brief moment I feel like running out of the office and over the lawns. But to *where?* The office door is large. I knock, its polished brass handle's cold beneath my fingers and there they are, seated, talking. They fall quiet as I walk towards them. Mrs Burke is ramrod straight in her chair, her large bust and ample hips sort of remind me of Nanna. Mrs Watson is lean and straight-backed, and they both scare me.

'Sit down, Beverley,' says Mrs Burke and points to a chair across from her desk. Sunlight filters through the window, small dust motes are floating about and I feel like I'm not here. Papers shuffle. 'Your end-of-term test results were excellent,' Mrs Burke says looking up at me. Mrs Watson nods her head in agreement. 'Your primary school reports did not indicate the potential you've now shown.' My heart is hammering.

'Mrs Watson and I have discussed this,' she says tilting her head towards her Deputy, who continues. 'We have one issue.' *What's wrong now?* 'As you've not studied French, and considering the catch-up work required, you will not be moved to the A stream, but to 1B1.' Mrs Watson hands me an envelope and says, 'This letter is for your parents to explain our decision.' My fingers tremble as they tighten on the edge of the envelope, and I can't believe what they've just told me. I'm *not* in trouble.

'Collect your belongings and go to Mrs Walker's form room. She's waiting for you and will give you your new timetable,' says Mrs Burke. It's over. The dust moats float silently. My legs won't move.

'Off you go now,' I hear. And I do. Out of the office, walking fast as there's no running allowed, across the quadrangle and into my empty form room. My footsteps almost tap dance with joy. Quickly, I gather my books, hurry back across the quadrangle and stop in the doorway of Mrs Walker's form room, out of breath. She smiles and points to a front-row desk. I feel awkward, we share the same surname, and she's a young, popular, teacher; everyone likes her! Now I'm in her form room and History Class. This is the best day *ever!*

I'm almost home from the bus stop, clutching my wonderful news close when Steyn's vicious large brown dog rushes snarling out of their yard towards me. The damn gate is open again! The dog terrifies me and we usually engage in a dance of my suitcase between him and my legs to the tune of my shrieks. Today, I've had enough of it and yell, 'Voetsak! Voetsak!' The dog stops in its tracks, as surprised as me. I stamp my feet and lunge forward swinging my suitcase and shout, 'Voetsak, voetsak, voetsak.' The dog retreats. 'You're ugly!' I shriek and start to giggle. That showed him.

It's Dad's day off. He will be seated in his favourite chair, surrounded by stamps, drinking coffee and I can't *wait* to give him the letter. I hurry inside and stop in the sitting room doorway, face flushed and breathless. Frances looks up at me, 'Goodness Bevlee, did that dog chase you again?' She shifts forward in her seat. 'If it did, I'm going down there to tell them to keep that gate shut!'

'Yes, it did. But I've got a letter from Mrs Burke for you,' I blurt out. Dad frowns and takes the letter from my hand. Frances stiffens. He tears it open and reads, slowly, then passes it to Frances. Her head is bent, lips moving silently as she reads the words, and over her head, Dad's eyes meet mine. Pride, that's what I see. He's *proud* of me. His lips twitch, he clears his throat and waits for Frances to finish. The letter drops into her lap. 'Well, I never! Bevlee, this is wonderful!' She shifts forward, stands up awkwardly, her left leg impeding her, and hurries towards me smiling broadly and pulls me into her arms. She's never hugged me before. Quickly she lets go. 'Lovely news, isn't it Dennis? I think we should have custard and apples tonight! Everything's so good now.'

Dad chuckles, 'Sounds excellent to me, Mrs Walker.'

'I even told Mr Steyn's dog to "voetsak" too. And it did!' We all laugh.

That night Dad and I pass in the hallway. His arms close around me, gathering me close to his chest and he hugs me hard. Frances is singing in the kitchen. I've got something *right* at last.

***

Form 1B1 is the best. I make a few friends and the popular girls fade into the background of my life. The bus ride home is still lonely. I sit at the front and all the Woodville kids socialise at the back. They know each other from attending the small primary school just behind our house. I want to join them but I'm so shy. Instead, I sit with a book open and study. We get at least two hours of homework every day, and often more.

A few weeks go by and I'm managing to keep up with all the house rules, when Dad appears one afternoon in my bedroom doorway. I'm surprised.

'Come to the sitting room, we want to talk to you,' he says, and turns away quickly. They're seated on the lounge together, side by side. Dad always sits in *his* armchair. I hover in the doorway and Dad nods for me to sit down. There's tension in the room, nausea instantly rises in me. Are they going to send me away to boarding school? I can't go back to Rusape. My fingernail slips between my teeth and I chew on it.

'Beverley, we have something to tell you,' says Dad. *He's holding her hand!* Yes, they are sending me away for sure. Frances controls things around the house, but Dad's talking to me now!

'There's going to be a baby in October.' They're both smiling, looking at each other in the way adults do, but I've not seen them do. Now they're looking at me. A baby! *Their* baby. There are only two bedrooms in the house. I wait for Dad to say more, but he's just watching me. Yes, they will send me away now for sure. My face is red, I don't know what to say. Mum had muttered once to Bill *they've only taken her because they have no children*. Their eyes are on me. Am I supposed to be excited? *Am I?* It's such a shock. Thoughts tumble in my mind of Susan and how it was before she was born, and how it is now. Bill doesn't want me there because we fight and I'm always in the wrong according to him. *I have to say something. But what?*

'OK, October,' is all I can mumble. Frances shifts forward and leans towards me. She's dropped Dad's hand. 'Just think, you will be a big sister and how lovely that will be.' She extends out the word 'lovely' and it sounds soothing. I look into her dark eyes. Mum's are light brown.

These eyes are soft as they watch me intently. Now I understand all the humming, dreamy looks and everything else. How dumb have I been not to see this coming? Over the years I've perfected the art of reading what adults are saying or not saying, their gestures, looks, and body movements. Living with different generations has given me a sixth sense of many situations. But this, I missed. I hear Frances, her voice sounds far away from me. 'We can sew baby clothes together and talk about names.' I nod my head and smile at her. Dad moves, gets up and limps towards his chair.

'Coffee, Mrs Walker.'

'I'll make it,' I say and hurry to the kitchen. Their muffled voices reach me before the boiling kettle obliterates them. They sound happy. The coffee aroma floats, I sigh, carry the cup to Dad and then retreat to my bedroom.

Baby, baby, the word rolls around in my mind and I reach for a book to read. I can't concentrate, and after a while give up and stare at the ceiling. Paint's peeling in the corner where a spider web hangs, and a large Daddy Long Legs is crouched there, oblivious of its dire circumstances if Lenid sees it and grabs his feather duster. Maybe he won't and it will stay in its home. Will I stay in this house? It's not my home, is it? Susan was born just over six years ago. I do the maths. I'll be almost 13 when this one arrives. I do love Susan, even though we fight like mad. She's my sister. I'm going to be a sister *again*. A small bubble of happiness rises in me, but behind it looms a larger one of how things are in Rusape with Bill and Susan. Will Frances be like him and want me gone when she has her baby? The spider has moved. This is all too difficult. I can't reconcile how I feel or don't feel. Anyway, there's another mystery to all of this. Where do babies come from? The hushed voices of new mothers say scary things like, 'Never doing that again,' and 'No one said it was that dreadful'. But they do have more babies. How does that even begin? The baby that is? It's all very confusing. Maybe I'll just read my book now. Be careful spider. Be *extra* good Bevlee. There are only two bedrooms.

***

A few days later I find Dad sitting at the far end of the dining room table with a large expanse of paper before him that's fighting for room with his partially done jigsaw.

'Beverley, come over here.' I squeeze past the high-backed chairs and stand beside him.

'Look, this is what I'm going to build,' he points to a drawing. 'See here, taking this wall down, putting up new ones along here and here…' His fingers move quickly over the paper; his voice is animated. 'This will be the new sitting room, and we'll have a larger kitchen. I'll make all the cupboards.' He looks up at me with a grin and sees my astonished face. 'I used to be a carpenter builder, remember? I put the toilet and bath into the farm.'

'Yes and Great Gran shouted the whole time!' We both laugh. I haven't seen Dad this animated for a long time. The last time was when I was with him in Durban.

'Here's another bedroom, it's going to be large with a built-in wardrobe. We have decided that will be yours and the smaller one will be for the baby.' *Mine! So I can stay, for sure? You wouldn't give me a new bedroom if I was going away. Would you?* Dad's so intent on his drawings he doesn't see my gathering tears. I blink rapidly and sniff.

'You two can sort out the colour I have to paint it.' He pretends to be angry but I can see he's so pleased.

'Will you do the baby's room too? The paint's peeling in the corner.'

'Is it? Well, we better get to that before October!' I wrap my arms around myself, lean forward, examine Dad's house plans and listen to him talking away. It's the most he's said to me since I arrived here—apart from talk about stamps. Frances is next door. Spider; you're evicted.

***

The winter school holidays are almost here. Friday night, it's drafty and dark at Bulawayo Station and I hang out the window to wave goodbye.

The past few weeks have been busy. Dad has demolished walls, covering us all in dust, and built new ones with John's help. Frances has been sewing baby clothes and talking about names. I've been allowed two budgies, one blue and one green—Rufty and Tufty—in a new second-hand cage. I think they're a concession because of the baby, to make me feel happy. But, it wasn't necessary. I'm happy about the baby, now.

The train jerks, its massive wheels turn, steam billows and slowly we depart and as it accelerates, my spirits lift. The confines of my Bulawayo life melt away with the receding city lights and darkness takes hold over the bundu, disturbed only by the click-clacking of wheels on the tracks. I'm liberated and yearn to hang my head out the window and sing loudly like I used to when Grandpa drove me home from school. It seems long ago now. I miss him so much.

Chapter 24
Susan Says Bad Things.

I hang out the window waving as the carriage glides past Mum. She sees me, waves and smiles. She looks beautiful, even glamorous, in high heels, with set blonde hair. Or is it that Frances is so plain, but pretty in her unassuming way? My feet fumble down the carriage steps and I race through the crowds and morning shadows on the platform and throw myself at her. Panache, I breathe in Panache, and Mum's mine for a few seconds. She lets me go and laughs. 'Goodness Beverley, you nearly knocked me over! Have you put on weight?'

I can't take my eyes off her. I've missed her so much and long to stay in her arms, that it takes a few moments for me to realise she's saying I'm fat, again. But I'm *not* fat! Bill and Susan appear. My excitement at seeing them again overtakes me and I try to hug them. Susan darts away as Bill turns saying, 'Come on then,' and heads towards the guard's van where suitcases are lining the platform. The air around me is chilly.

We go to Barbours Terrace Restaurant, perched on the third floor of Barbours department store. What a treat! Starched white tablecloths and napkins, silver tea service, and plush chairs. Waiters in white glide between tables and conversations hum. I just want to hug myself. I'm so happy to be home! Susan and Bill chat away, Mum's smoking and laughing at Susan's funny comments. She turns to me and says, 'Beverley, I've bought a pile of fabric so you can do some sewing over the holidays. Susan needs a few new things.'

'Sure Mum, I've been doing lots of sewing. We've been making baby clothes.' All three of them look at me. If I could slap my hand over my silly mouth I would. It's too late, and now I've ruined the wonderful morning. Around us cutlery clinks, but it's as if the entire room has heard me. My nerves get the better of me and I babble, 'Frances is having a baby. I'm going to be a big sister again.'

'We are not interested in them, or what goes on in that house. Or the apples and custard that have made you fat!' Mum says, her words are measured, hard, and her face is rigid.

Susan giggles. 'Wibby says you're not a nice big sister.' Bill frowns at her, folds his serviette and we all know it's time to go. Even the warm sun through the third-floor window feels cold.

***

Mr Markee is waiting at the back door for us. He hurries to the car, heaves my suitcase out, and is up the back steps, down the passage and into my room before we are all inside. I know he will unpack for me. I linger in the kitchen and breathe in the aroma of a freshly baked cake, and there it is, two vanilla layers cooling on a wire tray. Susan runs over, inhales deeply, sticks her finger into the middle of a layer, and licks it.

'Susan!' I yell, 'Don't do that.' She grins at me, raises her finger, and is about to poke the cake again.

'Susan!' Mum brushes past me, lifts the wire rack and places it on a high shelf. 'It's for afternoon tea.' Some things never change.

Before the afternoon sponge cake delight, I stand on a chair and retrieve from the top of the wardrobe two boxes of the precious things I packed away at the end of the last holiday. Dust drifts over me and I sneeze. Mr Markee hasn't been dusting up there! Slowly I unwrap my ornaments, special *display-only* dolls, and trinkets. They are old friends of mine, each with special meaning and memories, and after a three-month separation, I delight in arranging them around my bedroom. Susan hovers for a few minutes in the doorway, watching, then runs off to play. I just know she will sneak in and fiddle with things. There's nothing I can do about that, only hope she doesn't break anything.

***

On the old timber table at the far end of the partially enclosed verandah sits Mum's new Janome sewing machine. I run my fingers over its cream surface, admiring all the features that Frances's hand-turned Singer doesn't have: electric motor, buttonhole setting, zig-zag, gathering, stitch sizing and so much more. Fabric is piled beside it. A few beautiful David Whitehead prints of bright orange, yellow and green peep at me from their folded edges. And crimplene, Mum loves this fabric, a stylish monotone with a raised texture. There's no need to iron or oversew it. But I don't like it because it feels stiff to wear. Give me cotton any day.

Mum wanders out onto the verandah and perches on the edge of the table, cigarette smoke curling around her, watching me sort the patterns. I don't mention Frances's Singer machine. We choose several lengths of fabric for Susan's dresses. Mum picks up a pattern and runs her fingers over the details on the back.

'Add a bit on the sides, bodice length, and larger hems. These are all a size smaller than Susan is now.'

A few days later, Mum comes home with several dresses—*on appro*—for herself, and one for Susan. She has no intention of modelling any of them for Bill's approval, which is the point of the *on appro* concept: approval before buying. No, we don't do that. Mum tries them on, decides what she likes, draws sketches (she does this so well) takes measurements and examines all the details.

The *on appro* dress for Susan is expensive. We persuade her to try it on and she stands still for once. It's beautiful on her, and she's beautiful in it with her blonde hair, bright blue eyes and faded summer tan. The curved midriff bodice fits snugly while the back skirt is gathered onto wide elastic, which is secured with cross-over straps that fasten to the bodice front. The lightly gathered skirt falls to her knees. We turn her back and forth. The fit is perfect.

'See, these straps won't slip off her shoulders. Good to grow into,' says Mum, snapping the elastic across her back.

'Ouch! I'll tell Wibbly on you.'

'You do that and there'll be no new dress!' Mum whisks the garment over her head before she tries to run off. 'Bath time, off you go.'

We sketch the dress, measure the bodice, and Mum roughs out a pattern. We don't have any existing patterns in this shape, so we carefully examine how it's made.

'You got it all?'

'Yes, Mum. I'll return all the dresses in the morning.'

This is *exciting*, a new sewing machine and no hand-sewing of buttonholes!

The next day, I'm back at the sewing table to firm up the lines on Mum's pattern. Did she remember a seam allowance at the sides? After checking all the measurements, I'm still unsure. I need to re-measure Susan. There's no spare material if I get it wrong. I hear Frances's words, that it would be such a waste, and I have to agree with her!

I wander through the house looking for Susan and spot her outside playing French skipping using two chairs to hold the elastic. I call through the open window, 'Susan, come inside. I need to measure you.'

'No! Don't want to.' Her tanned legs straddle the elastic and she turns, wrapping the elastic around her ankles, then leaps into the air and lands with a foot on each strand. She's very pleased with herself.

'Come on, it won't take long. I need to measure you so I can make your dress.' She ignores me, executes another move and one chair falls over. 'Mum can make the dress. I don't want you to!' She shoves the other chair over in anger.

'Mum said I have to make it today. Stop being a brat.' I go down the back steps and walk towards her.

'I'm not a brat. I hate you!' Her fine features contort. Her blue eyes glare at me and suddenly there's a stone in her hand. Her arm swings back and the stone hits my chest.

'Ouch!' I shriek. I rush at her, my self-control is gone. I bring my hand up and slap her shoulder. Her arms become windmills connecting with my body. Now it's a fight of slapping and screaming. I try to grab her hands, but she breaks away from me, shouting, 'Shit, you are a shit!'

'I'll tell Mum on you for swearing. You need soap in your mouth!'

'Mum won't care!' She taunts me by running just out of reach before suddenly standing still in the dusty yard and looking directly at me, her fine blonde hair sticking out in a mess. I lunge forward to grab her.

'We don't want you here! Go back to Bulawayo and never come back!' I gasp. She's smug. For a moment, we hang suspended between my shock and her assuredness. The hot anger in me vanishes. Did she just say *we don't want you here?* She did. I watch her skipping away from me, singing, 'We… don't… want you here.'

I hug myself. The winter sun is warm, but I'm shivering. Naked jacaranda trees loom behind her small body, with branches stark against the cloudless blue sky. Their leaves lie in a swept-up pile that a quick breeze now disturbs. Susan throws herself into the leaves and tosses handfuls above her. The wind scatters them: dry, brittle, and hard. A cold ball of dread rolls through me. *They don't want me here.* Susan must have heard Bill and Mum talking. *Go back to Bulawayo.* She wouldn't have thought to say that, she's only six years old. Bulawayo, where Dad and Frances are having a baby. Will they want me when it's born? My chest is so tight that I almost vomit.

That afternoon, Mum fixes the pattern and I make the dress the next day. I don't tell her about my fight with Susan. I don't mention the taunts or ask for reassurance, not wanting to see the truth confirmed on her beautiful face. Susan doesn't tell tales to her Wibby either. I try to keep out of her way for the rest of the holidays and go out on my bicycle with Ant as much as possible.

***

On Saturday we will drive to Salisbury and I'll get the overnight train back to Bulawayo. We are just about finished lunch when Mum says, 'Just you and I are going to Salisbury.' My bottom lip is trembling but the thought of having Mum to myself for the drive stops it. 'Better get your packing done, we're going tomorrow.'

'But it's Friday tomorrow. The train goes on Saturday night!'

'Yes, you're going to stay a night with my friend Sheena and she'll put you on the train.' Mum's smile switches to a frown at the tears hovering in my eyes. 'You remember Sheena?'

No, *I don't*. I don't remember her. We are going two days sooner, a whole night sooner. The tears spill over now and Mum huffs, 'Don't start with the crying. What will Sheena think of me dropping you off with red eyes?' I brush my forearm over my face and push my chair back, it scrapes on the wooden floor, and I walk away. No one tells me to finish the cold cabbage because there are starving children in the world.

Aunty Sheena is bubbly and makes me feel welcome. After sandwiches for lunch, Mum leaves, and waving her lovely hand with pink painted nails out the window she calls out, 'Bye, Bye ….' I know I look miserable and Aunty Sheena puts her arm around me.

'Come on inside, we've got scones for afternoon tea and we can do some sewing too. Norma tells me you're very good at that.' She guides me through the house, chatting away and we reach the sewing room. I run my fingers over the fabric laid out on a table.

'I need to pin the pattern,' she says, passing me a folded pile of fine brown tissue paper, 'Here, how about you straighten the pieces out and we can start.'

I start telling her about making Susan's dress and suddenly I find myself saying. 'I got into a terrible fight with Susan…' Aunty Sheena says nothing, just listens and the more she listens the more my pent-up emotions bubble, boil, and spill with the tears running down my face. Words tumble over each other as I tell her about all the fights, arguments, Susan breaking my things, Bill getting cross with me, and finally I say, 'Susan said they don't want me there. I should stay in

Bulawayo.' I crumple like a rag doll into her arms.

'Sssh, it will be alright,' she murmurs and smooths my hair. Grandpa's words, his arms and hands. A scented hankie wipes my face. 'I think we'll leave the sewing and go into town for a special afternoon tea. Much nicer, a treat for us both.' And that's what we do. My eyes are burning, but somehow I feel lighter inside. Someone has listened to me. Auntie Sheena is lovely.

Chapter 25
Mum's So Mad with Me, and House Extensions.

Bulawayo Station is cold, and I follow Dad and Frances along the platform out into the winter morning sunshine. We drive home in silence without a mention of my time away.

It feels strange, and even though we argue a lot, I do miss Susan. She's so funny at times. Mum says, 'That child is like the rhyme, the little girl with the curl… and when she's bad—she's *horrid!*'

We pass through the city centre, over the intersections with dips and rises that make my stomach stay behind, past the shops—so much nicer than what we have in Rusape—and then into the suburbs. Past familiar houses I see on the bus trip home, with neat front fences, and Dad sometimes mutters, 'Look at the small yards!' There is the stretch where there's nothing but bush, tall grass and a ribbon of tar towards the airport. I'd love to go on a plane. But the trains are super too.

Auntie Sheena was so kind to me yesterday. My eyes are still a bit sore from all the crying. I don't understand why I get so upset every time I leave Mum, or why she gets so cross with me. I just don't understand. I wouldn't mind staying with Auntie Sheena again. We are almost home. Dad turns into the circular driveway, and I exclaim, 'Dad, you've knocked down the front door and half the house!'

Dad chuckles, and Frances says, 'Oh yes Bevlee.' She laughs her funny little laugh, sort of *he he he,* and continues, 'Dennis and John have been smashing down walls and buildings like crazy. You were lucky not to be here this past month!'

When I get out of the car, Lady starts barking and dashing around my legs, and Lenid appears at the back door, which has been moved, and I laugh. Dad has reused the old one with the too-small doggie hole that Lady struggles through. The inside of the house is a shambles. There's a temporary narrow sitting room with a black plastic wall at one end, the kitchen has been extended, the sink is balancing on two 44-gallon drums beneath a new window overlooking the backyard. There's no front door and the foundations for the new living area, third bedroom and front porch stand proud showing the large extensions Dad's building. Only my small bedroom and the main bedroom are untouched, but dust has seeped in and sits brown on everything.

Dad takes a few weeks off work to get a move on building and the house begins to take shape. For my new bedroom, Frances and I choose white paint with a hint of green, waffle bedspreads in soft green, and curtains in tones of green and white for the wide window front facing, with crisp white lace under them for privacy. It's a lovely room and it's *mine*.

***

Dad and John are busy laying bricks one afternoon when suddenly Mai appears at the back door screaming. Lenid rushes outside and follows her, running down the yard. John and Dad hurry after them. Frances tells me to stay inside; something awful is happening at the cottages.

A few minutes later, Dad comes inside and quietly closes the back door. His face is grey and he's trembling. 'The baby fell over into the fire, it's very, very bad. I'm taking them to the hospital now.' He grabs his car keys and heads towards the back door. 'Lenid won't be back today either.'

'You're filthy Dennis, change.' Dad looks back, shakes his head and is gone. Lenid and John's family are in the car, and Dad drives away faster than I've ever seen. I want to go to Mai, but I dare not. This is private time anyway, and what can I say to her? It's very late when Dad gets back. He parks and we watch Lenid helping John and Charity out of the car.

We don't speak, but make a coffee and put it next to Dad when he goes to sit in his chair. He reaches for the cup; his face is so pale. 'Charity wouldn't leave the baby in the hospital and refused to stay inside the building with him. It's very sad, I didn't realise how steeped in culture she is.' His hand shakes as it smooths over his hair.

'What are you saying, Dennis?'

'She insisted that the baby come home with them. It's a white man's hospital, and she refused … refused to stay. The African nurses tried to reason with her. The baby will die, that's what the Doctor told me.' Tears well up in my eyes. That beautiful, smiling, chubby little boy. Oh, this is too awful and I can't bear to think of the pain he's in and all the suffering they are all going through too. Frances shakes her head and wipes tears away. 'It's just the way some are. Dad saw it many times at the mission. They'd seek out the witch doctor first and then in desperation, maybe the hospital, and it was usually too late by then. So the white man's place killed their baby is the lie that's spread.' The baby died the next day. No one talked about the funeral in front of me.

***

Over six weeks pass and there's still no mail from Mum. Every day after school I hurry to my bedroom expecting to see an envelope with her beautiful writing. There's nothing. I know she's busy working. Finally, a letter arrives. I'm so excited to hear her news. I finger the envelope and gaze at Mum's handwriting and wish mine was that nice. The stamp's a recent one too, I'll soak that off for my collection. I'll write back and say how lovely Auntie Sheena was and ask for her address so I can send her a thank you letter too. I plop onto my bed and rip it open. There is only one page. The large words leap out at me.

How dare you tell Sheena all those stories about Susan. How dare you lie about your sister. The page trembles in my hand. I can hear her voice, see her face, and the bold words continue shouting at me.

Sheena called me to say how upset you were crying and telling her all the things Susan has supposedly done to you. What do you think she thinks of me now? I'm very angry with you and Sheena had plenty to say about the way we treat you! Well, if it's so awful here maybe you shouldn't come home for the holidays. Just think about that! Mum.

Frances is calling me; she's coming down towards my room. The letter is lying in my lap, the words are still not real, my subconscious sees them, hears them, but I can't acknowledge them properly. The denial of the truth they hold, the harshness and rejection seem removed from me. If I keep them away for a little longer, maybe they won't be there. But they are there in blue ink on white paper. My 12-year-old self can't deal with this now. Frances is at the door, 'Bevlee, Dennis, and I are having afternoon tea, come and sit with us.' She turns away adding, 'He's off to work soon.'

I slip the page under my pillow, hiding Mum there, to think about later. The following week I write to her and say sorry. I don't ask for Auntie Sheena's address. Every day, I hurry home from school and rush to my bedroom. There's no mail for me, week after week.

***

We shiver through winter in a sitting room that has been reduced to a drafty small corridor. Dad has rigged up black plastic that does little to stop the cold and wind. Dust coats everything and Lenid has long given up trying to clean it up. But by late July my new bedroom is finished. Two beds with green waffle spreads are recessed on either side of a large built-in wardrobe with lovely white doors. It's light-filled, big and I love it.

Dad embarks on getting the sitting room done and takes more time off work to keep the building moving forward. The baby is due in October and with the cold nights receding he and John work into the dark laying bricks. I spend hours after school helping pass bricks. It gives Dad and I time together and we make a big deal of slipping coins into the holes of some bricks before they are cemented together. We laugh about how one day people will maybe find these coins. Afterwards, we challenge each other to remember where the coins are. We can't always remember. And for a few hours, I forget the dressing table, now in its new room, that still has had no letters from Mum sitting on it.

Frances sleeps through the alarm clock several mornings and Mr Murray hoots in our driveway and scowls as I rush out with toothpaste on my chin and no breakfast. I've taken to putting a spare hairbrush in my school case.

The baby is due in about six weeks. Dad promises the sitting room will be done before that. Frances shakes her head and says, 'Oh Dennis, I do hope so!' I hope so too, but I've got other things on my mind. Frances hasn't said a word about only one letter in three months. I know she must be curious, but she's not going to ask. Some days I know she can see I'm upset and says things like, 'Come on Bevlee, let's sew cot sheets or baby clothes, and then have apples and custard!'

I know she's trying to be kind. Part of me wishes she would ask what's wrong, but then I'd have to talk about Mum, and we don't do that. Oh, why did Auntie Sheena tell on me? Lesson learned, *don't* say what I'm thinking! And now in the last few weeks before the holidays, I'm so worried and don't even feel like Eskimo Hut ice cream. Frances looks at me with raised eyebrows when I lick my ice cream cone slowly! It's such a treat, I can't enjoy it. I feel sick, the train leaves tomorrow night. Dad's taking me to the station. I want to say, I don't want to go. *But I do. No, I don't.*

***

The train pulls into Salisbury Station. I don't want to get off. Carriage doors slam around me, voices call out greetings, bodies hurry past the compartment and then it's quiet. I get off and follow the stragglers to the guard's van, my suitcase is one of the few waiting to be collected.

Soon, I'm the only passenger left. I perch on the edge of my large suitcase near the guard's van. Several porters are leaning against empty carts chatting, smoke plumes from their rolled cigarettes, tips glow in the shadows, and the smell of dagga (marijuana) drifts towards me. And their voices are echoing in the vast emptiness.

My anxiety rises. Dad had said a few days ago, 'You're booked on Friday night's train. I've got you into a first-class compartment. Your mother will pick you up.' That's all.

She's not here. I've got no money. If I ask the Station Master to call Dad he will, they all know each other on the railways, and Dad will be furious. What if someone sees me alone here and takes me to the Station Master's office? I'll have to say who I am and they will for sure call Dad, then he won't let me come to Mum again for the holidays. I shrink into the shadows. Fear ferments and I replay the words in Mum's only letter. *Maybe you should just stay there.*

'Missis, ipi wena humba?' (Misses where are you going?) The voice is close to me. I jump and look up. It's a porter. He's old: face folded in with life, eyes bloodshot, and smiling toothlessly at me. Suddenly Mum is here, cigarette between her fingertips, breathless and beautiful. 'There you are, Beverley! Why on earth are you all the way down here? Come on, hurry up, Bill's parked out the front.' She glances at the porter. 'Bring the suitcase please.' She turns and walks quickly away trailing cigarette smoke, her high heels clicking on the cement, long legs in fine stockings, a new crimplene dress with the hem well above her knees.

'Had a dreadful morning getting petrol, the usual garage had run out, Susan didn't want to get into the car. Traffic is so bad here on Saturday mornings.' Her words wash over me. I glance back. The old porter has heaved my suitcase onto a trolley and is hurrying behind us. Rattling wheels echo along the empty platform disturbing cooing pigeons, and they flutter upwards to perch on the metal beams above. We are walking fast so their poop won't land on us! I'm so relieved that Mum's here.

It's as if the letter never happened.

Chapter 26
The Baby Is Here!

Frances is upset; her face is burrowed into Dad's chest and his arms are around her. I watch from a distance. Uncomfortable. *Adults don't cry; or do they?* It's so hot, even in the shade of the trees on the hospital grounds, perspiration is trickling between my shoulder blades dampening my school uniform. Dad's shirt is damp too. That's something we have in common; we feel the heat. Frances glances over her shoulder, suddenly aware of me, and a small smile hovers unsuccessfully on her lips. She beckons to me. I move closer and hear Dad say, 'Don't worry Mrs Walker, it will be alright.' She wipes her eyes, sniffs and nods her head. *Why is she crying? Everyone has been happy until now.*

'Bevlee, Dennis, I think you should go home now.' We stand for a few moments in strained silence; there's so much going on that I don't understand. Dad clears his throat, kisses her cheek, and quickly turns to go towards the car. He looks anxious. We walk away—Dad's limp is more pronounced, he's tired—leaving Frances standing in the shade in her dressing gown. I'm allowed to sit in the front seat of the car. As we cross the Umgusa Bridge and turn right Dad says, 'The baby should be here tomorrow.' *How does it get here? This baby business is a mystery to me.* I stare out the window, we've just passed Redman's Garage—that's where Dad swaps almost expired petrol coupons for next month's, illegally. The roadside grass is tall, dead. Grandpa would be talking about the rains coming soon.

'If I'm not at home after school tomorrow, go to Linda's,' Dad says as we turn into our street, Seventh Avenue. *Home. Their home. Is it mine too, forever? I don't know. The baby is going to change things for sure.*

Questions I dare not ask rush through my mind. Dad is pale, his voice is different. He looks scared. *Yes, he is.* Now I'm scared too. But of what?

That night I lie on my bed and read, but I can't concentrate. I wonder if the baby will be a girl or a boy? I'd like a little sister. Yes, that would be nice and then I'll sew her dresses and play tea times with her. Is Frances alright?

The next day, in the late afternoon, Dad comes home, his face grey, and he hardly says a word. I go to bed and finally fall asleep, and in the morning, when I wake up, Dad's gone. But he picks me up from school. All the frown lines on his face are gone. The baby is here, and we are going to the Mater Dei Hospital to see her! It's a little girl! We arrive and walk together down long, brightly lit corridors, through doors. The smell of antiseptic surrounds us as we pass rooms of ladies with babies.

Dad says, 'Here we are.' Suddenly I feel shy and hang back in the doorway. Frances is sitting up, smiling, with a wrapped bundle in her arms. She looks fine. Dad has hurried forward, he leans over, carefully moves the baby blanket, peeps into the folds, murmurs soft words, and kisses Frances's cheek.

'Oh Dennis, the nurses told me to never come back for another one!' She chuckles and looks past Dad at me. 'Bevlee, come here.' She pats the bed next to her. I sit down, lean forward, and gaze at the baby. She's fast asleep: eyes closed, blonde eyelashes, button nose, a dusting of fair hair, tiny fingers and fingernails, so snug.

'She's beautiful,' I whisper, and Frances puts her into my arms. I'm surprised. 'Here's your little sister, we've decided to call her Sharon.' Sharon! *My best friend in Hartleys name. I'd said it when we were talking about baby names.* She's so light and warm. The smell of talcum powder fills my senses with memories of another baby. The one I couldn't hold. The baby that was going to die but didn't. *I almost say another little sister, but we don't talk about Susan.* Instead, I murmur, 'Hello baby Sharon, I'm your big sister.' I study her face. She moves in my arms and at that moment a feeling I can't quite define trickles through me.

Just over two weeks later I'm 13 and there's a card from Mum—there will be something waiting for me when I get home in a few weeks—and a small gift from Dad and Frances. Dad managed to get the day right, the 16th of November. Nearly every birthday card he's mailed me over the years said: *Happy Birthday for the 17th.*

Mum would mutter, 'You'd think he could at least get it right.'

Sharon is growing fast. Every day the school bus drops me on Seventh Avenue and I almost run to the house, even though my heavy school books slow me down. It's a wonderful feeling to see her and soon her large brown eyes turn towards my voice. It's just as exciting as a letter from Mum although I realise there haven't been many. I tell myself that she's busy working.

'She knows your voice already, Bevlee. We should get a smile soon and before we know it she'll be rolling around!' Frances laughs, that familiar *hehehehe* that makes me want to laugh too. A few nights later we are bathing Sharon. Her tiny arms and legs are exploring their freedom in the warm weightlessness, and her large eyes are watching me intently.

'I'm going away on Friday,' I say, and dribble water from my fingertips onto her round tummy. 'Are you going to smile for me before I go? Are you?' She kicks hard, water splashes. Frances and I laugh. Sharon smiles.

'Frances look! She smiled, smiled!' I tickle her, she smiles again. Frances grins, 'Well aren't you just too clever,' she says lifting the baby and wrapping her in a towel. 'Here, can you dry and dress her? I need to get dinner.' The damp bundle is in my arms and Frances limps away, down the passage towards the half-finished kitchen singing to herself. For a few moments, I stand in the bathroom clutching Sharon to my chest, a small trusting body. The previously undefined trickle floods over me, and I understand. All my pent-up love rushes out and finds a home—unreservedly—with this little girl.

Friday arrives and the thought of leaving Sharon doesn't overshadow my eagerness to see Mum. I packed days ago. My suitcase is ready near my bedroom door and I've got a small overnight bag for the train.

Dad and I drive silently to the station and in the closing evening, we arrive. Small brown birds are bustling, chattering, in the trees near the car park, and long shadows merge into deep grey as daylight suddenly vanishes. The lights under the awning bounce off cars parked beneath the *Bulawayo Railway Station* sign, and I follow Dad through the grand entrance and along the crowded platform. After the quiet of the car there's so much noise.

'I've booked you a first-class compartment,' he says. 'You've been good with the baby.'

I glance up at him. I wish he'd hug me and suddenly he does. *Daddy!* He moves back. 'The compartment's at this end, off you go.' I climb the metal steps, slide open the compartment door, drop my overnight bag on the green leather seat, and hang my head out of the window. Dad's looking up at me. He runs his hand through his hair. There's a funny look on his face, his brown eyes meet mine and words seem to be trapped in his throat. He coughs, 'I'd better get going. Goodbye, Beverley.'

'Bye, Dad,' I say. But he's already turned and is limping away. *I do love you, Daddy. I think you love me back.* And now the sounds and smells of train travel excite me: the hissing of the steam engine that billows clouds shrouding goodbyes, massive articulated wheels gathering momentum on shiny ribbon tracks, the banging of compartment doors, bedding that is rolled out—crisp white sheets and blue blankets. And I gaze through the etched '*RR*', Rhodesia Railways, emblem on the window. The city recedes. The sun's long gone over the horizon and darkness swallows the land. The gentle swaying and clacking wheels are taking me to another place. I feel light, free, and fall asleep. *Good night Daddy. Good night Grandpa.*

Chapter 27
Christmas, New Friends, and I'm In Trouble (1970-1971).

After visiting Aunty Anne for the night, Mum and I reach Rusape the following day. I'm chatting away in the passenger seat, 'Oh Mum the baby is so cute, you know what, she smiled at me just a few days ago!' I'm so excited about my new sister that I don't notice how quiet she is. 'Just the sweetest baby, by the time I get back she will be rolling around and—'

'Shut up!' Mum says without looking at me. 'I've told you before, we don't want to hear about that house, so shut up.' Her voice is hard and almost hisses between her teeth. We pull into the rear of the house, she turns the engine off and says, 'Well here you are, home again,' as if nothing harsh had just been said. *All I can think is that Mum and Dad's divorce must have been bad. But what's the big secret?*

Susan hangs out the back door and calls out, 'I've been baking rock cakes, come on.'

'Don't know what colouring she will have put in them, last week they were blue!' Mum says with a smile, 'Just pretend to enjoy them, they are like rocks. Dip them in your tea, it helps!'

Susan has arranged her rocks on a plate and is hopping from one foot to the other in excitement. 'This week they are pink, for girls,' she says leading us through to the sitting room where Mr Markee is placing a tea tray. He grins at me, flashing his fake gold tooth and nods. I know he will unpack my suitcase for me. It's as if I've never been away.

***

December 1970. The house smells of brandy-soaked Christmas cake, mince pies, and steamed pudding with hidden charms. Mum is icing the Christmas cake. I watch her deftly roll out the marzipan, and spread apricot jam over the cake—after adding an extra dash of brandy as you can never have *too* much you know—as she reminds me every year, and adds, 'Marzipan stops the icing going yellow.' I don't say, *I know and don't like marzipan*, because she knows I pick it off my slice. Royal Icing is beaten up and spread over the marzipan. We lick the leftovers off the beaters, our tongues twisting around the metal prongs. Soon the cake is iced, and peaks of snow cover the top with the ornaments we have saved over the years placed between them. Mum and I walk into the dining room and she puts the cake on the sideboard.

'I'm going to lie down for a bit,' she says, leaving me alone with my thoughts. Mum isn't as sad this Christmas, our third without Grandpa. I wasn't either, until yesterday when Bill, his cigarette resting on Grandpa's spin lid ashtray, started sorting out Grandpa's tree lights, untangling the green wires and checking each bulb: a snowman, Santa face, reindeer, little house, and more, just as we used to. How excited we were when they all lit up! Sometimes we'd search for ages screwing and unscrewing bulbs to find the dud one. Grandpa didn't mind. But Bill was frowning because they didn't light up. I kept quiet. They are blinking on the tree now.

At the end of the sideboard behind the cake is a crystal lamp. I love it, especially when Mum turns it on at night and the light streams through the round crystal shade casting images on the wall, over the crystal base and brown veneer sideboard. I lean forward. This is the lamp that matches the large crystal basket at Dad's house, it's on a sideboard too—that one's dark heavy timber. I can hear Dad's voice, 'That was a wedding gift to your mother and me.' Why would they keep them when they don't even like each other? I suppose the crystal's beautiful. *Is that it?* But Dad doesn't seem like the kind of person to think that way. I lean closer, Mr Markee needs to dust it. Suddenly glass smashes. My knee has gone through the sliding cabinet door. Large shards are lying flat around my feet, except for one—standing upright in my foot. *I scream.*

'What the hell have you done?' Mum's standing in the doorway. I point at my foot. 'For goodness sake Beverley!' With thumb and forefinger she plucks the long glass spear from just above my little toe. Blood fountains and she shouts, 'Mr Markee come here!' With a hankie in place over the tiny hole near my toe, I hobble to the bathroom in disgrace.

Mum has a few days off work from the Standard Bank between Christmas and New Year, which is just as great as Christmas. On New Year's Eve, us kids roam the town on foot or beg lifts from various sober to inebriated parents, between the Balfour Hotel, The Club, and the Crocodile Motel—which is a fair walk out of town. At each venue we help ourselves to whatever food is available, or con soft drinks and chips out of parents who suddenly realise they have more children than they thought. But they are enjoying themselves so much they just buy what we ask for.

Around 3am there is a champagne breakfast at the Balfour Hotel. By this time most of our parents have lost track of what we are up to, but know we will turn up for breakfast, and we sure do: for eggs, crispy bacon, toast, fried tomatoes, and onion, but not champagne.

In the balmy dark, before the sun rises, we all pile into vehicles and drive in a chain of flashing lights through the bush, out to the dam. From the car boots appear fold-up chairs, picnic blankets, flasks of hot water, teabags, coffee, bread rolls, and eskies holding meat and chopped-up onions.

The men have an ongoing supply of beer and the adults are soon seated while we kids lounge around on blankets. Fires are lit. Yellow and orange flames lick in the opaque grey before dawn, and the dam water lies pewter dark, slinking towards the shoreline. The sun rises fast and streams over the bush and water, promising a warm day.

Cape Doves coo, and flutter over the acacia trees; a wedge-tailed Go Away Bird's call echoes, *Go-awaaai*.

It's January 1st, 1971, and this is just great.

***

I have a boyfriend too, called Simon. He cycles into the backyard and I hop onto my bicycle, and we pedal off around town or out into the bush to explore. We buy chunks of watermelon from African sellers. And beneath the full-leafed acacia trees we eat them, spitting black pips with juice dripping from our chins, and later we pedal home like mad as rain clouds threaten above.

Susan thinks it's fun too. When Simon arrives she sings at the top of her voice, 'Beverley loves Simon, Beverley loves Simon…' over and over. And in the evening tells tales of how we'd left her behind. I'm so embarrassed and don't know what to do. Eventually, for a few afternoons, when Simon knocks on the back door I stay in my room. He gives up coming around, and I'm ashamed not to have told him that our bike rides were great. But at least Ant still cycles over, and we go to the swimming pool. We do have to take Susan with us, though.

Without Simon to amuse her, Susan focuses her attention on my bedroom again. She won't stay out of it and taunts me by fiddling with my things and occasionally breaking them. There's no point telling Mum because I don't want to remind her of the Auntie Sheena incident.So I outsmart her with an old trick she's never worked out. I wrap up my music keyboard and some dolls that she regularly undresses, leaving them sprawled naked around the room, in newspapers and tie string around each parcel with a long length attached. Then I lift the trapdoor under the bedroom mat and lower them by the string into the space below. She's never worked out the hiding place and doesn't dare ask questions for fear of giving herself away. She's quick to deny fiddling or breakages. It's just as well she never found the trap door because she'd probably have jumped down and then screamed like crazy, or worse still, hurt herself. Bill would have been very angry with me.

The holidays are nearly over. I've dragged my huge suitcase out from under the bed and it's lying open on the floor. I sigh and examine the dregs I've left in there for the past month. A few coat hangers, the wooden ones with *Walker* written on them, a cardigan that's too small now (but which I love because Mum knitted it), a skipping rope. *Now why have I still got that?* Unopened sanitary pads. I start to cry. My eyes are stinging and red. *Why, why do I do this at the end of my holidays here?*

'Will you just stop your snivelling, for goodness sake!' I didn't see Mum come through the door and swipe my hands over my face. She looks down and laughs, 'Still got some *Walker* hangers! And no sign of …' she says pushing the pack of pads into the corner.

'No,' I mumble and shove the jumper on top of them. Mum sighs, 'Oh well I suppose they will turn up, eventually! And do stop chewing your nails!' She draws on her cigarette, sits on the bed and says. 'Go on, start packing, hand me your blouses to fold.' I stare at my nails which I chewed off a few days ago. They were nice and long. Frances chews hers too.

I arrive back in Bulawayo with a cold. Frances is not pleased. I don't care because Sharon is just too cute, propped up on the couch, smiling at me. Frances says, 'You must keep your distance from the baby, Bevlee.'

Sharon's sleeping in my old room now. Dad's painted it white, new pink hessian curtains are hanging at the window, a cot on one side and a changing table on the other.

'She's sleeping through the night now,' Frances says, 'It's so good. You know how much I love my sleep!' Her little *he he he* laugh follows and I can't help laughing too.

'Yes, how many times have we both overslept and heard Mr Murray on our driveway hooting for me!'

Loud crying wakes me up. It's dark. I turn over and close my eyes, there's still crying. I flick on the light, cross the hallway and go into

Sharon's bedroom. A distraught, tear-stained face looks up at me. I scoop her up. Her nappy and night clothes are soggy.

'Shhh, baby, shhh baby.' She hiccups. I change her nappy and clothes and rock her back and forth. Maybe she's getting teeth. Finally, she's asleep; long eyelashes against plump cheeks, no longer red, and a small sigh escapes her. The same thing happens on many nights. Frances likes her sleep and doesn't hear a thing.

***

There's a new girl in our class. Everyone's looking at her and whispering. She's very pretty and she walks towards the front of the classroom and me!

'Hi, I'm Janet,' she says lifting the desk lid and dumping a pile of books down before easing into the seat beside mine and grinning. 'Before you ask, I've come *down* from A2!' She draws out the word 'down' with delight. I raise my eyebrows and murmur, 'Last year I came up from 1D!'

She laughs, a light tinkling sound, and her eyes are full of fun. 'Well they had no choice, you see, I'm dismal at French, only got 3% in my last exam! That was for writing my name, neatly!' I want to laugh out loud but the Form Mistress has arrived. Janet wriggles in her seat, pulls her dark ponytail over her shoulder, and feigns attention to Roll Call. Goodness, I don't think my waist-length ponytail will ever be as long as hers—she can almost sit on it!

And there's another new schoolgirl, on the bus home. I'm still not part of the Woodville group and am too shy to join them all at the rear of the bus. They talk to me, but I just don't fit in and it's lonely sitting on my own, so to cover up feeling left out, I study. Today I'm aware of those behind me, in particular the new girl. Her laughter, clear and unrestrained, lifts above the other voices. She's fitted in just like that! *Why can't I?* My stop is one of the first in Woodville. I glance at the retreating bus, belching fumes and see the new girl waving out the rear window. I smile, wave and hurry down the shimmering tar road to see Sharon.

The next day, at recess, Janet strolls across the lawn in the quadrangle, folds her knees gracefully, and sits opposite me. I've got a book in my lap. I stare up at her, no one has ever joined me at recess.

'Come on, get your face out of that! What are you doing this weekend?'

'Well, for sure we aren't going to church on Sunday night!' I say laughing

'Church! You're kidding!' Her dark eyes are alive with mirth.

'Yep, that's what we used to do but not anymore. I've got a new baby sister, and besides petrol is sooo short you know.' I say mimicking my father's voice.

'Well, my parents never go to church. They go to the Churchill Arms Hotel instead. Us kids stay home and have fun.' Soon we are chatting and laughing, Janet is my first friend at school.

The next day the other new girl is in front of me at the bus stop. Her boater is balanced on the back of her head, her shoulder-length hair is loose, her uniform too short, and as she clambers up the bus stairs I think she has shaved her legs too! If the Prefects see her, she will be in trouble, *big time*. I slide my boater onto the back of my head, and stand taller, making my regulation-length dress look shorter.

'Come on down the back with us,' she says glancing at me on the step below her, 'I'm Diane.'

'Bev,' I say, not Beverley. I hate my full name. She makes it easy. No one seems to notice that I've joined them. Everyone is laughing and talking, and for the first time, I'm sorry we are turning off Drayton Avenue. My stop is around the corner.

'I'm going to the pool this arvie, around 3, see you there,' says Diane. I grab my suitcase and hurry down the aisle towards the exit door.

'Sure, great!' I call over my shoulder. This is the first time anyone has asked me to the pool. It's so exciting! *I can't wait*. Wonder how long it will take to walk there; wish I had a bicycle. Frances is in the sitting room. I fling my suitcase down in the entryway.

'Frances! Guess what?'

'Goodness Bevlee, what happened? Calm down.' Sharon shrieks at my excitement, 'I've made another friend, her name's Diane. I'm going to meet her at the pool this arvie! Isn't that great?' Frances stares at me. I babble on, 'Have to be there at 3, what towel can I use?' I turn to leave the room. 'Will the old blue stripe one be OK?'

'You're not going.'

'What?'

'Don't *what* me, I said you're not going.'

'Why not? Diane's expecting me. She said to be there at 3.'

'Because I said so, that's why. Don't be rude. Your budgies' cage needs cleaning. I let Lenid do it while you were away.'

'I'll do it. Then I'll go.'

'No, you will not. You Didn't Ask Permission.' Her words are spaced out and each one is defined. I realise that she's very angry: her face is stern, her lips compressed, and red blotches are blooming on her neck.

'Get changed, there's a sandwich in the fridge for you.' I go to speak, but the look on her face shuts me up. I turn towards the passage that leads to my room, and her voice follows me.

'Don't leave your case there!'

Quickly, before the tears hovering on my eyelashes fall, I grab my case and retreat. Rufty and Tufty flutter when I peer into their cage. It does need cleaning. Maybe if I do that Frances won't be cross anymore. The conversation replays in my mind. No, it's not the dirty cage, is it? *Ask permission.* What and why? That's made her angry. Mum goes to work every day and never says anything when I go out, as long as I say where I'm going. Sometimes she will say, 'Don't be out late,' or, 'Got a hat?' And, 'Don't forget to take Susan with you.' But here I do have to ask before opening the fridge, taking food, and even if it's OK to wash my hair. I suppose I should have known. Today was the first time that someone here has asked to meet up, and I was so happy. Then I have an even worse thought. Dad will be getting up at 3.30 after his night shift and Frances will tell him. He won't speak to me for days again and Frances will ignore me too. Even though I know she will only manage to do that until tomorrow because she likes chatting too much. Somehow, I have to show that I'm sorry even though it wasn't all my fault, was it?

Cage in hand, bird wings flapping, I hurry through the kitchen and out the back door towards the tap near the 100 fruit trees Dad's so proud of. Lenid follows me with sheets of newspaper to line the bottom tray I'm washing under the tap, along with the seed and water holders. In a few minutes, it's done.

I carry the fresh-smelling cage inside, open the bedroom window, sweep up the seed husks scattered on the bedroom floor, tip them in the kitchen bin, and wash my hands. Now I have to say sorry, but it doesn't feel right. After a few moments, I realise that I'm not sorry at all. I truly didn't know. If we talked about my life in Rusape, Dad and Frances would understand how hard it is to remember all *their* rules and work out what's expected. But then again, if they did know how relatively free I am there, Dad might stop me from going home for the holidays. A flicker of resentment ripples through me, then I hear Grandpa's words, *'It will be alright, child.'*

I stand up straight like Nanna taught me to and walk into the sitting room with my lunch sandwich. Sharon has fallen asleep on the couch and Frances is sewing. Her left hand turns the manual handle while the other guides the material for a new dress. She's concentrating. Jim Reeves's voice drifts from the record player. That's a good sign. I stand, waiting for the song to finish, and as it does I say, 'Sorry for not asking permission, I will next time.' *Half a lie, sorry Grandpa.* She looks up and smiles, 'See you've got your lunch, come, sit. You can make your father's coffee just now. I want to get this dress finished.' *She's not going to tell Dad!*

'I can do the hem if you like,' I add and start eating, crusts and all. We don't have to do that in Rusape.

'That would be nice, I'll bathe Sharon while you do that.'

Am I allowed to go to the swimming pool another day?

***

Diane pokes me in the ribs, 'Where were you yesterday? We had so much fun!' The metal steps vibrate beneath my feet, the idling bus engine drowns our conversation as we shuffle toward the rear. From behind, Diane nudges my legs with her suitcase to move faster and giggles. We plonk ourselves down on a bench seat and I start telling her what happened. She listens, tips her head sideways and pulls her ponytail free—we are supposed to keep our hair tied up in uniform—and her face screws up in disbelief. 'Permission! You're kidding!' Her laughter erupts, unrestrained, and her brown eyes, filled with amusement, stare at me through an overlong fringe. 'So, what now?'

'I don't know,' I say and lift my shoulders to my ears. 'My Mum's different to Frances.'

'Frances?'

'My stepmother. I'm probably never going to be allowed out now!'

Diane rolls her eyes, 'Tell you what, my Mum can call and invite you over.' She grins at me, 'Sorted!' And it is.

Just like that. Mrs Vaughan phones Frances, invites me over, insists that Diane come to our house to collect me and walk me back too. She arrives at the kitchen door wearing a knee-length dress, hair tied up neatly, floppy fringe bobby pinned back, and with a demure look on her face. I almost giggle, she's even wearing her school shoes!

'Hello Mrs Walker, my Mom has sent me to pick up Bev for a visit.' I almost expect her to shake hands with Frances. 'I have to bring her back too, Mom said.' Frances smiles at her. Diane's obviously made a great impression. We leave, sedately walk the length of the acreage, aware of eyes following us, climb over the rear low wire fence, and take a narrow winding path into the tall dry grass. As soon as we're out of sight Diane rips off her shoes, pulls her hair free, slips the bobby pins into her pocket, and bursts out laughing.

'Please tell me that's not your dress?' I splutter, pushing her shoulder.

'Yuck, no way, it's my sister's. She's sooo proper you know! Come on, let's go. Saw a great lemon tree on the way. I think we can nick a few!'

We almost get caught *picking* lemons and arrive at her house giggling. Mrs Vaughan is just like Diane, smiling, relaxed, and welcoming. Two huge German Shepherd dogs lounge on their cool concrete verandah, one heavily pregnant. 'That's Simba,' says Diane, 'Her pups are due any day.' Simba flops down, tongue lolling, and my body relaxes.

Diane's 'proper' sister, Lorraine, is home studying in her room. She's so quiet compared to Diane. I wonder what her three older brothers are like. A younger brother and sister are home from primary school and are running around outside, which leaves the sitting area and record player to us. We play records, loudly, all afternoon. Sometimes the same track, over and over again, and Mrs Vaughan doesn't stop us. I wish I lived here.

Chapter 28
Bill and Mr Markee are Gone.

My life settles into a slightly different routine in Woodville. At last, I'm allowed to go with Diane to the swimming pool, and to her house, and we secretly visit the Rodrigues boys. Dad wouldn't like that, and I'm not sure why, so I simply don't mention it. Anyway, he's not friends with their parents or anything like that!

Janet's mother invites me to stay for weekends and Dad picks me up. I have to make sure he's on the day shift for Saturday or Sunday, otherwise I can't go. I love their house. Her Dad and Mum go out on Saturday nights and drop in to check up on us four girls. Sometimes Uncle Mike just comes on his own and we all like that. He's so much fun and talks to us like we are adults. Janet loves him to death!

The rules at home stifle me even more. I find it difficult to comply with a smiling face.

I must remember to turn the lights off too! It drives Frances *mad* and she shouts, 'Bevlee, you've left the bathroom light on, again!' (Or whatever light it is). Mum leaves the lights on all over the house, so I just don't *get* it. And then there's: 'You didn't ask permission to open the fridge and take whatever.' I can't say 'Sorry, I just got back from Rusape and have been opening the fridge *whenever* for four weeks.' That would be 'cheeky.'

And money is always an issue. Mum never talks about money; she just puts everything on the 'Account' and writes 'post-dated cheques' towards the end of the month. But Frances never does any of that. Every cent spent is considered. I'm allowed $2 pocket money a month and no amount of begging for an extra 10c gets me anywhere.

Sometimes that's all I need to afford a little extra material to make a dress. Mum opened an account for me at Meikles last month that I'm not to mention to anyone, and I'm allowed $5 a month for 'essentials'. Mum's essentials are stockings, perfume and makeup. My essentials are records, books and a deodorant I like. I'm very careful not to spend over $5, ensure my purchases aren't obvious, and could have come from Rusape with me!

Dad only talks to me when Frances is out, or about stamps, which is fine because they interest me. Occasionally when we pass in the dining room, where his jigsaw puzzles lie on the table and the wedding gifts from another marriage sit on the sideboard, he will hug me quickly. But Sharon is a darling and I adore her. She is 10 months old when I leave for Rusape.

***

It's a Sunday in the August school holidays. Mum and I are on the verandah sewing a summer dress for Susan who is growing so fast. She has long skinny legs that have stretched beyond the let-down hems of last summer's clothes. She's just turned seven and has all her new front teeth, but her hair, which she still refuses to brush, is still a mess.

Mum's playing her LPs. 'Camelot's on the turntable and Franco Nero's words *If ever I would leave you,* drift out onto the verandah. We know all the tunes and words to this record, 'Mary Poppins', 'Sound of Music' and more. I watch Mum's fingers feed fabric under the foot of her new Elna sewing machine. It's green with a funny knee-control handle rather than a pedal and is not very easy to get used to. Mum's not humming or murmuring the words like she usually does. And come to think of it, I've noticed her heels are moving slowly over the wooden floor. And then it comes to me. She's sad. My beautiful, vibrant Mum is sad. Sad like she was when Grandpa and Nanna died. I might know why!

'Mum,'

'Mmm…' Camelot's finished. The next stacked LP falls, and the arm moves automatically into place.

'Ant wrote to me. Her Dad died in July, a few weeks ago. She said they'd just moved to Salisbury too.' The haunting prelude to 'Sound of Music', an all-time favourite of Mum's, reaches us and instrumentally crescendos to Julie Andrews' voice, '*The hills are alive…*' She flips open the Peter Stuyvesant box beside her and wedges a cigarette between her fingers.

'I thought Antoinette would write to you, she's good like that.' The lighter flame licks the cigarette tip, and it glows. She inhales deeply, tips her head back, and exhales. 'It was very sudden, you know,' and then almost as a whisper, 'Just like that he's gone.' Her head shakes slowly and as if I'm not there, she stops talking and gazes through the gauze towards her Flora Bunda roses. 'So sudden,' she murmurs. I wait. Ash grows like Pinocchio's nose on the cigarette now sitting on the crystal ashtray. Something's unsaid.

'I went to Salisbury, to help them. Lily was a mess. Ed was just home from University…poor Antoinette was at boarding school.' The medley overture is running fast through the tunes we love. Mum rests her elbows on the table and cups her chin. I dare to ask, 'Mum, is that why you don't work at the Bank anymore, because Uncle Mike was transferred?' The soft voices of nuns waft over us. Soon bells will ring and they will sing 'Alleluia.' Softly, her words come, 'Mike wasn't here anymore, it wasn't the same. Now he's never going to be here again.'

The nuns' voices rise, joyously, and Mum says. 'Turn that off, will you.' She straightens her back, and her voice lifts like a shrug, 'Besides, I couldn't stand the new Manager! I'm going to find Susan, she needs to try this on.' She stands, and walks away; away from Julie Andrews and so much more.

Mum's found Susan, who is now in her new dress and standing still, for once, in front of us. Mum kneels on the red rug to measure the hem. She takes the final pin from between her clamped lips, stabs the fabric, and says, 'There, done.' Deftly the garment over Susan's head, scoops the leftover pins into a tin and begins to stand. Susan doesn't move. Normally she runs off, fast. Today, she's standing still, very still, and I watch her toes curl in the red plush pile.

In a small voice, she says, 'I want some shoes.' Her feet shuffle, and she remains in the middle of the carpet. Mum looks up in disbelief, 'Sure thing, so you can bury them in the lane for the picanins to take!' Head down, her eyes focused on her bare feet, she says again, 'I want shoes. Please.' She starts to cry. Quietly. There's none of her normal shouting, crashing, and thrashing around. I watch large tears drip from her blonde lashes and over her cheeks. Mum's about to laugh but stops, glances at me, and I make my eyes wide. Topaz eyes watch us now. Mum's brow furrows, thoughts flit over her face, and she makes a decision.

'Well, I think we'll walk into town and find you some then. Put your school ones on. Let's go!' That night, without a fight, Mum washes Susan's hair, brushes out the knots, and it dries in gentle curves around her lovely face. In the morning, she emerges, like a butterfly from a chrysalis. Her hair is brushed and she's wearing her new dress and white sandals. She's beautiful. To me, it's the day 'Susan' moved out and 'Sue' moved into our lives.

But Mum's high heels still walk slowly over the wooden floors. It's as if someone has switched off her happy light. However, she has made a new friend, Shauna Kelly, who makes her laugh.

I like the Kellys. They're a vibrant family of Irish heritage with burning copper hair and freckles on pale skin. Shauna has four kids: Shannon and Aiden, who are older than me, Liam, a bit younger, and a toddler, Kayleigh, with gorgeous curls. We got to know them last school holidays and even better after an incident in the laneway late one night that woke us all up. It was dark and cold. Mum had run through the house and out the back door shouting, 'It's Shauna. Bill, call the police!' Susan and I hung out my bedroom window. Someone was screaming in the laneway, loudly. The police arrived and suddenly it was quiet. Mum eventually came home and didn't notice us lurking and listening.

'Oh Bill, it's too awful. Her ex-husband turned up and tried to take the baby away. He was in the laneway holding a knife. Poor Shauna.' Mum then lowers his voice, 'The bastard slashed all her clothes in the wardrobe. I'll have to take her a dress in the morning…' And that's what she did and now they're great friends.

So some nights I jump out of my bedroom window and walk down the lane to the Kelly's flat. Shauna works two jobs, one at night as an usher at the flicks, and so that's when we listen to records, talk and cook dinners of mashed potato and tomato sauce. It's great and I love the crowded noise. It's just like Diane's house on the weekends when everyone is home!

The only problem is my window is too high to climb back in easily, and one night, with my fingers straining to pull me upwards, Bill's face appears above mine. He's supercross, and without a word, points to the back door. He's standing in the kitchen when I get inside and says, 'I've told you before. Do… Not… Jump out the window. No sneaking off to the Kellys. Do you hear me!' I'm scared. Bill stalks off, the floorboards creak, and the bedroom door slams.

Mum sticks her head out of the bathroom, hands over her mouth and eyes wide. She's laughing! So now Mum leaves the back door open and I sneak back in, making sure to skirt around the creaking floorboards. But all too soon I have to leave again. And Frances is cross when I arrive home because I've returned with a cold. 'Again' she reminds me.

I love school. Especially as I've made a few friends and sit in the quadrangle with Janet or Mel at recess, and Diane on the bus. And finally, October's suicide heat gives way to the November rains that pelt down most days at 1pm and 5pm. The tar steams and water gushes down the drains. I think of how wonderful it would be to run barefoot on the farm.

***

In December, Mum makes everything that we always have: iced Christmas cake, mince pies, and fruity pudding. She's tried very hard, but it's not the same without Grandpa and Nanna. Aunty Lilly, Ed—he's older and I'm a bit shy of him—and Ant come to stay for a few days to share Christmas with us. Ed has to sleep over at Kelly's flat because we just don't have enough room here. I think he likes Shannon, so he will be fine over there! It's super of Mum to invite them.

New Year's Day dawns over low campfires and party-jaded people waiting on the shores of the Rusape dam for the sunrise. Cautiously, a yellow ball floats over the horizon, swathed in clouds of muted greys and ash white. It finds a crack and slices a brilliant yellow highway over the deep stainless-steel water, bordered by black one-dimensional trees and bush. In the distance, Henrietta the Hippo lifts her head, snorts, and moves like a lump of shiny lead towards us, gliding through mirror images of clouds, with ripples moving ever outwards. The dawn of 1972 shines on us all.

But the waters are murky with shadows of sadness still around Mum. I don't dare ask her *why*.

Then it's time to leave, yet again, with my red eyes and a snivelling nose that I try so hard to hide from everyone.

***

Mum hasn't written for ages. Today, there's a letter! I'm so excited until I get to the second page. She says they can't meet the Salisbury train because there are no spare petrol coupons. She tells me to write to her work address so that she will get my letters before going home. Isn't that nice, she looks forward to my letters too! But Dad's not happy with this suggestion. 'Apparently, according to the letter, there's suddenly a shortage of petrol coupons to be had.'

His tone remains flat as if it's painful to speak of them in Rusape. Why did Mum write, I wonder. The occasional contact is usually when she rings Dad at work. I can tell when she has. Dad comes home white-faced and tells Frances, whose lips vanish even more, and she nibbles on her fingernails.

Today, there's an undercurrent I don't understand, and before I can think about it further, he adds, 'I'm not happy about the suggestion you wait alone for two hours at Salisbury Station for the Umtail train.' *Two hours!* I'm scared. Frances is watching me with narrow eyes. She agrees with Dad. Why hasn't Mum asked Auntie Anne to pick me up? She would, I know, and it's only a few hours. Dad's frowning, turning stamps over and says, 'No, you're not going.' I find my voice, 'It's fine, not that long, honest.' *Yes, it is and I'm terrified.* Salisbury Station is huge and cold and I'm only 14 years old. If Dad and Frances sense this, they will not let me go and I just *have* to see Mum. I miss her so much and can almost smell her perfume.

So, here I am on Salisbury Station, in the early morning hours recalling Dad's 'this is not right' face, perched on the edge of my large cream suitcase, examining the silver spring locks, bored out of my brain, *and* nervous. The late winter chill surrounds me; porters' voices echo as the sun gradually lightens the shadows and gleams on the metal train tracks. An engine shunts in, passenger carriages with *RR* etched into their windows line up, and porters no longer slouch, but hurry back and forth carting luggage to the guard's van. I grab one, 'Please tell the guard, I'm off at Rusape.' I say, and help load my suitcase.

'Yehbo.' A tickie slips from my fingers into his creased palm, and he touches his forehead. 'Thank you,' I say, and nod my head.

For a moment, I wonder where he lives and how far he travelled to be here before dawn. Does he own that all-important bicycle? It's not proper to ask, is it? At least he doesn't have to bother about petrol coupons! But then again, pedalling is hard work too, just like hauling these carts and suitcases is, but they all chat with each other, laughing from time to time. Are they happy? I don't know, and do they wonder about us too? Are these people milling around unhappy and just not showing it?

Bodies surge around me, carriage doors hang open, my feet find the metal steps, and I walk along the polished wood corridor to my compartment with its green seats.

Mum's standing on the platform when I arrive, and I run into her arms. Youth Dew all around me. Her arms are around me. If only I could linger here. But no. 'My goodness Beverley, you nearly knocked me over!'

We walk down the platform chatting, 'Mum, I'm starving. All I've had is an apple and a soggy peanut butter sandwich!' She laughs, 'Won't do you any harm! You need to lose weight!' It's hot, the sky's so blue, and on the horizon, large clouds loom with the promise of an afternoon storm. Summer is almost gone and soon Rusape will be bone-jarringly cold. I shiver, thinking of winters here, and how mild they were in Hartley.

We weave our way along the crowded platform, between groups of Africans towards the guard's van, past men carrying bundles, women with small babies tied on their backs, some with sleeping heads lolling and a few with snot running from their noses, and children clinging to outstretched hands. The noise is intense. Africans tend to talk loudly and joyfully when seeing people they know. *I love it!* This is what the farm sounded like and a warm feeling creeps over me. I wish I could speak Ndebele or Shona instead of this hybrid language we use, Chilapalapa, that everyone in Rhodesia seems to understand. I asked Dad once about it, and he said it's a language born of need because thousands of people come to work in Rhodesia and there has to be a common language. It's quick to learn and we all understand it.

And now all these rich voices swirl around me. Happiness, clutter, disorganization, chickens in baskets hanging their heads out, parcels balancing on women's heads, and suddenly we are past them all, past the carriages they are disgorging from, past Africans hanging out of windows, and as the crowd surges away only a few vendors are left, selling food through the carriage window. I've never seen this before. There were always vendors at the stops along the way, but the ladies in the compartment closed the windows and refused to buy from them. I couldn't look out and didn't dare ask questions.

'Mum, all these people?'

'What about them?'

'They're all down this back end of the train, lots of them.'

'Yes, in third and fourth class.'

'Third and fourth class?'

'Oh, Beverley, stop asking questions. Come on, grab that porter, and let's get away from all this!' I'll ask Dad about the classes when we are alone. We drive through town, past familiar shops while Mum chats away about how easy it was for me to just wait in Salisbury. There's a lightness about her. Restraint is gone and suddenly I realise that she's *happy*. I'm happy *too*.

In the rear lane just before we reach our back gate, Mum swerves right and parks facing the flats where the Kellys live. Why stop for a visit rather than go home, where Mr Markee will unload my suitcase and unpack it for me? Joy of joy, he will do that and all my washing and ironing for the next month! And make sponge cake while we chat. Who cares, this is Mum all over: impulsive. She interrupts my thoughts. 'Come on, hop out.'

I follow her up the stairs and walk briskly along the open-air corridor. We don't stop at the Kellys. Mum's got keys in her hand and is opening another door.

'This is where we live now,' she announces.

'We've moved. Again!'

Mum pushes the door open. 'Yes. Just me. Bill is still living over there.' Her arm waves in the general direction of our old house. Her heels click on the parquetry floor, and she opens another door, 'This is your room, nice isn't it? Sunny and all your stuff's here.' And it is, transplanted in perfect Mr. Markee-order, right down to my special doll standing on the dressing table.

'Kitchen,' says Mum and I peer inside. There's a new second-hand fridge, 'Sitting room.' Oh, thank goodness, Grandpa's favourite chair, a new-old couch, and our red carpet!

'My bedroom,' she says opening doors, 'Susan's, bathroom and that's it! All mine!' She smiles and flings her arms wide. There's a shuffling noise in the hallway, and an African appears with my suitcase. 'Thanks, Solomon, can you just put it in there?' Soloman nods his head at me and slides my large case into my bedroom. Mum drops a coin in his hand and he's gone.

'Mr. Markee's day off?' IMum flips open a Peter Stuyvesant Box and lifts out a cigarette. I just hate her smoking.

'No, he defected to Bill! He was here and then Bill offered him more money to work over there!' The last words spit from her lovely lips. 'Traitor!' This is all too much, not only has Mum left Bill—which is sort of OK—but Mr Markee with his gold tooth, wonderful face and cakes is gone too.

'Mum, he's been with us *forever*, from Grandpa's time, way back. He knows us, me… he can't go!'

'Well, I told him in no uncertain tones that he's not going in my compost heap now.' She grins. 'The old bugger laughed. I had to laugh too, it's OK, we can get Sue to order us a casserole and sponge cake!' And that's another thing I'm going to miss. Mr Markee and Mum sort of disagree and it ends with Mum telling him he's old and must go to his kia (traditional home in the bush) to rest and die, and he says, 'Ikona, no kia, put me in compost heap!' And they'd both laugh like crazy.

The thought makes me sad. Deep down, I realise that I love Mr. Markee. He's part of what makes home, *home*. He's always been there, for as long as I can remember. He knows the farm, Dad, Great Gran, Grandpa, Nanna, Noddy, everything. We talk about all of that. I suppose I can visit him over there, but it's not the same. He's part of the family. We keep a compost heap for him! And even the thought that he will die one day is sad. Even though we all joke about it. I'm sure he has a kia!

'Mum, where's Sue?' Maybe out with a friend. It's strange, I'm sure she would have asked to come to the train station. Mum turns the kettle on. 'She lives between here and there.' Again her arm flicks towards the old house, 'Wherever she feels like, especially if she's cross with me and then she says, "I'm going to Wibby's!" She knows you're here so will no doubt be back tonight, with rock cakes!' We both start to laugh. What else can I do, there's no point in being serious about this, Mum *certainly* isn't!

'Oh, and we share a maid too!' Great, my washing will be done!

And suddenly it's all very clear: her slow, sad steps, the writing to her work address, the not fetching me from Salisbury, and only two letters in three months. But Mum's happy, again, so it's OK. I'm not going to ask her the divorce question again. On that first night, Sue turns up as Mum said she would, and stays the night.

After coming to terms with the loss of Mr Markee, the new arrangement doesn't bother me because I can visit him when Bill's at work. The Kellys live next door so there's no more climbing out of my bedroom window, even though I have to admit that was fun. We are all happier. But I'm not so sure about Bill, as I've kept out of his way; or even Sue, who comes and goes according to her moods. If we upset her, or lunch isn't to her liking, she takes off over the laneway saying, 'I'm going to live with Wibby and Squibb. So there!' We laugh and call after her, 'See you when you get back!' That will be when she's bored, or Bill upsets her.

The following Sunday dawns sunny, and after a few hours, Mum suggests we go to the Crocodile Motel for a swim and a jump on the trampoline.

'And a Brown Cow (Coke and ice cream drink) too!' says Sue, her pixie face eager for a treat.

'Sure,' says Mum, and with that, Sue's out the door calling, 'Just going to Wibby's for my costume!'

Soon, we're at the Motel, climbing in and out of the pool, swimming under the Crocodile mouth spurting water, jumping on the trampoline, dripping wet, and laughing as I double bounce Sue. Her lithe body flies high into the air, fine blonde hair flies around her shoulders and she shouts to me, 'Time for Brown Cows!' I stiffen my knees, her bouncing stops, and she darts off the black mat and runs across the lawn towards Mum, who is sitting in the shade of an umbrella. I hurry after her. She suddenly stops. We almost collide. A tall, dark-haired man is relaxing in a chair next to Mum, ankle propped on one knee, beer in hand, and they're chatting. Sue glares at him. 'Who are you? Why are you sitting with my mother? What's your name?' She's like an automatic gun, firing words and scowling at him. I try to pull her away, back towards the pool, before she says anymore. She digs her heels into the grass and stares at the man. He returns her gaze with amusement in his dark eyes.

'I'm sitting here because your mother said it was fine to keep her company. That's why. My name's Cliff.' His Rhodesian voice (so unlike Bill's posh accent) is deep and playful in contrast to his serious face, and there's not a grey hair in sight amongst his curls. One eyebrow rises, and waits. Mum looks as if she could strangle Sue. Sue frowns, her blonde brows furrow together above blue eyes, and I hold my breath. She's always so bold and will say whatever she's thinking.

'If you buy us Brown Cows, you can stay!' Cliff gives this mock serious consideration and says, 'Deal!' He grins at Sue, who claps her hands and turns a cartwheel.

'Call me when it's here!' She says and dashes across the lawn. I follow her long brown legs and we flop onto the trampoline and lie there, sun on our faces, giggling.

We lie beside each other, Sue's fingers fiddling with my long hair. It's so peaceful. For the first time in years, I could almost roll around with joy. Mum's not consumed with what I now know was an unhappy marriage. How long had she been sad? I think on this for a few moments and realise it was from when Uncle Mike died, that a huge cloud rested on her, hidden, but I knew it was there.

Now we are living in a super flat. I love it. Mum comes home from work and just the two of us spend nights watching TV, talking, and reading magazines. Sometimes Sue calls in and stays all night, and in the mornings we cook breakfast, laugh, and play around. We don't ever fight now. If only there were a high school here. I could stay with Mum and everything would be great. Now, Mum just has to tell Dad that she's left Bill, and all my worries about that will be gone too. This is perfect. I'm so happy, and this is my home now. I belong at last. *You were right, Grandpa, it will be alright!*

I flip over, and through the bushes and leaves, I can see Mum. Her perfect profile is tipped back, she's laughing. I can't hear her. Cliff leans forward and lights her cigarette. I can't see her. He's in the way. The waiter's walking towards them carrying a tray with Brown Cows and beers. He's almost there. I feel something, what is it? And after a few moments, I understand what I'm seeing and for the first time in my life, the future slaps me in the face, before it happens.

I disconnect from my body, float over the pool with its crocodile fountain and look back at myself lying on the trampoline mat. I look serene.

The corrugated iron roof is warm, and its undulations curve beneath my bare feet.

Grandpa, are you there?

Grandpa calls to me, 'Bread's out of the oven —come down from there, Child.'

I'm somewhere I shouldn't be.

Chapter 29
There is a Beginning, and There is an End.

The Beginning Journey: Bulawayo, Rhodesia 1959.

The two-year-old girl is sobbing in the car seat beside him. Her chest shudders with every breath. Huge brown eyes observe him, her rumpled body shifts nearer, her tear-stained face burrows into his lap, and chubby hands reach up to his chest. He can't touch her. Self-control will desert him if he does. He won't be able to let her go.

He has arrived. Before him is a familiar house, a keeper of hopeful memories. The engine's cut. Silence. Tight fingers uncurl from the steering wheel.

He'd left with the sun setting, now it's rising. The car had broken down, overheated, and had a flat tyre. The worst was the child. She'd alternated between sobbing briefly, dozing and throwing herself at him, hysterically crying, 'Mummy, Mummy,' causing the car to veer.

A sigh leaves his body. How could this have happened? He can't think about it now.

The front door opens. They are hurrying towards him, worry etched on their aging faces.

'Denny, we are so sorry! We just don't know what to say.' Iris's voice sounds far away, but she's right before him and reaches out. He steps back. His tightly held facade will splinter if he embraces her.

Eric, her husband, gathers the soggy hiccupping child repeating, 'Mummy, Mummy,' into his arms. She clings to his neck, and he murmurs soothing words in her ear.

'I've got no one else to leave her with.' His hand hovers towards her small dark head, then falls away. 'I've got to go, I can't stay here!'

He turns, gets into the car, quietly closes the door and drives away.

His daughter's now screaming, 'Daddy Daddy!' Clouds of dust and her words chase after him. He can't look back.

Iris and Eric carry the child inside. They are, after all, her maternal grandparents. No one thought I would remember.

***

My Father, Denwood William Walker (1926–2012)
Australia, 2012

Have you ever looked at the seed pod of a jacaranda tree? Maybe not. They're interesting; at three inches round they are fully grown. They're green and then mature to brown. This is where nature is clever: these dried-out pods snap open, warp and fling small round gossamer-winged seeds into the wind which then float away. Some fall too close and die, unable to compete; others ride the breeze and settle far away, take root and flourish. These grow tall, magnificent, and burst into abundant purple flowers, before leaves shoot each spring, to proclaim their presence in the harsh heat of October, before the November rains.

Our family has been flung like these seeds. Some landed near our Rhodesian home, others in Australia and New Zealand. We are a complex family tree, each with our opinions; but now we are united.

Dad to some, Uncle Denny to others, is probably going to die tomorrow. And we all love him. How can this be? Well, tomorrow, under local anaesthetic, as that's all his heart can withstand, he's having a hip replacement. To my mind, he's committing medical suicide. The other family members are in varying degrees of distress. My cousin Cindy sobs on the phone to me in Sydney from Ladysmith, South Africa. 'Uncle Denny's going to die. You have to stop him. He'll listen to you…'

You're probably right, but do I have the right to do that? Cindy is clinging to her Uncle Denny. Dad's brother, her father, has passed away.

My half-sister Elaine, who lives with Dad in Ladysmith, quietly says, 'Dad's afraid, but has made up his mind. Do you think we can try to talk him out of it?'

Yes, Cindy says that too. We could try, but should we? Poor Elaine, she'd nursed her mother, Frances, to the end: this is so difficult for her. Regret and recriminations consume her. They shouldn't: she did her best.

My half-sister Sharon, in New Zealand, says, 'Dad's going to do what he wants, he's so damn stubborn. No point trying to change his mind.'

Yes, you've nailed Dad's attitude! Sharon's had enough of long-distance problems; she has to deal with her aging in-laws too! So, here we are, an international family, and we all agree, that Dad, Uncle Denny, is probably going to die tomorrow. For sure.

***

My Father. Ladysmith, 3rd June 1941—Denwood William Walker. Age 14

Gradually there is an awareness. It's warm; he's on a bed, a sheet resting lightly over his body; he savours the sensations but keeps his eyes closed. Is it dark beyond them? He can't speak. There's no memory, or wait—*is there?* He was feeling very sick. He never gets sick. His brown eyes open and he stares at the white ceiling, white walls and the sun tunnel boring through an open window where dust motes are dancing on a warm breeze.

A man in a white coat appears at his side. 'Welcome back, young man. Let's have a look at you.' He flashes a light in the boy's eyes and moves a cold stethoscope over his chest. 'You've been waking up for a few days now!' There's a waft of disinfectant as the doctor moves away.

'What happened?' He's finally able to ask his mother. 'It's going to be alright,' she says, 'You've had meningitis and been in a coma for months.'

The nurses wash him. His skin is translucent white and his veins run like bush paths over his body; every bone is defined. The nurses try to amuse him and teach him the names of the bones he can see. They joke and say his beautiful eyelashes are wasted on a young man! He can't sit up without help, walk or lift his arms. His body has wasted away, but his mind races out of the window and into the sunlight.

It was cold, very cold when he was last out there. Snow smothered the grey slopes of the Berg—the Drakensberg Mountains—and the wind carried ice that gathered on his gloves as he cycled to school. His long legs spun the pedals, lungs sucked in frigid air that escaped as misty puffs of laboured breath. His lean body swung from the bicycle and he jogged, fringe falling forward on his brow, towards the athletics field. Fourteen years old, fit and awake to manhood. Then nothing. Now it's warm outside. *Where did winter go?*

The doctors say, 'Mrs Walker, Denny will never walk again. Take him home and make the best of it. Buy a wheelchair.' Rebecca Walker straightened her five-foot-two-inch spine. It had been stoically straight since her mother abandoned her in an orphanage in Cape Town when she was about three years old. Her father was dead. She was not going to buy Denny a wheelchair. He still had one good leg. And walk Denny *did*.

His mother massaged, bullied and cajoled those muscles in his left leg that pretended to be dead. How dare they try that on her watch! In an era before physiotherapy, she used intuition and common sense and Denny stood tall again, limped proudly using limited leg muscles with a foot that never met the ground flat. He rode his bicycle but never ran again. He smiled and grew up to be an honourable man. And now, 70 years later, his right hip has retired itself after a lifetime of service. No gold watch!

Now there's something I need to ask him. It's been over 40 years since I last asked the question that predictably went unanswered. Today is my last chance. *Am I selfish?* I'm going to ask again, one last time.

The phone receiver is sweaty in my hand. I loosen my grip and wait for my half-sister Elaine to answer. I can visualize her and Dad in their villa, with the grass outside and paths that meander around the complex. Beyond the shrubs and trees, the sun will have risen over the still snow-tipped Berg, even though it's January and stifling. Here in Erina, Central Coast, New South Wales, Australia, evening lorikeets are chattering in the trees and the cicadas will soon cease their drone. Dad will be hot, too, perspiration soaking his shirt. Dad's *always* hot, even when it's cold. Maybe because of meningitis, he tells me. I wipe my hand on my T-shirt. I'm glad they finally succumbed to an air conditioner. Strange how insignificant thoughts pop into one's mind. Elaine answers. Her voice is clear and flat, she's resigned to Dad's wish.

'Elaine, I'd need you to talk to Dad for me... to ask him...' She agrees.

The waiting is overwhelming, crushing my chest, silently squeezing my breath that leaves in shallow sounds. That's *all* I hear. My breath. Slowly, the significance of the situation laps unwanted at the edge of my thoughts. I want to deny them, but can't. A near-empty bowl metaphorically sits in my mind; it holds my father, alone. He is the last of my five parents. My mother, Norma; stepmother, Frances; stepfathers, Bill and Cliff; all live safely now in the created cemeteries in my mind.

Early the next morning the phone rings. It's dark; I stumble to reach it. Dad has gone. He survived the operation and then had a massive stroke. Elaine is consumed with guilt, she cries and says, 'I should have done more!'

You couldn't have, my dear sister, let him go and join your Mum in peace. It's what he wanted. Truly. He was lonely, worn out and sad. Then, as she hangs up, she mumbles, 'I did ask him... I'll write to you.'

It's Australia Day, January 26, 2012. Dad had always dreamed of living here. The bowl is empty.

***

My Mother—Norma Erica Walker (3 April 1935–9 March 2003)

Mum was beautiful; to be blunt, stunning! Perfect features, nipped-in waist, long shapely legs that cellulite never dared invade. She was vivacious and had a wicked sense of humour. One of her three husbands once told me, 'Your mother has the most spectacular legs I've ever seen.' But, boy did she *hate* the Germans! Just the thought of them made her compress her lips and scowl, but even *then* she was gorgeous! 'It was all the fault of the Germans!' she used to vehemently say.

***

Northern Rhodesia: 1939

The bed's snug, warm, *too* warm and suddenly it's too late. The little girl rolls out and under it, her fingers lock around the spring base above her and then they arrive. They remind her of big black birds, with mean eyes. Hands grope for her, grab her leg and pull. She won't let go. *Whack!* 'Ouch!' she shrieks grabbing her caned ankle and is yanked into the light. Her small body is lifted and flung face down onto the bed.

Whack! 'You dirty girl!'

Whack! Scream.

Whack! High-pitched scream.

The smell of fresh pee fills her nose as it's pressed into the wet patch. Her pyjamas are wet too. The nun stands over her panting. Smacks the cane against the bed frame and shouts, 'You can sleep in that tonight. You dirty child!' And then she is gone, a mean raven retreating towards the door. It's the same every morning. She's only four and a half years old. It was all the fault of the Germans.

Everything had been wonderful until a few weeks ago, before Mummy, Daddy and she, went to the train station. The huge steam train was hissing and there were people everywhere. Mummy was squishing her hand, smiling. Daddy had picked her up, squashed her against his chest, and kissed her lots. Then he was on the train, all the men were on the train and all the mummies and children were waving... waving until the train became a small dot *way, way, away*. Then they stopped and the mummies cried quietly behind their hankies.

'Where's Daddy gone?' She asked that night. *Who's going to read me a bedtime story?*

'Burma, far away,' said Mummy holding her close.

'Why?'

'To fight the Germans in the war. Time to sleep now.'

That was the last night she slept in her lovely safe bed. The next day Mummy had taken her to a big building where ladies in black dresses with white faces smiled at her and said she was going to stay with them. They smiled at Mummy too and said, 'She will be fine.' *Liars they turned out to be!* She didn't want to let go of Mummy's hand and wanted to know why she was leaving. 'I have to work. So you have to go to boarding school,' she replied, 'Because Daddy's gone to fight the Germans.'

Daddy stayed away for a long while. He came home a few times, but he didn't want to play. Mummy was very sad. The little girl was too, but things got a bit better when she stopped wetting the bed and discovered some of the big black birds were kind. *See, I told you, it was all the fault of the Germans.* But they weren't responsible for her stretch marks; that was my fault.

'I gained 60 pounds when I was having you!' she'd say. 'Ate way too much liquorice. Dad used to buy me as much as I wanted!' And there were the silver streaks on her hips to prove it was true. So, I was born in 1957, short, with dark hair, and wearing rolls of fat. A beautiful baby that screamed constantly with colic. Mum would say, 'You know, we travelled by train from Ndola to Bulawayo, and you bellowed all night in a compartment for six!' She'd look at me laughing, 'As we crossed the Victoria Falls bridge, I seriously considered tossing you out of the window. I think the entire compartment would have cheered!' Mum taught me many things, among them how to sew, knit, crochet, and eat fast!

'If I didn't eat fast in the convent I starved!' She used to tell me. So, I ate fast to keep her company. Which was fine, as I like my toast hot, with melted butter.

'Yuck!' She'd say as I quickly ate mine. She loved her toast cold, with butter sitting on top. But then she loved dripping (Cold rendered fat from roast meat) on slabs of bread too. I just couldn't eat that, no matter how much she shoved a slice towards me. And therein began the differences between Mum and me.

***

Australia: 9th March 2003

A crocodile has been, for weeks, sunning itself on my chest—heavy, lazy, and unmoving. I can't breathe properly, it's crushing me and even though I push, it won't move; it's too comfortable. If I irritate it, sharp teeth sink into me and pain radiates; best I leave it to slumber. It's hot for March, maybe it will slide off me and cool off in the river; soon.

It's quiet in the hospital room. The nurses have closed the curtains to nosy eyes and a fan is blowing too fast. Mum was OK yesterday; sick yes, but now she's dying. It's Sunday. What's that saying she has? Oh yes, 'Sunday's child is full of grace.' That's Sue, born on a Sunday! Yes, that suits my half-sister Sue, with her blue eyes and blonde hair. And then laughing she'd add, 'And Beverley was born as Saturday's child, who works hard for its living!'

It's difficult to believe we are here now. We were supposed to have another four years together, not hours. Mum was admitted on Thursday with pneumonia and on Friday I walked into her hospital room to find Sue, who is here early from Sydney, seated beside her.

'Mum's coming home today,' she says.

A hello would have been nice. It's possible. Mum looks better.

'She has to be back in again Monday for a blood transfusion,' I say, 'Maybe she should stay, just to be safe.' Two united, determined faces confront me. They knew I wouldn't agree. They've been plotting.

'I'm coming home. Today.'

'Mum's going home,' Sue says.

'Sue, I need to talk to you outside.' I turn away from my thoughts. They have already got this all worked out for sure.

'Nothing to talk about. Susan, get me out of here!' Mum says. *Ah, it's Susan, is it? Mum means business.* In the empty corridor, I tell Sue that my family is worn out. We are Mum's full-time carers and we're also trying to run a business purchased four months ago. We need a break. And I *don't* say, you're both forgetting it's my family's home too.

'Well, it's not up to you,' says Sue. 'Mum wants to go home and I'm getting her out of here. That's that!' She turns and hurries away.

I watch her retreating. Oh goodness, I see her as a child again. Blonde hair, the funny walk she shares with her father, feet slightly out-turned, knees slightly bent that don't fully straighten as they walk, with short flat-footed steps. This is how she's *always* walked in times of frustration, disappointment, and anger. I hear Sue's voice from all those years ago, upset with Mum and me, 'I'm going to find Wibby' (Bill, Dad)

She's now walking away, again. Years of suppressed words gather on my lips, threatening to spew forth. *Don't do this.* It's always been Mum and you together, she loves you so much—two kindred spirits—I'm the thorn in your sides. She loves you best. But is that your fault? No. I call out, 'Sue!' She stops, her shoulders sagging slightly; her back remains facing me. She straightens.

'Sue! Come back! I love you.' Her knees bend and I run, down the antiseptic corridor, and pull her into my arms. 'Let's see what the Doctor suggests.' She nods in agreement.

The Doctor says Mum needs to stay. That was Friday, and now it's Sunday. Two days ago, just two days ago she was fine, and today she's lying beneath a creased sheet—why would I notice that? *Oh yes, Nanna loved ironed sheets,* so long ago on the farm, where we boiled them outside in a huge tub over a fire lit on red dirt, Rhodesian earth.

Mum's restless, hot, and her lovely feet extend from beneath the sheet, her toenails are painted with deep pink nail polish. She loves to have her nails painted all the time She could have modelled hands, feet—in fact—her entire self.

'Bev, Bev...'

'Yes Mum, I'm here.' I lean over and touch her face. She's partially deaf now.

'Bev, is this what I think it is?'

You know I won't lie to you Mum, that's why you're asking me, isn't it? In the end, it's the sensible Saturday child you turn to!

Breath catches in my chest; even now she's circumspect. I whisper close to her ear, 'Yes, Mum, it is. Just go. It's OK to go.' Her eyes fly wide, shock registers on her face, a myriad of emotions reflect in an instant and she focuses intently on me. 'Oh, oh!' she mumbles and blinks. The crocodile's teeth sink into my flesh sending pain down my arms. I wish the bloody thing would slide into the river. Leaning over her I wait. Is it acceptance I see now? Yes, and so much more. After a few moments, I say, 'Mum, I'm going home to Laura, it's her birthday today. I'll see you later.' My lips brush her cheek, her soft brown eyes meet mine. I nod at Sue seated beside the bed and leave to buy a chocolate cake for our little girl who was born at 6.33pm this day, nine years ago. I need to be with her at that time.

***

My husband and I are outside Woolworths, I'm holding a cheap chocolate cake—lucky there's one even *left* at this time—in its clear ugly packaging. Suddenly the lights dim around me. A cold damp sheet is falling over my head, it drifts to my feet cloaking me in a fog, a clammy clinging shroud muffling sounds—distorting them. *I'm cold. I can't see.*

A creeping sensation trickles upwards from my feet, into my stomach, and with it comes nausea. I'm going to vomit. Faint. The ugly cake is gone from my hands; reality is gone. I'm lost, lost in a fog—disconnected, alone. In the distance a phone rings. My husband's muffled voice answers it. I know. The crocodile seizes my body, crushes my chest, and death rolls me into the dark, dank water. I can't fight back. But I must, and light nine candles on my Laura's cake. I'll see you later, Mum.

***

Frances Mary Ellis Walker (nee Wright). My Stepmother (14 September 1942–20 March 2009)

Frances died today, too young, and far away in South Africa. I loved her dearly in the end. After we had travelled together in disharmony during my teen years, we found a clear calm pool to sit beside. And that's where we stayed for the remainder of her life, metaphorically seated at the edge of the Nyangombe Falls in Nyanga, where the river tumbles over a long stretch of sloping rock into a large pool. That was our relationship in the beginning; ever-moving and turbulent. But then we reached a mutual place beside that river, where it lapped clear against the sandy shore, calm and peaceful—Frances and I. The past was mutually forgiven.

***

Early 2000s Phone Calls from Sydney To South Africa.

'Frances, we can only talk for half an hour. OK? When we hear the beeps we must hang up, we only have 30 seconds to do that!' I remind her and myself as well.

'Oh yes Bevlee, the beeps! We will hang up. Definitely.' Her voice lifts on that final word. I visualize her head nodding, her dark side fringe, now slightly sliver, flopping forward into her eyes.

'*Beep – beep – beep.*'

'We'd better hang up,' I say. Too late! The 30 seconds have lapsed. 'Let's just chat for another half an hour!'

'But this is costing you another $20!' she says, 'I should've stopped talking! *Hehehehe*... I do talk too much, don't I!' That *hehehe*, a laugh that trembles her entire upper body, her cheeks bunch up towards her eyes and it's just Frances. I can visualise it!

'Doesn't matter... I'm just as bad,' I counter. 'So tell me about...'

That's how it was, back then, for a phone call from Sydney to South Africa. We paid by the half hour.

***

Over the years Frances mentioned how her left leg came to be the way it was. She told me the story of her father taking her to get medical assistance. I've written below an account, slightly fictionalised to catch the essence of the time, and Grandpa Wright's strong beliefs.

The Methodist Mission Waddilove lies 13 miles from the settlement of Marandellas, remote in the Southern Rhodesian bundu (bush). Their youngest child, Frances, is very ill, and now lying on the seat, beside her father, who is driving on a rutted road. She is perfectly still. He brakes hard and places his hand over her heart, there's no beat. Silent prayer moves his lips, and his palm pushes down over and over, on her small chest. She comes back. Her father says another short prayer and restarts the engine. God will take care of her. The Right Reverand Morely Wright firmly believes this.

***

Frances also spoke to me of her father's diary and her fervent wish that it be published one day. She felt so strongly about this, and appreciating that I love writing, she asked me to do 'something' about it. Towards the end of her life, maybe she knew it was close, she became quite adamant about this.

Now as a tribute to her, I'm adding direct excerpts, as they are written, that relate specifically to Frances.

Excerpts from the Diary of Reverand Morely Wright: June 1944 Waddilove. Southern Rhodesia

When I was called back home from Pathfinder Camp, I found that Frances was indeed very ill. She had had several attacks of malaria, but this was very different. Her right knee was very hot. Dr. Greenwood, the local government Doctor said it was urgent she be taken to Bulawayo Hospital and suggested Dr Strong be called. Hilda and I drove up to Bulawayo .... Dr Strong diagnosed the trouble as osteomyelitis. It could mean her death. We left her in the hospital and trusted everything to God's care.

Hilda stayed and sent me the following letter about Frances and the operation.

My Darling, I fear it will have been a shock to you to receive the telegraphic news I sent. The Dr. made two incisions, one on each side of the knee, and removed a great quantity of pus. The Doctor came to speak to me, he said it is very, very serious and 'the best I can promise you is a permanent stiff knee.' When I went to the hospital yesterday morning she was crying and crying and calling 'Mummy, Mummy,' while they were preparing her for the operation. When she was ready, they let me see her, she put her little arms tight around my neck...

Petrol is a difficulty... there is a bus up to the hospital and in any case I suppose it is not wise to go and upset her. So much love my darling...it is good to know that whatever difficulties may come we meet them together and with Him. God bless you, Mummy.

On Monday, December 18th (1944) we took Frances to Groote Schuur Hospital (Cape Town) for further operations by the Specialist, Mr Hamilton Bell. He was confident that he could improve the straightening of her bent knee.

Hilda and I called at Groote Schuur a couple of times to see our little one there, but it was clear we only upset her by visiting. We made arrangements for Frances to be left at the Lady Michaelis Home at Plumstead, where she could be under the care and observation of the medical people.

From the diary, there is a note that an operation was performed on 8th February, 1945.

On July 2nd (1945) during the school holidays, I set out for Cape Town to get Frances from Lady Michaelis House. She surely looked well as she stood in her playpen. Alas, she did not know me or was able to talk to me in English. Alas, I knew no Afrikaans.

It was indeed so strange that I could not talk to my own daughter. I had to ask the bedroom steward on the train to translate for me.

When Frances called her mother 'Nurse' Hilda nearly broke down.

***

In 1947 the family travelled to England, and Grandpa Wright's diary entry records the following, …about Frances and her admittance to the Children's Hospital in London to see if a further operation on her leg would straighten it:

We soon got Frances into Great Ormond Street Children's Hospital and Mr Hulbert, as Registrar of the main surgeon took charge of Frances, who was later sent to their country Nursing Home at Hemel Hempstead where she stayed for quite some time.

***

Authors Note: There are many references to the family throughout Grandpa Wright's diary. I know Frances didn't read it and she never spoke to me about the long hospital separations from her family. I believe she didn't remember and that her parents didn't discuss them with her. However, the profound loss she suffered with the death of her little brother, Colin, are written in the diary. But she never spoke of that either. All her siblings excelled academically, and Frances always said she felt inferior to them.

I believe that she found *her* home with my father, and was happy. But all the suppressed memories and emotions did impact her life. I wonder how she would have felt, if she'd read the diary.

Afterword

I returned to the farm in 1980. Carl drove us out there. We couldn't stop. Instead, Carl turned fast circles over what was once our lush lawn, past the barren hard earth where the house once stood beneath towering trees, and behind them, Grandpa's now stunted fruit trees clung hard to life. Beyond, the brick chicken runs still stood, now filled with human squatters, living clustered together, and as we did a final third spin, there they were: the tree where Daddy hung my swing, the red brick Post Office standing alone and derelict. Then we sped away. I was heart sore.

Today, almost 45 years later, my mind takes me back to that farm and the mango trees. I'm up there, climbing between the branches, where the sun spotlights through the darkness and lands on mangos, ripe, yellow and blush. I pick one and flick the skins at the strutting turkeys and look out for Grandpa. It's serene up here, amongst the green and breeze, and in the distance I hear the laughter of women coming to fetch water.

I understand so much now. By my early 30s, I'd reached a peaceful place about my childhood, but there remained the whys. *Why was I treated the way I was?*

The day before my father died, free to do so because my other parents were all gone, he told a story. For me, it answered all the whys and closed the door that was ajar.

'Grandpa, why are the white turkeys the best?'

'Don't know. Are they?'

'Never found out, but I like to think so.'

Christmas 1965, our first without Nanna

Dad and I at Palmerston Hotel 1965

Sue and I at the Wilkinson's house

*Grandpa, Mum and Nanna.
circa 1951*

*Bill and Mum, Balfour Hotel,
Rusape, 1970.*

*Sue and I, Rusape.
circa 1971*

www.ingramcontent.com/pod-product-compliance
Ingram Content Group UK Ltd.
Pitfield, Milton Keynes, MK11 3LW, UK
UKHW010700070625
6266UKWH00013B/49